# THE NEW MANAGEMENT SCENE

**Joe Kelly,** a management professor at Concordia University, Montreal, Canada, and organizational behavior consultant, has published more than 20 articles for business journals and six books, among which is another Spectrum book titled *How Managers Manage.*

**V. V. Baba,** an associate management professor and member of several management associations, has conducted numerous conference presentations and written articles for business journals.

A SPECTRUM BOOK

Prentice-Hall, Inc., *Englewood Cliffs, New Jersey 07632*

JOE KELLY
*and*
V. V. BABA

# THE NEW MANAGEMENT SCENE

## Readings on How Managers Manage

*Library of Congress Cataloging in Publication Data*

Main entry under title:

The New management scene.

    A Spectrum Book
"Designed to accompany J. Kelly's How managers
manage"—Pref.
    Includes bibliographies.
    1. Management—Addresses, essays, lectures.
I. Kelly, Joe.    II. Baba, V. V.    III. Kelly, Joe.
How managers manage.
HD31.N454      658.4      81-23485
                     AACR2

ISBN 0-13-615393-3

ISBN 0-13-615385-2 {PBK.}

This Spectrum Book is available to businesses and organizations
at a special discount when ordered in large quantities. For
information, contact Prentice-Hall, Inc., General Publishing
Division, Special Sales, Englewood Cliffs, N.J. 07632.

1  2  3  4  5  6  7  8  9  10

Editorial/production/supervision
and interior design by Kimberly Mazur
Manufacturing buyer: Barbara Frick

Prentice-Hall International, Inc., *London*
Prentice-Hall of Australia Pty. Limited, *Sydney*
Prentice-Hall of Canada, Ltd., *Toronto*
Prentice-Hall of India Private Limited, *New Delhi*
Prentice-Hall of Japan, Inc., *Tokyo*
Prentice-Hall of Southeast Asia Pte. Ltd., *Singapore*
Whitehall Books Limited, *Wellington, New Zealand*

# Contents

M any people in our society want to play a larger part in controlling their affairs and take a more decisive interest in influencing the people, groups, and organizations that run their lives. We believe that lurking inside most people there is a manager who wants to show his or her genius for organizing things, directing others, and controlling outcomes.

This book, which is designed to accompany Joe Kelly's *How Managers Manage* (Prentice-Hall, 1980), is an introductory reader to start the student in the management field. We recognize management as both an art and science, and we emphasize that organizational analysis is a joint province of practicing managers and social scientists. We examine the economic and social significance of management theory in practice. This introductory reader is neither definitive nor complete; it is presented as a developing montage of new departures, concepts, and practices. We refer to the work of a number of managers and management theorists. With few exceptions, the books and

papers mentioned have much more to say than can be included in an introductory text. The reader is not intended to obviate the need to read the books and journals from which the readings have been taken, but rather to stimulate the student's interest in the field. We hope to provoke debate and to encourage the exchange of information among managers, social scientists, and students.

We hope that you will actively scrutinize and select some of the concepts and ideas that follow to improve your problem-solving skills as managers. But skill in diagnosing management problems is achieved only through persistent effort and careful analysis. As you move backward and forward through the text, you will begin to look at corporate behavior in a different light.

This book can be used to expand on the ideas offered in regular text courses in management. It is also our intent that this book of readings be used to add a new existential dimension to courses in the principles of man-

# Preface

agement and personnel management. An existential emphasis should make these courses more relevant and meaningful for today's students.

Finally, this book's structure encourages the student to take a trip with the authors into this burgeoning field, to experiment with new ideas and to relate these ideas to managerial life. The study of management is more than an exploration of great theories or a chilling tale of executive stress. It is also an exciting experience, or, in Hemingway's term, "a moveable feast." This collection is offered in the hope that some of the magic and mythology of the study of management will be transmitted to the student.

We wish you well on your quest.

The article comprising Chapter 1, "In Search of a Paradigm," by Kamran M. Khozan, is an original work printed by permission of Kamran M. Khozan. © Kamran Khozan.

The article comprising Chapter 2, "Systems Thinking in Management Circles," by J. Pierre Brunet, is an original work printed by permission of J. Pierre Brunet. © J. Pierre Brunet.

The article comprising Chapter 3, "An Alternative to Macro-Micro Contingency Theories: An Integrative Model," by Laird W. Mealiea and Dennis Lee, is reprinted by permission from the *Academy of Management Review*, 1979, Vol. 4, pp. 333–45, and by permission of the authors.

The article comprising Chapter 4, "Dreams of Humanization and the Realities of Power," by Walter R. Nord, is reprinted by permission from the *Academy of Management Review*, July 1978, pp. 674–79.

The article comprising Chapter 5, "Management by Objectives: A Critical View," by George Strauss, is from *Training and Development Journal*, Vol. 26, No. 4 (April, 1972), pp. 10–15. Reprinted by special permission from the editor. Copyright 1972 by the American Society for Training and Development, Inc.

Michael B. McCaskey, author of the article comprising Chapter 6, "Goals and Direction in Personnel Planning," would like to thank Fritz Steele, Luise Cahill Dittrich, John Kotter, and Richard Boyatzis for their helpful comments on an earlier draft of this paper. He also acknowledges the support for this research, provided by the Division of Research, Harvard Graduate School of Business Administration. Reprinted by permission from the *Academy of Management Review*, July 1977, pp. 454–62.

The article comprising Chapter 7, "The Design of Work in the 1980s," by J. Richard Hackman, is reprinted by permission of the publisher, from *Organizational Dynamics*, Summer 1978, 7, pp. 12–17. © 1978 by AMACOM, a division of American Management Associations.

The article comprising Chapter 8, "Toward a Paradigm Shift in Selection: The Assessment Center," by A. Bakr Ibraham, is an original work printed by permission of A. Bakr Ibraham.

The article comprising Chapter 9, "Lower Participant Power: Toward a Conceptual Integration," by Richard S. Blackburn, is © 1981 by the *Academy of Management Review*.

# Acknowledgments

The article comprising Chapter 10, "The Poverty of Management Control Philosophy," by Geert Hofstede, is reprinted by permission from the *Academy of Management Review*, July 1978, pp. 45–61.

The article comprising Chapter 11, "Improving Executive Decisions by Formalizing Dissent: The Corporate Devil's Advocate," by Theodore T. Herbert and Ralph W. Estes, is reprinted by permission from the *Academy of Management Review*, Oct. 1977, pp. 662–67.

The article comprising Chapter 12, "The Ideological Character of Organizational Work," by Harry Abravanel, is an original work printed by permission of Harry Abravanel, Bishop's University, Quebec. © Harry Abravanel.

The article comprising Chapter 13, "Mutualism between Management and Behavioral Science: The Case of Motivation Theory," by Craig C. Pinder, is an original work specially prepared for this volume while the author was on leave at the University of Minnesota.

The article comprising Chapter 14, "The Experimenting Organization: Using the Results of Behavioral Science Research," by James A. Waters, Paul F. Salipante, Jr., and William W. Notz, is reprinted by permission from the *Academy of Management Review*, July 1978, pp. 483–92.

The article comprising Chapter 15, "A Behavioral Theory of Management," by Thomas A. Petit, is reprinted by permission from the *Academy of Management Review*, Dec. 1967, pp. 341–50.

The article comprising Chapter 16, "Four Perspectives on Conflict Management: An Attributional Framework for Organizing Descriptive and Normative Theory," by Ralph H. Kilmann and Kenneth W. Thomas, is reprinted by permission from the *Academy of Management Review*, Jan. 1978, pp. 59–68. This article is based upon a paper presented at the 34th Annual Meeting of the Academy of Management, August 18–21, 1974, in Seattle. The authors' names are in alphabetical order to indicate the collaborative nature of this work.

The article comprising Chapter 17, "So You Want to Be an Executive: Be Androgynous," by Monica Belcourt, is an original work printed by permission of Monica Belcourt.

The article comprising Chapter 18, "The Management Theory Jungle Revisited," by Harold Koontz, is reprinted by permission of the *Academy of Management Review*, 1980.

# THE NEW
# MANAGEMENT
# SCENE

Having chosen to study management, you decide to take stock: just what are you getting into? To some the study of management includes useful tips on Machiavellian manipulation, handy mnemonics such as "Management equals POLE" (planning, organizing, leading, and evaluating), and much reading about Battleship X or Company ABC. The more serious student, however, expects to learn how to design organization charts, write role descriptions, formulate policies, and prepare plans. When he has mastered this organizational anatomy and physiology, he will be well on his way to mastering not only the principles, but also the practice of management.

In the 1950s, a course in management—aside from introducing you to Frederick Winslow Taylor, Elton Mayo, and Herbert A. Simon—would have taught you how to slice a problem into its component parts through case analysis. The essential steps would (and still do) include the following: define the problem, specify causes, develop, assess, and select an alternative, and recommend a plan for implementation. This sequence, which is the classical route to effective management, is still appropriate. However, the more recent influence of behavioral science on management education, encouraged by the Carnegie and Ford Foundations, has been widespread in the latter part of the twentieth century. Critics of the behavioral science influence said it took the snap out of the analytical bite. Nevertheless, management benefited from the study of individual motivation, group dynamics, and organizational development. In our zeal, it seems, we had taught the student how to analyze problems into bits, but not how to put the bits together into a synthesis. The last step of implementation had either been ignored or glossed over. To remedy this deficiency, the modern approach tries to find a balance between analysis and synthesis, between task achievement and human satisfaction, between efficiency and effectiveness.

# INTRODUCTION

## THE ORGANIZATION: A GIANT AMOEBA

If you regard an organization as a giant amoeba, how do you figure out what it is going to do?

In the world of organizations, social scientists are employed to make up stories about future events. Such stories are called scenarios. Herman Kahn at the Hudson Institute at Croton-On-Hudson developed the scenario technique as a means of studying the future.

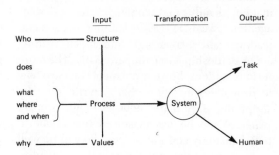

FIGURE I-1 *A Simple Model for the Study of Organization.*

### Creating Scenarios and Inventing Models

A scenario might be described as a narrative describing a probable, possible, interesting, or illustrative sequence of events. These events may be simultaneous or sequential and grouped into a manufactured story, case history, or parable. The purpose of the scenario is to clarify certain points or explore the branch points or decision loci that may exist in a series of events or policies. Its advocates claim that if one relied upon real events only, plausible or obvious implications of a decision might go unnoticed. Both executives and social scientists have a consuming and extended interest not only in scenarios, but also in models and metaphors which simplify the real world just enough to make it manageable.

A model is a relatively simple system that is used instead of a more complex one in order to generate conclusions that can be tested against actual events to come up with a good betting average in terms of successes. To be useful a model does not need to be always right. A theory is expected to be always right. For example, job descriptions and organization charts may be thought of as models which help managers talk about organizational problems.

A useful and simplified model for studying management is shown diagrammatically in Figure I-1.

The model in Fig. I-1 has three input varia-

bles: structure, process, and values. These variables can be thought of as *who* (structure of actors), did *what, where, and when* (process of events), and *why* (values and myths).

### Structure, Process, and Values

Structure describes the political shape of the system: its rules, roles, and relations. If the rules are understood by everyone, the need for supervision is reduced. Roles describe one's expectations in regard to duty and obligation; a person's role is the behavior and attitude appropriate to a particular position regardless of who occupies it. Relations are used to describe how one role fits into another.

While structure is rigid, process is dynamic, and is usually concerned with information exchanges. The management process consists of the following elements: Objective Setting; Planning; Organizing; Staffing; Leading; Evaluating and Deciding (OPOSLED).

The management process begins with the formation of goals and objectives. Plans are developed and performance is measured on the basis of objectives. Planning is concerned with the formation of goals required to achieve a course of action. Organizing consists of preparing organization tables which delineate the relationships of various functions, jobs, and personnel to each other. Organizing also provides a set of roles which must be filled through staffing, which requires recruiting, selecting, training, developing, and directing people in a way that helps the firm achieve its objectives and gives employees a sense of growth and development.

Management measures the degree of success by checking performance against standards and taking corrective action if necessary. This is referred to as the process of evaluation and control.

Decision making ties all functions of the management process together. Systematic decision making necessitates the application of scientific methods and the use of mathematical techniques to make problem solving more precise. Participative decision making uses employee participation and results in a high sense of employee morale and effective implementation of decisions.

Values hold the structure and process of an organization in position and help managers make decisions. The traditional system values science and technology, aggression, achievement, affluence, and alienation. The new existential system values self-actualization, interdependence, participation, creativity and commitment.

To achieve the integration of structure, process, and values for corporate efficacy, a new type of manager is needed, one who can handle the modern corporate problem of free will within a framework of determinism of economic and technological forces. This manager must balance his own needs with his colleagues' needs for awareness, authenticity, and self-expression.

## THE ROLE OF THE MANAGER

A manager is a person who sees his destiny in directing others in important discretionary work, where choice is critical. A manager's work is usually nonroutine, potentially creative, and nearly always profitable. To do this work effectively, two things are required. First, a manager must possess a particular attitude which sets him apart from professionals and entrepreneurs, and which structures his behavior and attitudes so that he sees the world as *something to be managed*. A manager must believe he can significantly change the course of events through his influence in a way that will generate both profit and visibility. Management education seeks to inculcate students with this sense of destiny.

Secondly, the manager must acquire a range of problem-solving skills that have emerged like arithmetical results from the application of the scientific method to organizational matters. The capacity to recognize problems, to develop models with explicit assumptions, to mobilize facts, to separate the essential from the nonessential, and to take action after a careful review of the relevant data, is a complex ability which management education seeks to develop. This means developing a paradigm.

One of the most important issues that has been raised in management is the question of to what extent a management paradigm is applicable across a wide range of organizations. It is increasingly argued that management style in public and private organizations is converging. But it would be facile to believe there are no differences at all. What is being argued is that we must make a more careful examination of the differences; ultimately, perhaps enough data will be available to spell out the actual differences in management style between the private and public field.

## MANAGEMENT THEORY

The most important thing to know about management theories is that every manager carries one in his head. These theories are dependent upon the cultural weather, they tend to be oversimplifications of reality, and they can be a lot of fun. There are three kinds of management theories: classical, human relations, and systems.

One strand of classical management theory called scientific management, and invented by Frederick W. Taylor, introduced the concepts of work study, time study, production planning, and budgetary control. Another strand, administrative management theory, was developed by Lyndall Urwick and Henry Fayol; they thought in terms of defining the objectives, dividing the task into functions, drawing up organization charts, and writing job descriptions.

Classical management theory works very well in the military and in large corporations, but "red tape" can easily cause problems. Human relations theory has attempted to solve some of those problems.

Elton Mayo, whose original research was responsible for the human relations movement in management, was primarily interested in management as it affected the shop floor.

Mayo began to scientifically examine the relationship between productivity and illumination. To test this relationship, he isolated two groups of workers. One worked under constant illumination; the other worked under varying illumination. Production records were kept. Both groups increased their output, because the workers felt somebody was taking an interest in them.

The systems approach to management is concerned with how a system fits together, and how one part affects another. An example of how a system interlocks can be seen in the following situation on a hot summer day in New York. In office suites high up in the glass-windowed skyscrapers stenographers and clerks turn up the air conditioning. The demand for electricity increases, more power stations are needed, more pollution is emitted from the smoke stacks of the power stations, and the office workers demand more and bigger air conditioners. If the skyscraper's office management and the power generation planners try to solve their problems separately, each will face the other with a succession of escalating demands that could go on indefinitely. The systems approach requires both parties to get together and find solutions that recognize the need to build windows that open in tall buildings as well as the need to build pollution control devices into power station stacks.

The systems approach has been widely used in the analysis of organizations. J. Pierre Brunet points out in *Systems Thinking in Management Circles* that the systems concept was developed by a biologist who wanted to treat organizations as open systems. Brunet defined a system as a set of parts which has as its mission the accomplishment of a set of goals. Whether a single-celled bacteria or a multinational corporation, an organization interacts with its environment. Brunet provides the manager with a new perspective, one which will help him see his organization as a system.

## MOVING TOWARDS EXISTENTIAL MANAGEMENT THEORY

The new existential attitude in management theory represents a commitment to rediscover a philosophy of personal value and self-realization, a dream of an ideal organization or community in which individuality will not be subsumed in and sacrificed to "the system", but fully developed and expressed. In a society undergoing future shock, people are turning to existentialism in increasing numbers in an attempt to enhance their personal freedom, to expand their potential for self-actualization, and to make society and its organizations a medium for the full free growth of man.

The student of management must necessarily be interested in what happens when human beings try to break out of the traditionally assigned, prescribed roles in an organization, and develop existential values. For the manager, this process is one of reconciling traditional values with existential values.

Classical Values: Rationality and perfectibility

Human Relations Values: Feelings supersede thinking, openness, awareness, horizontal cooperation

System Values: Gestalt within Gestalt, nonlinear logic, openness

Existential Values: Back to mysticism, magic and mythology in a world of good faith; genuine contact with human perceptions

It is important to note the effort a manager must make to bridge the gap between systems as organization without people and individuals as people without organizations. Human organizations can only operate effectively when the manager has his eyes on the boundary conditions, keeps the organization on course, and mobilizes his full resources. All this can only be achieved when there exists some social contract (commitment) which has been entered into freely with full knowledge of what is implied. Organizations can only fully function as existential systems when human beings are recognized as the critical and decisive elements in the system.

Kierkegaard wrote of an absent-minded professor who was so wrapped up in abstractions about life that he hardly remembered he existed, until one fine morning he woke up to find himself dead. Uneasy as we are about methods of management, we choose to remain as absent-minded as the man in Kierkegaard's story on the crucial question: what is management? One reason we do so lies in the curiously remote position which modern society has relegated to such philosophical questions, leaving them to academicians to ponder. We ask ourselves, instead, whether ideas should indeed be the subject matter of the management student; perhaps our central subject should be the singular experience of the individual manager who claims to be a "practical" man, above all theories. Does this mean we should confess methodological bankruptcy,

pack our bags, and head for the nearest corporation to see what is happening?

But what happens when the student of management is left at the entrance of an organization, with no conceptual system to which he may refer, and with this instruction: be more of a witness than a thinker. Henri Bergson tells us that abstract intelligence is insufficient for grasping the richness of experience. To call intelligence the scientific method, as John Dewey does, is to ignore that deepest center of the human being where fear and trembling start.

There is a curious incompleteness about the present theories on management. Less than a handful have ever really come to grips with the central subject: the manager herself. The meaning of "management" and "manager" must be recast now in terms of the individual, with human faults and shortcomings.

# 1

# Basic Theories of Management

*In Search of a Paradigm*
KAMRAN KHOZAN

## THE PURPOSE OF MANAGEMENT

What is the purpose of management? A medical doctor can tell you with no hesitation that the purpose of medicine is to cure sick people, or a psychologist might tell us that her field of study will contribute to a deeper understanding of the human psyche, and so on.

Is the purpose of the science (or art) of managment social welfare? Good of humanity? Is it a device to help organizations, or the managers within those organizations? Or all of the above? Floyd Allport offers a significant anecdote regarding this question:

At a meeting of the faculty of a certain large university a proposal for a new administrative policy was being discussed. The debate was long and intense before a final vote of adoption was taken. As the professors filed out of the room an instructor continued the discussion with one of the older deans.

"Well," observed the latter official, "it may be a little hard on some people; but I feel sure that, in the long run, the new plan will be for the best interests of the institution."

"Do you mean that it will be good for the students?" inquired the younger man.

"No," the dean replied, "I mean it will be for the good of the whole institution."

"Oh, you mean that it will benefit the faculty as well as the students?"

"No," said the dean, a little annoyed, "I don't mean that, I mean it will be a good thing for the institution itself."

"Perhaps you mean the trustees then—or the Chancellor?"

"No, I mean the institution, the institution! Young man, don't you know what an institution is?' "(1)

To distinguish the significant variables from the insignificant ones in human societies is virtually impossible. However, one significant criteria that all societies—regardless of their particular cultures and traditions—have in common is that of survival: this is the core around which human endeavours revolve. Survival is the deepest and the most primitive craving of humanity.

We can conclude, then, that the purpose of "management" is to help managers survive. Now what about the theories that build a structure around this purpose to support it and help our managers to survive and hopefully prosper?

There are numerous rival theories of management. Each view has its staunch advocates and sworn enemies. Yet these theories are not really rivals at all. They may be different descriptions of the same phenomena, but to choose one to the exclusion of others does not mean that one is correct or true and the others incorrect or false. It simply indicates that one particular theory serves a special purpose at a given time and situation, while others are more helpful at other times.

Let us now investigate, very briefly, what the major theories and points of view are in this field.

## THE SEVEN FACES OF MANAGEMENT

### Management as a Formal Process

Robert Michels proclaimed, "Who says organization says oligarchy." This is what has come to be known as the classical or formal model of organizations, and most of our present institutions are still structured according to this model. New developments in organizational theory are usually assimilated into this structure.

The formal process in organizations has been with us since at least 165 B.C. In China, officials were chosen by examination. Today we have assessment centers that will "scientifically" choose the right person for the job.

After the French Revolution in 1789, that country was immersed in the red tape of bureaucracy, and soon this new political mode was adopted by the Prussians which eventually was formalized by Max Weber whose ideal organization was given the name "bureaucracy".

The dictionary of the French Academy's 1789 Supplement defines "bureaucratie" as "power, influence of the heads and staff of government bureaus". Balzac popularized the word in his novel, *Les employés* in 1836. John Stuart Mill in *On Liberty* (1859) and *Consideration on Representative Government* (1861) compared bureaucracy unfavorably with democracy, concluding that the former is a threat to representative governments.

For Weber, the bureaucracy was the major element in the rationalization of the modern polity. He argued that "increasing complexity of civilization" necessitates bigger and more efficient administrations; this complexity inevitably pushes such administration towards bureaucratization.

Weber's bureaucracy was based on five major principles: 1) division of tasks, 2) hierarchical structures, 3) formal set of rules, 4) impersonality between superiors, subordinates, and their clients, and 5) employment for life, and promotion by merit.

Is management a formal process? Weber told us it should be. Frederick W. Taylor followed his advice and in his attempt to adapt business enterprises to the bureaucratic principles, Taylor created the "scientific management" based on the Protestant work ethic, economic rationality, and individualism.

Based on his actual work experiences at the Midvale Steel Company, Bethlehem Steel Company, and as a consultant to many firms, Taylor formulated specific solutions to the problems of management, including:

1. selecting the right man for the job;
2. deciding by method study on the one best way to do the job;
3. developing differential piecework plans that reward effort;
4. careful planning of the actual work process;
5. developing line and functional specialization. (2)

Taylor's scientific management brought time and motion studies into the work place; he standardized the process of factory work to such an extent that these principles have become part of most of our organizations today. However, scientific management focused on the shop floor worker, while administrative management theory—developed by Lyndall F. Urwick—was directed to the managers and the managerial levels. This change in direction began with Henri Fayol's *Administration Industrielle et Générale*, published in 1916. Fayol divided administrative activities into five elements: planning, organizing, command, coordination, and control.

Following in Fayol's footsteps, Luther Gulick and Lyndall Urwick edited *Papers on the Science of Administration* in 1937. "Integral to Urwick's approach was the paradigm of rationality—the idea that logical analysis rather than personalities should determine how organizations should be structured" (3). Thus we ended up with line, function, and staff relationships within a firm, each with different spans of control in the breakdown of operations and unity of command. All this gave rise to the role description and organization charts that have become an integral part of any organization's setup.

What Fayol started and Urwick perfected, Chester Barnard adopted for his three principles of work and task specializations in an organization. These principles are:

1. Defined roles, promotion by merit, and establishment of informal lines of communication so that formal channels are seldom used.

2. Maintenance of morale through incentives, control, supervision, training, and education.
3. Formulation of purpose and objectives by management and its application to all levels of the organization.

Professor Joe Kelly in *Organizational Behaviour* pinpoints a major factor that is often overlooked by the classical theorists of management. The state of technology dictates the number of workers, the nature of their jobs, and organization of the work and the workplace. Yet, as Professor Kelly so eloquently brings to our attention:

In spite of the complexity of technologies, management theorists have ignored the technological factors in thinking about structure. For many, Weber's idea of a bureaucracy was considered to provide a universal plan for all organizations irrespective of the specific technology. The human relations school considered both the technological and economic factors to be so well developed that they could be ignored. In fact, as anyone who has ever used a copying machine knows, technology has had a tremendous effect on behavioural systems, including the way people think. (4)

The "rational actor" and the "paradigm of rationality", as G.T. Allison calls them, are integral to the classical theory of organization. Allison's basic assumption is that logic, rather than personalities, dictates the structure and process of an organization, which ultimately leads to the illusion of logic in action, and an absence of actors. Goals and objectives are given and the most logically efficient way of achieving them—which minimizes cost and maximizes profits—is thus selected. This system of "rational decision-making" led Alfred Krupp to conclude that in such an organization, nothing should depend on the life or existence of any particular person; nothing of importance should happen without the foreknowledge and approval of management; and the past and the determinable future of the organization should be retrievable from the files (5).

Success in such an organization would, therefore, depend on efficient and controlled use of resources for attainment of the set objectives.

However, human beings are not always rational, nor do they necessarily act in the best interest of the organization. Pecuniary interests are not always of prime importance; the Calvinistic work ethic is, in fact, alien to human nature; profitability does not spell success; tight rules are by nature dysfunctional; poor morale reduces productivity; and finally, goals cannot be of primary importance when the process of achieving them is subject to human interaction. It is true that many people, to a greater or lesser degree, aspire to be as efficient as machines; in addition, many people are conditioned to behave like machines. But we should not forget that irrationality is also a primary characteristic of human nature.

## Management as an Interpersonal Process

It was not as a pious hope that managers turned to human relations, but in the hope both of bringing about a better understanding between management and labour and of reducing frustration and conflict. (6)

The idea of management as an interpersonal process dates back to F. J. Roethlisberger and W. J. Dickson's studies at the Hawthorne plants of Western Electric Company near Chicago. Though the experiments were methodologically unsophisticated and at times quite incorrect, the findings—especially what came to be known as the "Hawthorne effect"—were quite revolutionary in their own right. The Hawthorne study found that increased productivity depends not so much on any particular incentives as on workers' interpretation of change as evidence of management's interest and good will (7).

The Hawthorne experiment was heavily

criticized. Almost sixty years later, we have come to the conclusion that conflict is good for the organization; F. E. Fiedler tells us that the most successful manager is psychologically distant from his subordinates (8). Have the bases upon which this approach to management was built crumbled? Is the human relations approach to management bankrupt? By no means. This is the richest and the most widely researched aspect of management in general, and of organizational behavior in particular.

By now psychologists had become sovereign in the field of management. Theories of management based on the psychology of leadership and motivation have been offered which are based on different psychological schools of thought. But the bulk of psychological investigation of organizations is concentrated on how to manage an organization, how to fit human beings into a group, and how one can function within organizations. Scarcely any attention has been paid by organizational psychologists to the effects of organizations on the society in general and the individual in particular.

In their attempt to investigate the effect people have on organizations, organizational psychologists have labeled human beings as hedonistic consumers, because such a definition suits organizational structures. A different model would not fit the structure of organizations so neatly, and thus would be useless or at least cumbersome to deal with. It does not matter whether the model thus presented is real or a distortion of reality; as long as such a model is practical enough to be manipulated by the management and organizational psychologists, it is used without further contemplation.

Too many organizational psychologists, it seems, have become the instruments of the very organizations they investigate. They analyze how an organization should be flexible in the face of changing environments without taking into account the impact of organizations on the environment. It is, however, the respon-

sibility of organizational psychologists to investigate the nature of that influence.

But how and from where should they start their investigation? From the top of the organization, of course; where else! And there lies the concept of "power," in three categories: economic, political, and cultural.

Organizations define what is to be regarded as normal or desirable within our societies. The values of industrial society that are based on notions of ambition, achievement, acquiescence, and conformity are created and sustained by the dominant institutions in our societies. Educational, industrial, religious, and governmental institutions shape our values of loyalty and conservatism, which are so crucial to the survival of those institutions in their present state. Therefore, those institutions restrict our attempts to see beyond the present social organizations of our societies, and the interpersonal approach to their management is but an instrument for them to achieve goals.

## Management as an Economic Process

Joan Robinson in *Economic Philosophy* poses the question:

With all these economic doctrines, decaying and reviving, jostling each other, half understood, in the public mind, what basic ideas are acceptable, and what rules of policy are derived from them? (9)

She concludes that there exists one "lump of ideology" that remains unchanged over the years, and she refers to it as "nationalism". The very nature of economics is rooted in nationalism, she proclaims (10). This declaration reminds us of the old mercantilists such as Antonio Serra, Gerard de Malynes, and Thomas Mun. But on the other hand, we remember Edgworth who proposed to add up units of happiness, and the neoclassists with their utility functions breaking through frontiers, announcing that "utility knows no frontiers".

Joan Robinson with her discovery has not solved the dilemma, she has only managed to create a new set of problems based on the same old set of problems. From a practical point of view, we can easily observe that the universal benevolance of neoclassicists is measured in terms of National Income Accounts. Now is it a theoretical dichotomy or merely hypocrisy on the neoclassicists' part? Paul A. Samuelson, Nobel laureate in economics, told us that the consumer is "king". John Kenneth Galbraith asks whether that means that the corporation has no power, since "anyone subject to sovereign power can have no power of his own" (11).

But corporations do influence their markets, shape the taste of the consumers, and lobby in the corridors of power. The old concept of profit maximization went by the board when William Edward Rothschild's concept of "survival" crept in, and finally William J. Baumol declared that the objective is to create customers, not to maximize profits. It was left to George Katona to perform the daring feat of bunching all the previous unitary declarations together to produce instead a series of factors or goals that were to be maximized. Profits, sales, market share, liquidity, managerial comfort, and even survival were to be maximized! Survival maximized? It is not surprising that hardly anyone took him seriously. But that does not mean that the same idea was not promulgated over and over again, each time dressed up in a new form. A. Papandreau, in *Some Basic Problems in the Theory of the Firm*, discussed preference functions; he gathered all those factors that Katona had so meticulously placed under the umbrella of "general preference function" and sent the whole package sky high with his notion of "maximization".

The next shot was to be directed at the only concept that had hitherto stayed constant: maximization. This task was left to Herbert A. Simon who shot down the concept of maximization and reduced it to his notion of "satisficing". Now we knew that all those years we were "satisficing," not "maximizing".

By 1965, managerial scientists and economists had begun to realize the following:

Although it is appropriate to consider firms and individuals in them as having objectives, it is not true that these objectives are pursued in the maximizing mode . . . The idea that firms or their decision makers have objectives for which a preference ordering of the states of nature always results in the choice of the most preferred alternative is unrealistic . . . Maximizing is virtually impossible because the information required and the time and money to obtain it are limited. (12)

So much for the assumption of "perfect information". Simon told us that we have "bounded" capabilities and cannot have all the information needed in order to decipher all the alternatives.

The gap between what the theoreticians thought they knew and what the managers were busy doing in their offices was gradually becoming more and more evident. Both the traditional and the new theories of the firm had little to do with reality.

Gradually the whole methodological approach to the study of firms was brought under scrutiny. R. M. Cohen and Richard Cyert in *Theory of the Firm* declared that organizations formulated goals by the "coalition" of certain individual goals of people affiliated with the organization. Therefore, " . . . the decision on the final set of goals of the organization is in some sense a political decision . . . To understand organizational goals it must be realized, first of all, that all resolutions of goals within the coalition are not made by money. Rather, many side-payments to members in an organization are made in the form of policy commitments" (13).

Recently we have begun to look at the firm as a complex organization in which economics plays a major part, but not the only part. The predictive powers of the theory of the firm, according to Milton Friedman, cannot be overlooked. After all, we are dealing with an organization that is allocating scarce resources through a price system, and economics is and will remain at the core of that system. But rigid, theories cannot be applied to the day-to-day functioning of such organizations. At best, they remain a vague shadow of the reality, leaving out many human and organizational variables. A *Behavioural Theory of the Firm*, published in 1963 by Richard Cyert and James March, was the first attempt to move away from purely economic theories of the firm into the realm of organizational behavior and theory. Today, factors such as the value systems inside and outside the firm, its structures, internal dynamics, and the way policies are formulated or evolved, are all considered to be as important and decisive as the economic factors. The firm is no longer viewed as an economic unit only. Therefore, its management cannot be merely an economic process.

## Management as
## a Decisional Process

The recent movement in administrative thought calls forth the image of an antiintellectual, rough-and-ready pragmatist who will maneuver his own life and that of his organizations by his political wit, rather than his logic.

However, Simon still insists on turning the traditional bureaucrat and the semimodern corporate person into intimate bedfellows who believe in the limited capacity of humans to process information in their complex environment where total comprehension of all available information is beyond their grasp. Yet, human beings need order in their lives, Simon tells us, and order, direction, and objectives are outcomes of rational planning. Once "the plan" is ready, human beings will fit into it like nuts and bolts in a machine, and each will do what the plan requires them to do. As such, in an or-

ganizational structure, human beings can be positioned so that they will help the organization to achieve their objectives.

Therefore, the behavior of people within an organization, relative to that organization, and with respect to the overall goals of that specific organization becomes "rational". This "rational" behavior is thus governed by the authorities, but under the condition that one adheres to the rules of the game.

Thus rationalism can pervade the whole organization to the point where individuals within that organization give up creative thinking altogether, and instead let the "fundamental" ways and "routines" guide their actions. Organizations thus turn into factories where the information is fed in and, inside the "black box," (organization's process), the corporate workers stand on each side of the process's conveyor belt, rubber-stamping everything according to the "plan".

## Management as
## an Analytic Process

In order to provide a quantitative and organized approach to management, and to conceptualize an array of activities that an organization encompasses, it is necessary to "analyze" the system, and, in turn—if the system is to be effective in solving the problems and finding alternative solutions according to some standard—select one final solution over the others.

The main element to be considered in such an analytical approach to the management of organizations, especially in the practice of system dynamics, is the organization's structure. That includes the policies, decision-making styles, time lags, information feedbacks, and so on, that come about as a direct result of the structure of the organization. In a system dynamics model, all these variables are put into a cause-and-effect model in the hope that a better understanding of the problems facing the organization will result. This is, of course, a counterintuitive approach to organizational problem solving. This is what has come to be known as a multiple-loop nonlinear feedback system.

People would never attempt to send a spaceship to the moon without first testing the equipment by constructing prototype models and by computer simulation of the anticipated space trajectories. No company would put a new kind of household appliance or electronic computer into production without first making laboratory tests. Such models and laboratory tests do not guarantee against failure, but they do identify many weaknesses that can then be corrected before they cause full-scale disasters. (14)

Herbert Simon tells us that we go through four phases in order to solve a problem or make a decision: finding the problem, finding alternative courses of action, selecting one alternative among these courses of action, and going through a feedback session in order to evaluate our choices (15). Each one of these phases, in turn, consists of many complicated steps. But to simplify the matter, we can say that a manager makes two types of decisions: programmed and nonprogrammed.

The programmed decisions rely on the established routines and standardized procedures that exist in any organization. The nonprogrammed decisions come about when the manager is faced with new and previously unknown problems. Obviously a decision made according to a tested program of action has a better chance of success in the complex environment of today's organization.

Model building is not a new phenomena: human beings have always used this technique in solving their day-to-day problems. The only difference between the mental models of human beings and the programmed decision making of an organization, as Jay Forrester tells us, is that mental models are usually very fuzzy and have not been tested for accuracy (16).

The more complex the organization, the more complex are its problems, and hence the manager becomes an integrator of many parts. In such a position, an analytical approach to problem solving becomes more urgent. However, not all decisions are programmable; intuition, as we shall see, plays a major role in some managerial decisions. Yet one cannot deny the fact that an analytical approach to problem solving becomes more necessary as the organization grows in complexity.

## Management as a Political Process

Rational man is dead, long live the Machiavellian man, Allison cries (17). Very few of the mind-soothing concepts of management against which administration practices were thought to flourish now apply, and much of the background against which those writings were produced no longer exist.

There is much speculation as to what management is now all about. The African chief comes face to face with the vote-seeking, hand-shaking, baby-kissing politician; the politician is at the mercy of the press; the managing director is told that the profit motive is passé; the supervisor is inhibited by the unions; and the headmaster is intimidated by the parents. All around us cherished values change. The manager's dilemma is whether to stick to the old values that she knows so well, or to take "proactive" decisions in order to interfere with an undesired process, and reject all ethical questions completely.

The evolution of the manager's image from shifty-eyed miser to authoritarian leader to person within a system shaking the "black box" to the smiling humanitarian to the twentieth century Machiavellian character (with or without shifty eyes) who shakes the "black box" with authoritarian smile—it makes one wonder if the efforts of social scientists and management experts since the industrial revolution has not been a wasted attempt in describing and prescribing managerial behavior. It seems that we have come full circle. After all, the medieval merchant knew very well what we have just "discovered": that managing is a political game based on the individual bargaining skills of the players. Although the game has become more complex, the nature and process of the play still remain the same.

## Management as an Intuitive Process

In *The Origin of Consciousness in the Breakdown of the Bicameral Mind*, Julian Jaynes tells us—based on recent laboratory studies of the brain functions, and use of some archaeological evidence—how ancient people of Mesopotamia and Peru were not able to "think" as we do today. They were unable to introspect, and were not "conscious" the way we are; when the right hemisphere of their brain wanted to contact the yet underutilized left hemisphere of their brain, these people experienced auditory hallucinations or "voices of gods". These messages told a person what to do in circumstances of novelty or stress (18).

Can we say, then, that if intuition is the "voice of gods", it must be superior to logic, the voice of humans?

Laboratory evidence shows that the right hemisphere of the brain, associated with intuition, solves problems at a much faster pace then the logical, scientific, linear, left hemisphere. The manager is a generalist as well as a specialist; a holistic approach to problems is the trademark of the right hemisphere of our brain. The modern manager works at a relenting pace on a variety of activities, and prefers nonroutine functions, as Professor Henry Mintzberg tells us in *The Nature of Managerial Work*. The manager deals with incomplete information, spending an average of ten minutes on each issue. She has no time for reflection and analysis (19). Thus, everything—time, money,

information—conspire against the left hemisphere of the brain in a managerial job. The manager is forced to rely on her feelings and hunches. Intuition helps bring all the fragmented pieces together, and allows the manager to "see" the whole thing and make a decision speedily and, most of the time, correctly.

Contrary to most approaches to the study of management, however, we are still unaware of any process that could be stated explicity about intuition. Usually the process involves only one person, and there is no documentary evidence to show us the process step by step. All we know is that the bits and pieces of information received are somehow put together and a decision is made. The executive's "gut" feeling in preferring one alternative over another still remains a mystery. She cannot tell us why she has this feeling or why she is so confident about her hunches.

In *The Conduct of Inquiry*, Abraham Kaplan differentiates between the method of inquiry—or, as he calls it, "logic-in-use"—and the hypotheses we make about such a method, the "reconstructed logic". We use scientific methods of inquiry to arrive at a decision, and then sit back and talk about the process we went through (20). Unfortunately, we cannot do this with our intuitive decisions. Thus we have no "reconstructed intuition", only "intuition-in-use".

This is why books on management usually tend to ignore this element in the practice of management. It would turn the definable steps of the *science* of management into the undefinable vague forms of an *art*—and you can never tell an artist how he should do his job.

But, "When we foreswear MANAGEMENT, do we forego rationality?" asks Albert Shapero in an article entitled, "What Management Says and What Managers do." He concludes:

No! Never have we had more need of rationality, but the kind of rationality rooted in observed phenomena. We need to return to a rationality tuned to the natural messiness of life, and not one dedicated to neat abstractions. There are no straight lines in nature, and despite the linearities depicted by MANAGEMENT, there are no straight lines in management either (21).

## THEN, WHAT IS MANAGEMENT?

A formal process, maybe? Interpersonal, hesitantly? Economic, sparingly? Decisional, possibly? Intuitive, shiveringly? Analytical, reluctantly? Political, delphically?

All these theories, dare to confront the depth of the management experience, but to no avail. One can scarcely subordinate theories and the problems they pose, logically, one to another. Each participates in all the others, and they circulate around a common center. That center is the manager herself.

Who is this person who "manages"? What does she do? Mitzberg answered the question by an intensive study of five chief executives. The manager's job characteristics, as Mintzberg states them, are: much work, at an unrelenting pace which is brief, various, and fragmented. The manager prefers live action, is attracted to verbal media, and acts as a contact between the external environment and the organization (22). The essence of managerial work roles according to Mintzberg's findings are:

1. Interpersonal Roles
   - Figurehead
   - Leader
   - Liaison
2. Informational Roles
   - Monitor
   - Disseminator
   - Spokesperson
3. Decisional Roles
   - Entrepreneur
   - Disturbance Handler
   - Resource Allocator
   - Negotiator

So much for the manager. But, is management what managers do? Yes and no. Here we must differentiate between the "business of management" and the "management of business". If, by management, we mean management of business, then what managers do is what management is. However, the business of management has a lot to do with what managers do.

If the business of management—in other words, the academia—has to do with training and influencing managers and thus "management", then the concept of management should also be analyzed from this point of view.

But as soon as we start analyzing management from an academician's point of view, the dichotomy of science and art creeps in. Where should we place management; in the arts or sciences?

All the formulas and theories in the world are of little use if certain elusive and essential human qualities are lacking in the manager. The technical and administrative part can be taught, the human part must be experienced.

The difficulty, however, arises when the very phenomenon to be explained tends to be identified in terms of a current explanatory theory; in other words, by explaining an explanation. For example, there are several theories that try to explain what management is all about and we have reviewed seven of them. But the very term "management" already has certain theoretical and practical connotations.

The student of this field who rejects these points of view would naturally refuse to use the term "management" unless she purposely wishes to be misunderstood. She will have to use some other term. But unfortunately most of the alternative terms have already been used and each carries its own connotation. So how is she to identify what she wants to explain? If she says there is no such thing as "management", she may be misunderstood, although she is not rejecting the phenomenon, but the theory. Yet we continue to make judgments that this manager is better than that manager, presupposing the existence of certain qualities applicable to certain situations and presupposing the existence of a paradigm.

## MANAGEMENT: AN ART OR A SCIENCE?

The academician, as a detached observer, asks: "What is management?" It is not surprising if she comes up with a logical, scientifically verifiable answer, thus turning "management" into a science by asking, then answering, the question. Another manager may approach the question by asking: "Who am I?" or "What makes me a manager?" The answer to these questions cannot be scientific. Here a person confronts her own self, where feelings, emotions, intuition, and style, are involved. She cannot reduce her functions into rigid, cold, empirically proven terminologies. She is most likely to describe her job—management—as an art.

Therefore, study of management is a scientific endeavor; practice of management is an art. Management has a technical and a human aspect which inevitably overlap. Management is, in fact, a human affair, but it is also a job, and a highly technical one.

We know what a good manager is intuitively. She has certain qualities that we feel most managers should have. But what are these qualities? The problem arises when we try to explain an insight that is intuitive.

In order to explain the truism of a paradigm, three things have to be defined: the identity of the phenomenon, its recurrence, and its description. Yet, the element of faith has a lot to do with embracing a new paradigm: not faith in the solved problems, which are self-evident but faith in the future. We may know only that the old paradigm has failed and the new paradigm has resolved only some of the problems; our faith may be in a future promise that could as easily betray us.

Albert Einstein once said that a physical theory was not determined by the facts of nature, but was a free invention of the human mind. If this is true, then we must ask ourselves: "How much of science could be otherwise?" This leads directly to the question of "objectivity" and "truth" in science. Do we "discover" things or "invent" them?

To enhance our knowledge, we choose a method; every choice brings with it a loss—the loss of that which we did not choose. Social sciences, by their very nature, rest on human judgment, and human judgment is rooted in human perception and prejudice. In the absence of a controlled experiment, we must rely on the interpretation of evidence. Statistics based on the pattern of past events might predict the future accurately. But are we *really* sure that the sun will rise tomorrow morning? We have no reason to believe so, except the probabilities we attribute to our past experiences.

A paradigm cannot play the same role in social sciences as it does in other sciences or it will turn into a religious dogma, hindering our vision and our progress.

## REFERENCES

1. Floyd Allport, *Institutional Behaviour* (Chapel Hill: University of North Carolina Press, 1933), p. 3.
2. Joe Kelly, *Organizational Behaviour* (Georgetown, Ont.: Irwin, 1974), p. 61.
3. Ibid., p. 79.
4. Ibid., p. 76.
5. Ibid., p. 79.
6. Ibid., p. 90.
7. Ibid., p. 92.
8. Ibid., p. 91.
9. Joan Robinson, *Economic Philosophy* (New York: Penguin, 1962), p. 117.
10. Ibid., p. 125.
11. John Kenneth Gallbraith, *The Age of Uncertainty* (New York: Houghton Mifflin, 1977), p. 257.
12. R. H. Cohen and Richard Cyert, *Theory of the Firm* (Englewood Cliffs, N.J.: Prentice-Hall, 1965), p. 331.
13. Ibid., p. 331.
14. Jay Wright Forrester, "Counter Intuitive Behaviour of Social Systems," *Technology Review*, 1971, p. 212.
15. Herbert A. Simon, *The New Science of Management Decisions*, rev. ed. (Englewood Cliffs, N.J.: Prentice-Hall, 1977).
16. Jay Wright Forrester, "Counter Intuitive Behaviour of Social Systems," p. 212.
17. Graham T. Allison, *Essence of Decision* (Boston: Little, Brown, 1971), pp. 144–84.
18. Julian Janes, *The Origin of Consciousness in the Breakdown of the Bicameral Mind* (Boston: Houghton Mifflin, 1976), pp. 117–18.
19. Henry Mintzberg, "Beyond Implementation: An Analysis of the Resistance of Policy Analyses," *OR '78*, K. B. Haley, ed., North Holland Publishing Co., 1979, pp. 106–62.
20. Abraham Kaplan, *The Conduct of Inquiry* (New York: Chandler, 1964), pp. 3–11.
21. A. Shapero, "What Management Says and What Managers Do," *Interface*, February, 1977, pp. 106–8.
22. Henry Mintzberg, *The Nature of Managerial Work* (New York: Harper & Row, 1973), ch. 3.

The rapid rise in the popularity of the systems approach in the analysis of organizations of all types—from the lowly amoeba to complex multinational enterprises—indicates that it must be an effective and widely applicable tool for analysts in many fields. Some of these fields are scientific in their orientation, but others are not. The systems approach has become so widely used, in fact, that practitioners and teachers in fields from anthropology to nuclear physics to zoology assume that the notions are common knowledge. The study of management is no exception. We have applied the systems approach to just about everything we can think of, and most of us applaud its usefulness.

Such blanket acceptance, however, often indicates the need to raise a red flag of caution. Surely there are some limitations to consider. Perhaps people in different fields have different notions of what constitutes the systems approach.

We will try to explore these questions in three sections. First, we will define the concept as it was developed by two of its originators; then we will examine current debates and disagreements about this subject in the field. Finally, to put the whole question into perspective, we will give the systems approach a place in the study of management.

Although we will not attempt to make any definitive statements about the subject, we hope to raise a number of issues for the student of management to ponder.

## THE SYSTEMS CONCEPT

The first author who we know viewed the world as a system or an interrelated group of systems is Ludwig von Bertalanffy (1). He explains that in his early years as a scientist studying biology, he recognized organization in organisms. It became useful for him to distinguish between

# 2

# Schools of Management

*Systems Thinking
In Management Circles*

J. PIERRE BRUNET

"open systems" and "steady states". The generalizations that naturally followed from these specific applications became known as general systems theory. Von Bertalanffy first outlined his ideas in a speech in 1937, but because theory was not well received in biology during that time, he did not publish material on general systems theory until after World War II.

The objective of von Bertalanffy's general systems theory was to provide a framework for studying any conceivable level of science, from a single cell to the most complex of societies. His idea was to view every organism as an open system, which means that it interacts with other organisms in its environment. It is obvious that from this point of view, every system is part of a larger one, and so a natural hierarchy develops among systems. The aspect of openness is important in general systems theory. Without openness, the concept loses much of its descriptive power. Interactions with the next higher level system are crucial. Von Bertalanffy has cited several developments that seem intended to meet the needs of a general systems theory as evidence that his thinking was in line with that of other scientists. These are 1) cybernetics; 2) information theory; 3) game theory analysis; 4) decision theory; 5) topology, or relational mathematics; 6) factor analysis; and 7) general systems theory, in the narrow sense (2).

Subsequent to von Bertalanffy's work, general systems theorists developed the notion that the theory was applicable, not only to the natural hierarchy in biology, but also to relationships in any science. This was a departure from the practice of rigidly upholding the barriers between sciences. Here was a sort of science of science, a theory whose postulates held true in virtually any application in virtually any field of endeavour (3). The similarities involved methods of handling information overloads, the crossing of system boundaries, coding of subsystems, feedback, and the transactions of input, throughput, and output. These relationships could be validated in any scientific discipline (4).

## APPLICATIONS TO THE MANAGEMENT OF ORGANIZATIONS

Management thinkers and writers have spent a great deal of time and energy developing applications of general systems theory to their fields of endeavor. It is virtually impossible to read a book on any part of management without somewhere coming across the systems concept. Some groups, in fact, have based their major research efforts on the basic concepts of the systems view of the world. The Tavistock Institute of Human Relations is one such group. The Institute has developed a tool of analysis for organization researchers called sociotechnical systems, which has spawned many developments and other refinements in our thinking about systems.

This sociotechnical system does not limit itself to the technical inputs into an organization's operation. It also recognizes several levels of social interaction among members of the organization, both with each other, and with elements of their particular organizations' environments. Three categories of interactions are commonly identified. These are: 1) The executive system, which includes the formal structure of the organization. Interactions of this type follow the formal hierarchy by using official channels of communication; 2) The representative system, which includes the informal interpersonal relationships that evolve from people in an organization getting to know and like or dislike each other. Unlike the executive system interactions, these are not planned by the organization. They emerge, rather, as a result of people's attitudes, values, and so on; and 3) The legislative system, which groups together all of the outside influences on an organization. Included in this category are interactions with groups such as unions, shareholders, government legislative bodies, consumer advocate groups, suppliers, and customers. These are partly planned and partly emergent, and take their direction from both the executive and representative systems.

Another major effort toward applying the systems concept to organizations is that of Daniel Katz and Robert L. Kahn. Their book champions the cause of the open system approach and looks at virtually every aspect of management from power and authority to health and change, through the systems filter (5).

Before management discovered systems thinking, developments were achieved mostly in the pure sciences, such as biology and mathematics. Hence, the writing became rather heavy with its own particular technical jargon and inside examples. We read about cybernetics and relational mathematics and saw examples that included carbohydrate molecules and second-order derivative functions. The first person to outline the concept in nontechnical terms was C. West Churchman (6). He coined the phrase "the systems approach", which is the title of one of his books. His objective is not so much to defend the systems approach in the book, as to provide a clear statement so that it may stand or fall on its own merit, much along the lines of Karl Popper's suggestion for testing a theory (7). Popper argues that the best test of a theory is to expose it to every conceivable way of falsification, in order to retain only the fittest among them, *rather* than trying to save the lives of untenable systems. Churchman defines a system as " . . . a set of parts coordinated to accomplish

a set of goals". Based on this definition, he specifies that the aim of the management scientist is to spell out the detail of a system, including its objectives, its activities, and its environment. Churchman bases his view of systems on five aspects that analysts should consider, though not necessarily in order of presentation. These are:

1. The total system objectives and, more specifically, the performance measures of the whole system
2. The system's environment: the fixed constraints
3. The resources of the system
4. The components of the system, their activities, goals, and measures of performance
5. The management of the system

He makes rather lengthy statements about each of these, which we may summarize as follows.

A system's objective can be outlined by a management scientist by determining what other goals the system will willingly sacrifice in order to attain the objective. The measure of performance of a system is a kind of score that tells us how it is doing relative to its objective.

The environment of a system is what lies outside the system. Furthermore, not only is the environment outside the system, but "it" is also something that determines in part how the system performs. Churchman suggests two questions that we must answer in order to determine a system's environment: "Can I do anything about it?" and "Does it matter relative to my objectives?" If we answer no to the first, and yes to the second, then it is in the environment.

The resources of a system are inside it. They are the means the system uses to do its job. These resources are typically measured in terms of money, work hours, and equipment.

The components of a system include the rational breakdown of the tasks that the system must perform. Breaking a system down into relevant components helps the analyst determine whether or not the system is operating properly, and what should be done next. It does this by providing information in a form that lends itself readily to analysis.

Finally, the management of a system sets the component goals, allocates the resources, and controls the system's performance. This is in part the control function for the system.

Churchman completes his description of systems with the input-transformation-output view. The transformation part of this model, or the "black box" as it is often called, is a central part of his description. Churchman explains the five steps of the systems approach in terms of their impact on the workings of the black box.

Let us give an example here to clarify the notion of transformations. A general hospital in a large city will serve us well.

In Figure 2-1, we have our hospital viewed as a system with inputs, transformations, and outputs.

Inputs into a hospital are many. They include:

1. Money (from governments, private donations, research-granting agencies, patients' fees)
2. Patients (with whatever types of problems the hospital is equipped to handle)
3. Medical Staff (including doctors, lab technicians, nurses who are looking for work)
4. Support Staff (including orderlies, cooks, maintenance people, clerks, and so on, who will facilitate the work of the hospital)
5. Managers (who will represent the owners of the hospital, and make decisions on their behalf)
6. Suppliers (including drugs, equipment, food, communication systems, and so on)

Transformations are the activities that occur in the black box. For our hospital, they would include:

1. Allocating resources
   - Assigning people to departments and tasks
   - Committing funds to the various sectors
   - Allocating space and equipment to needed units
2. Treating patients
   - Ensuring that each patient receives the care and attention needed to alleviate his problem
   - Allocating drugs and other medical supplies
3. Maintenance
   - Keeping the plant and equipment in good working order
4. Research
   - Developing new machinery, drugs, techniques, and so on, that can improve the level of patient treatment and care

Outputs, or the product of all the work, includes:

1. Treated patients (who are either better off or worse off than when they were inputs)
2. New procedures and/or equipment (which can be adopted by other hospitals in their transformation)

Churchman finally takes the larger perspective and explains that each system is part of a larger system; finally we can envision a complete hierarchy of systems that includes everything we can think of. This is, of course, the basic notion of general system theory: what constitutes the environment of one system becomes an integral part of the next larger system. In our hospital example, we could view the city as the system, and the hospital as that element of the city system that provides health services.

Conversely, we could reduce the size of the system we analyze. We might look at treating patients as a system. In that case, research, support services, maintenance, and so on

TRANSFORMATIONS

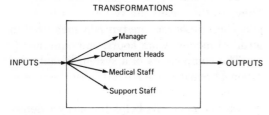

FIGURE 2-1 *The Hospital Viewed as a System.*

would be inputs; we could look at more specific transformations in areas such as neurosurgery, obstetrics, pediatrics, emergency, outpatient care, and others.

Churchman concludes his book by saying that science and the systems approach are really methods of deception about the real world. This deception turns out to be no more than another type of filter on human perceptual processes (8, 9). The filter provides a bias to observers, which Churchman argues is necessary for analysis and opinion-making. His final comment in the book is an endorsement of the systems concept. He says: "And finally, my bias: . . . the systems approach is not a bad idea" (10).

Churchman's work was a major stepping stone on which systems thinking crossed from the so-called pure sciences to social sciences, and especially to management.

## SOME DEBATES IN THE FIELD

One of the points made by general systems theorists that is questioned by critics is the categorization of openness when, in fact, applications seem closed. Systems science, which was spawned as a result of the use of general systems theory in applied sciences, includes three specific fields:

1. System engineering
2. Operations research
3. Human engineering

Often, in analytic treatments of real life situations, users of these concepts will make unrealistic assumptions about the stability of relationships in order to make the pieces fit.

Another difficulty with the approach is its preoccupation with biochemical and biological aspects of phenomena (11). One writer has described a hierarchy that is applicable in the science of science tradition, to the study of the world. The eight levels of his hierarchy include:

1. Frameworks of static structure
2. The clockworks of physics and astronomy
3. The control mechanism or cybernetic system
4. The cell or self-maintaining structure
5. The genetic or plant level
6. The animal level with purposive behavior and self-awareness
7. The human level
8. Social organization or individuals in roles (12)

The problem, say the critics, is that if we are to apply general systems theory to one aspect of a particular science, we may not take advantage of the hierarchical nature of the theory, and concentrate only on the study of analogous phenomena at the same level of development.

We must realize, of course, that because it is a theory with such far-reaching applications, general systems theory is vulnerable to attack from a great many sources and on a great many fronts. Probably the main criticism is that there is no clear and precise definition of "system", which is at the core of the theory. Critics say, in this regard, that it is precisely because of the vagueness of the definition of system that general systems theory seems so universally applicable (13). But any precision would necessarily limit applicability, so the generality must remain. To the extent that precision is lost, scientific reproducibility is also lost, and this—in the eyes of rigorous scientists—is a grave fault.

Supporters, on the other hand, argue that the generality that is deplored by the critics is really not a shortcoming at all. It rather illustrates the almost universal applicability of general systems theory. The argument sounds familiar: a rigorously scientific approach versus broad applicability. It certainly will not be resolved in the near future.

## A PERSPECTIVE FOR MANAGEMENT

While management writers certainly recognize the potential of systems thinking, few agree on its most suitable applications to the field. There is a message in this disagreement, although it may not be very clear. We could rationally assume that each author has his own bias about the most important application of systems thinking, and therefore presents a different perspective. The message, however, is deeper than that.

Could it be that management theorists fail to see the systems approach as a type of metaconcept, one that has a much higher level of applicability than those we normally find in management, such as management by objectives, or scientific management? It seems that two aspects of systems thinking give it this lofty position. First, the emphasis on interrelationships between systems and environments greatly broadens its general applicability. Second, its notions of a hierarchy of systems means that any discipline can be understood within the broad perspective of others in the same family of disciplines. The systems approach, therefore, involves analysis of a hierarchy of interrelationships among all possible systems at the limit. Management, or finance, or fine arts, or politics, or any other field of endeavor fits onto the hierarchy, but does not constitute the whole hierarchy.

Jay W. Forrester's life work began with *industrial dynamics*, went on to *world dynamics*, then to universal dynamics, and now everyone is waiting to see the next step. Perhaps it will be "existence and the system approach."

These lofty thoughts may be fine for academicians, but they do not do much for the practicing manager. Can systems thinking help him? The answer must certainly be yes, but how it helps is another matter. It is probably most useful to him in providing a general framework of how the various parts of his world fit together, but it cannot make his next decision. It is an orientation, a way of thinking, rather than a specific management tool.

## REFERENCES

1. Ludwig von Bertalanffy, "The History and Status of General Systems Theory," *Academy of Management Journal*, December, 1972, pp. 407–26.

2. Ludwig von Bertalanffy, *General Systems Theory: Foundations, Developments, Applications* (New York: George Braziller, 1968), pp. 90–91.

3. James G. Miller, "Toward a General Theory for the Behavioral Sciences," *American Psychologist*, 10, 1955, pp. 513–31.

4. James G. Miller, "Living Systems: Basic Concepts," *Behavioral Science*, 1965, 10, pp. 193–237.

5. Daniel Katz, and Robert L. Kahn, *The Social Psychology of Organizations*, 2nd ed. (New York: John Wiley, 1978), pp. 14–29.

6. C. West Churchman, *The Systems Approach*

(Lasalle, Quebec: Delta Canada, 1968), pp. 29–30.

7. Karl R. Popper, *The Logic of Scientific Discovery* (New York: Harper & Row, 1968), p. 42.

8. Fred Luthans, *Organizational Behavior* (New York: McGraw-Hill, 1977).

9. Edgar F. Huse, and James L. Bowditch, *Behavior in Organizations: A Systems Approach to Managing* (Don Mills, Ont.: Addison-Wesley, 1973).

10. Churchman, *The Systems Approach*, p. 232.

11. Katz and Kahn, *The Social Psychology of Organizations*, pp. 14–29.

12. Kenneth E. Boulding, "General Systems Theory: The Skeleton of Science," *Management Science*, April 1950, vol. 2, pp. 197–208.

13. Ida. R. Hoos, *Systems Analysis in Public Policy: A Critique* (Berkeley, Calif.: University of California Press, 1972).

Now that we have introduced a frame of reference, we begin the exercise of looking at the structural variables of our model, that is, the rules, the roles, and the relations of the management game. Here we are concerned with an overview of the structure or anatomy of the management system. Following our discussion of management theories, essentially four different kinds of structures are considered (See Table II-1). The classical structure is concerned with organization charts, authority, and delegation; the human relations structure turns the classical one upside down and is concerned with participation and "bottom-up management"; the systems structure is concerned with how information is processed and directed; and the contingency structure means that different forms of organization are needed for each type of task; it all depends on the contingency.

Having disposed of the idea of authority which presupposes legitimacy, we turn to nonlegitimate authority, or power. What we are concerned with here is organizational politics, which is exclusively concerned with who gets what, where, and when. The Realpolitik of or-

Table II-1  Four Types of Structure and Management Theories

| Structure | Theory of Management | Characteristics |
| --- | --- | --- |
| Structure of Authority | Classical | Organization Charts Role Descriptions, Line and Functional Management |
| Structure of Affection | Human Relations | Participation, Democracy |
| Structure of Information | Systems | Switches to Connect And Disconnect Information Circuits |
| Contingency Structure | Contingency | Mechanistic versus Organic |

# II

# THE STRUCTURAL VARIABLES

ganizations takes as its point of departure the question "What does it take to succeed in management?" After a swift look at the manager as a political animal, and at cliques and cabals, we turn to the conspiracy theory of organizations.

A useful paradox to keep in mind is that authority and power are in juxtaposition. Both are needed, but they must be kept in balance. Perhaps this section of the book will make managers more aware of how this balance may not only be maintained but exploited to make good things happen.

## THE STRUCTURE

The most important thing a manager should know about how to manage the organizational structure is that firms need different structures at different stages of their development. Classical structure revolves around such practical desiderata as organization charts, role description, and rule books. But to get further into structure in a more fundamental sense, it is necessary to know something about authority. Exercising authority is essentially a study in moral geometry.

The rule with authority is legitimacy, that is, a shared value base exists between the supervisor and subordinate, so that when the boss gives an order, her subordinate's critical faculties are suspended; one does what one is told. Speaking in terse terms, the order is seen as legitimate and credible.

### Two Models of Organization

Business organizations are usually structured either by function, by product, or by area. The basis of this system is the hierarchical pyramid with the presumption that a certain amount of authority inheres in each level. This authority is exercised according to due process and company policy. According to Stanley M. Davis in *Two Models of Organization: Unity of Command Versus Balance of Power*, businesses follow the pyramid model in principle, while in reality they manage things according to the balance of power model.

This structural dilemma raised by Davis creates many interesting paradoxes. For example, there is a paradox generated by having product and area managers whose authorities neither coincide nor are perfectly balanced; the organization deliberately creates such a structure which increases the need for conflict management which in turn means managers must work harder to achieve coordination by working through these conflicts. Davis quotes a brilliant example: Alfred Sloan developed General Motors as a decentralized line operation with the various divisions such as Chevrolet, Buick, and Pontiac; all were decentralized but coordinated through a central policy and centralized staff function. Davis argues for a better balance of centralization and decentralization.

Since the early 1960s, considerable effort has been expended to develop a contingency theory of management which presumes that no one way of managing is right in all circumstances. Now, Laird W. Mealiea and Dennis Lee in *An Alternative to Macro-Micro Contingency Theories: An Integrative Model* have come up with a novel point of view. They developed an integrative model that incorporates both macro and micro variables to assess the interactive relationships between these two levels and how this interaction affects organizational performance. This new model will help managers develop a more useful concept of the relationship between size, structure, and technology of organizations.

It is now necessary to return to the subject of organizational power which is concerned with what happens when the authority breaks down and coercion starts.

## Organizational Politics

There are numerous definitions for the term "organizational politics". One definition centers around the idea of the manager who has an unlimited need for power. Other definitions emphasize the idea of coalitions, or the war among organizations. One early definition focused on the idea of organizations as places where a fight goes on for the allocation of scarce resources. Some insist the term refers to policy preferences. Bronston T. Mayes and Robert W. Allen in *Toward a Definition of Organizational Politics* set out to catalogue a wide variety of definitions of organizational politics and ended up with the concept that organizational politics is the management of influence to obtain ends not sanctioned by the organization or to obtain sanctioned ends through nonsanctioned influence means. The authors then proceed to analyze the management influence process that links strategy and tactics.

The most important thing a manager should know about organizational politics is that they are important, interesting and ubiquitous, and she must learn to love the game of organizational Realpolitik. Learning to love the game means developing not only a successful managment style, but a commitment to success. A manager must develop an intense need for power if she wishes to make her way to the top. There is considerable evidence to support the view that managers with a strong need for power produce superior performance and morale. According to David C. McClelland, this need for power can be developed.

A manager with strong political sensitivities recognizes the importance of forming or joining the right coalitions and realizes that cliques and cabals control both the good things and the bad things in organizations.

## Managing Political Behavior

Typically, we tend to think of political behavior in organizations as being subversive. But, in fact, the modern bureaucratic organization is so powerful that it is able to mobilize, direct, and focus political behavior to further its own ends. As you will recall, bureaucracy strives to maximize efficiency through hierarchical authority relations and the application of calculable rules, all carried through by loyal members of a meritocracy. In developing the theory of bureaucracy, Max Weber expanded Karl Marx's thesis to focus on the means of the administration.

For Weber, bureaucracy is a "power instrument of the first order."

The most decisive thing here is the leveling of the governed in opposition to the ruling and bureaucratically articulated group, which in its turn may occupy a quite autocratic position, both in fact and in form (1).

The basic issue in organizational politics is whether, in fact, the exercise of power can be humanized. Employees want to be treated as ends rather than as means; they want to engage in meaningful challenging work, be encouraged to develop their uniquely human abilities fully, be treated justly and with dignity, and be able to exercise substantial control in organizational decisions, particularly those decisions which affect them directly. So argues Walter R. Nord in *Dreams of Humanization and the Realities of Power*. Nord makes a powerful case for the need to develop organizations in a way such that people can live in them. This means that organizations must be redesigned so that power is exercised in a more considerate way.

Unfortunately, the inner life of organizations is highly competitive. Somehow there must be a degree of power sharing so that employees can live in a more democratic context. Unfortunately, where industrial democracy has been introduced in business, it has always had as its primary objective the increase of efficiency or the improvement of productivity. Nord makes the point that it is necessary for management to come up with a more fundamental solution to the problem of industrial democracy.

## REFERENCES

1. Hans Gerth and C. Wright Mills, ed., *From Max Weber: Essays in Sociology* (New York: Oxford University Press, 1958), pp. 196–244.

This article points out the inherent weaknesses of developing and utilizing contingency theories that fail to integrate both the macro (size, technology, environment ⟷ structure) and micro (structure ⟷ employee behavior) dimensions. We develop an integrative model incorporating both macro and micro dimensions, and describe the benefits derived from a truly total systems perspective.

Since the early efforts of Burns and Stalker (4), Dill (8), and Woodward (44), considerable attention has been directed toward contingency theories of organizational design and behavior. Kast and Rosenzweig (16, p. ix) identify the underlying theme of contingency theories saying:

The contingency view of organizations and their management suggests that an organization is a system composed of subsystems and delineated by identifiable boundaries from its environmental suprasystem. The contingency view seeks to understand the interrelationships within and among subsystems as well as between the organization and its environment and to define patterns of relationships or configurations of variables.

Although current contingency theories are heavily dependent on systems concepts, they have failed to fully integrate a total systems perspective. Van de Ven (41, p. 66) argues that a thorough analysis of the internal behavior of the organization cannot be obtained.

by either focusing upon aggregate structural characteristics of organizations as many researchers have done or (focusing) at the departmental work unit level as some others have. What is needed are theories and research which (a) identify and distinguish the relevant properties of macro and micro organization context, structure, and process, (b) measure and compare the unique structural patterns of departments that are differentiated vertically and horizontally within the complex organization, and (c) examine how these differentiated components are linked together as a macro-organizational network.

# 3

# Structure of Management

*An Alternative to Macro-Micro Contingency Theories: An Integrative Model*

LAIRD W. MEALIEA and DENNIS LEE

Van de Ven only developed his conceptual model to the point of describing characteristics of organizational climate resulting from interaction between the organization and macro components; that is, environment, size, and technology. Consequently, he fails to describe the appropriate employee behaviors given an existing organizational climate.

Luthans and Stewart (19, p. 181) have argued that "a comprehensive theoretical framework for contingency management has been lacking." However, when constructing their General Contingency Matrix, they failed to (a) develop specific examples for stated functional relationships between performance criteria, situational, and management variables; and (b) clearly articulate resulting behavioral requirements, or consequences, for individuals performing within an existing system.

Those researchers interested in the micro approaches to the study of organizational behavior have likewise been guilty of ignoring the work of contingency theorists. For example,

Schneider refers to the failure to link the macro contingency theories with the more micro personnel approaches when he states that personnel specialists "have generally failed to consider the potential effects of the larger environment on the way the organization behaves and the kinds of people it attracts" (37, p. 5). Schneider says:

The purpose in addressing the larger environment issue is to emphasize the fact that jobs and organizations do not just independently exist: They are caused by understandable phenomena. This leads us to the conclusion that organizations operating in different kinds of larger environments will develop different kinds of jobs. It follows that these jobs will require different kinds of people (37, p. 22).

We will develop a model for the integration of the macro contingency theories with the micro level of behavior and illustrate the impact of macro variables on the micro aspects of organizational behavior.

## CONTINGENCY MODELS

To facilitate construction of this model one must describe a number of contingency models that have had a significant impact on current theory and research. The first was developed by Thompson (38) in an attempt to explain how and why organizations behave as they do. Thompson depicts the complex organization as a rational entity that must function as an open (indeterminant) system. In an attempt to reduce the uncertainty which results from interacting with the external environment, the rational organization seeks to isolate, and thereby protect, its technical core. This technical core represents the specific technology utilized by the organization to achieve desired goals. This allows the organization to produce a

quasi-closed (determinant) system when operating its technical core.

Surrounding the technical core are boundary-spanning units which, by definition, interact with the external environment. "The crucial problem of boundary-spanning units of an organization is not coordination (of variables under control) but adjustment to constraints and contingencies not controlled by the organization—to what economists call exogenous variables" (38, p. 67). When describing the external environment to which the boundary-spanning units must adjust, Thompson utilizes two dimensions, stable $\longleftrightarrow$ shifting and homogenous $\longleftrightarrow$ heterogeneous. The structure or design of the boundary-spanning units will be a function of the external environment with which they interact. When considering Thompson's model, one must remember his basic underlying assumption that organizations (and subunits) with similar technologies and/or environments will exhibit similar behavior in the form of structure or organizational design.

In this way, the rational organization (implying the successful organization) structures its boundary-spanning units in response to environmental conditions. Such structuring produces a unique and identifiable organizational structure.

A model similar to Thompson's was developed by R. Duncan in an attempt "to identify the characteristics of the environment that contribute to decision unit members experiencing uncertainty in decision making" (9, p. 313). A decision unit is any formal work group under the direction of a superior charged with the responsibility for attaining organizational goals. What is significant about Duncan's approach is his basic argument that factors both internal and external to the organization will have an impact on the perception of decision unit members. Duncan says that the structure/behavior of a particular organizational unit or subsystem is a function of three things: What happens (a) within the unit, (b) external to the unit but within the organization, and (c) external to the organization.

When describing the environment of the decision units, Duncan utilizes the dimensions, simple $\longleftrightarrow$ complex (the number of factors considered when making a decision and their degree of similarity), and static $\longleftrightarrow$ dynamic (the degree to which relevant factors change). The impact of these dimensions results in different levels of perceived uncertainty by decision unit members.

Lawrence and Lorsch (18), like Thompson, built their model around environmental uncertainty. Based upon empirical evidence they argue that organizational success depends on

the correct levels of differentiation and integration required to adjust to demands within the environment. Specifically, they divide the organization into three subsystems which interact with three external subenvironments. The subsystem/subenvironment interfaces are research $\longleftrightarrow$ scientific; sales $\longleftrightarrow$ market; production $\longleftrightarrow$ technical-economic.

Application of contingency logic indicates that subsystem behavior will be a function of the degree of uncertainty found with the relevant subenvironment. An example would be the sales subsystem responding to the degree of uncertainty found within the market subenvironment. Furthermore, the greater the differentiation between the external subenvironments, the greater the need for internal differentiation. Concomitantly, the greater the differentiation between internal subsystems, the greater the need for sophisticated integration strategies. Only when the required levels of differentiation and integration are achieved can the organization hope to be successful.

More relevant to the development of our model is Lawrence and Lorsch's prediction of varying subsystem orientations (that is, structure, time perspective, interpersonal relationships, and goals) in response to varying degrees of uncertainty in the respective subenvironments. There predictions are presented in Table 3-1.

The model developed by Perrow (28) emphasizes technology as the major determinant of organization structure. Viewing technology as the means employed to transform raw materials into desired goods and services, Perrow describes two specific dimensions of technology. They are the degree of variability of raw materials and the degree to which search procedures (determining required response behavior) are analyzable. This breakdown allows Perrow to describe four distinct environmental situations in which "organizations wittingly or unwittingly attempt to maximize the congru-

Table 3-1   Resulting Subsystem Orientations in Response to Subenvironmental Uncertainty.

| | Low Subenvironment Uncertainty | | High Subenvironment Uncertainty |
|---|---|---|---|
| Internal Structure | Highly Structured | to | Highly Unstructured |
| Interpersonal Orientation | Task Oriented | Relationship Oriented | Task Oriented |
| Time Orientation | Short Term | to | Long Term |
| Goal Orientation | With respect to goal orientation, the potential exists for each subsystem to have different goals because each responds to a different subenvironment. | | |

ence between their technology and their structure" (14). Structure is conceptualized in terms of (a) the discretion of subgroups, (b) their power, (c) the basis of coordination within the group, and (d) the interdependence of groups.

One of the most comprehensive, empirical studies of the relationship between contextual variables, organization structure, and behavior at the group level was undertaken by the Aston Group in England (29, 30, 31, 32, 33). Based on comparative data collected from fifty-two organizations, they found that bureaucracy takes on different forms in respect to different contextual settings; that is, size, workflow integration, dependence, location in terms of number of sites, and operating variability.

Having empirically determined the existence of specific structural dimensions and their relationship to contextual variables, the Aston Group classified the organizations studied on a three-dimensional taxonomy (see Figure 3-1). What is important is that each type of bureaucracy represents a different organizational climate in which the employee must function.

Finally, in an attempt to integrate environment, technology, and structure, Jelinek (15) constructed an elaborate contingency model which incorporates multiple environments and multiple technologies. She argues that infrastructure must accomplish a dual fit by adjusting to both the core technology it protects and the external environment. Thus, the design, or behavior, found within buffering elements will be contingent on (a) interactions with the external environment, (b) interactions with the organizational core, and (c) other internal interactions.

## AN INTEGRATIVE MODEL

When reviewing contingency literature we were confronted with conflicting results and criticisms of research methodology (5, 6, 11, 12, 23, 34, 35, 40, 43), making predictive validity of contingency models suspect. We believe that inconsistencies result from past researchers'

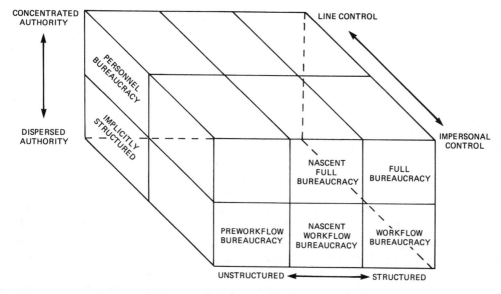

FIGURE 3-1 *An Organizational Taxonomy Based on Structural Dimensions.*

failure to fully integrate micro and macro dimensions. Consider, for example, the prediction of organizational success based on the degree of congruence between external environment, structure, and employee behavior. Eight potential matched pairs actually exist, rather than the two traditionally considered, that is, A-1 and D-1 in Figure 3-2. Here congruence implies that the conditions existing on each level are consistent across levels, that a decentralized structure is congruent with a dynamic-heterogeneous environment. Conversely, an incongruous situation implies that the conditions existing on each level are inconsistent across levels, that a highly centralized structure is incongruent with a dynamic-heterogeneous environment (38).

From these eight matched relationships we can envision situations which would produce conflicting results. Contingency theory predicts that an organization whose structure is congruent with the requirements of its external environment will be successful: conditions A-1 and B-1. However, a researcher studying firms under condition A is likely to obtain perform-

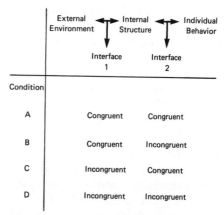

FIGURE 3-2 *Potential Relationships between Micro and Macro Levels.*

ance results dramatically different from results obtained by studying firms under condition B. Although both types of firms have established organizational structures consistent with environmental requirements, only A type firms have obtained the concomitant congruence between structure and dominant behaviors expressed by employees.

For example, assume that two firms (A and

B) have adopted a centralized organization structure in response to a stable and homogeneous environment. Further assume that B's employees tend to be young, aggressive self-starters, while A's employees tend to be followers. Such personnel differences may result from differences in selection policies, firm location, or conditions in the labor market. It is significant that while firm A has achieved congruence on both the macro and micro levels, firm B has achieved congruence only on the macro level. As a result, there exists a conflict state between the dominant behavior of B's employees (aggressive self-starters) and the firm's centralized organization structure. Consequently, while holding other factors equal, firm B is likely to perform at lower levels than firm A (3, 7, 24, 25, 26, 27, 36, 42). Similar conflicting results are likely to be found when studying conditions C and D.

Therefore, to improve the predictive quality of contingency models, it is necessary to consider both the macro and micro dimensions. The following model (Figure 3-3) incorporates both dimensions in a total systems model to overcome the weaknesses of the models described above. Specifically, it assumes that the organization is an open system which actively interacts with its environmental suprasystem through permeable boundaries. In addition, the organization is envisioned as a system composed of interrelated constituent subsystems which both support and are supported by the total organization. Furthermore, the organization's primary goal is survival within its environment.

## Interpreting the Model

When interpreting this model, one must remember several points. *First*, it is assumed that the employee, when performing within the organization, is pressured to behave in a manner consistent with organizational requirements. Based on contingency logic, congruence is required both on the macro level (size, technology, environment ⟷ structure) and the micro level (structure ⟷ employee behavior). Only when this occurs can one expect the organization to perform at desired levels. However, it must also be realized that the employee brings to the organization a unique personality which is reflected in dominant behavior unique to that individual.

*Second*, when referring to employee behavior, we are most interested in the more general types of behaviors which may represent dominant behavioral patterns of the organization's personnel, rather than with technical competence. The general behaviors presented in Figure 3-3 are the critical behaviors which must be congruent with the structure of the organization given equivalent levels of technical competence (2, 10, 13, 17, 20, 21, 22, 39).

*Third*, the direction of predominant influence is from size, technology, environment to structure; and from structure to employee behavior (9, 15, 18, 29, 30, 31, 32, 33, 38). The term "predominant influence" implies that organizations can affect their environment, and employees can affect organizational structure. The stronger direction of influence, however, is from size, technology, environment to structure, and from structure to employee behavior. It is at the structure ⟷ employee level that congruence must be achieved between existing job characteristics, structure, and employee behavior. Congruence may be achieved in three ways: (a) select employees with congruent behaviors; (b) modify existing behavior through training and development or transfers and (c) change the structure of the organization to match the dominant behavior of unit members. Any alteration to the structure of the organization must be made within the limits specified by contingency design in order to match structure with size, technology, and environment.

*Fourth*, the variables utilized under each of the main categories are considered by the contingency models presented above to be the

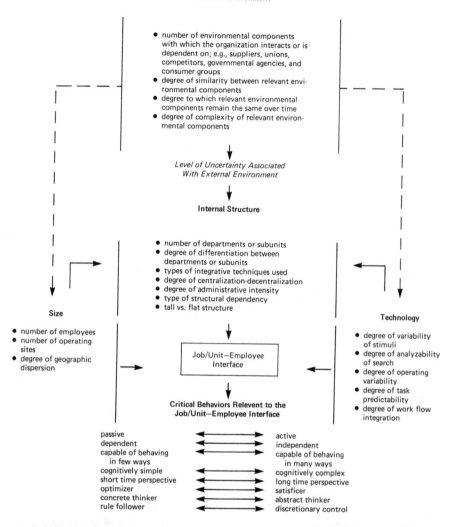

External Environment

- number of environmental components with which the organization interacts or is dependent on; e.g., suppliers, unions, competitors, governmental agencies, and consumer groups
- degree of similarity between relevant environmental components
- degree to which relevant environmental components remain the same over time
- degree of complexity of relevant environmental components

*Level of Uncertainty Associated With External Environment*

Internal Structure

- number of departments or subunits
- degree of differentiation between departments or subunits
- types of integrative techniques used
- degree of centralization-decentralization
- degree of administrative intensity
- type of structural dependency
- tall vs. flat structure

Size
- number of employees
- number of operating sites
- degree of geographic dispersion

Job/Unit—Employee Interface

Technology
- degree of variability of stimuli
- degree of analyzability of search
- degree of operating variability
- degree of task predictability
- degree of work flow integration

Critical Behaviors Relevent to the Job/Unit—Employee Interface

| | |
|---|---|
| passive | active |
| dependent | independent |
| capable of behaving in few ways | capable of behaving in many ways |
| cognitively simple | cognitively complex |
| short time perspective | long time perspective |
| optimizer | satisficer |
| concrete thinker | abstract thinker |
| rule follower | discretionary control |

FIGURE 3-3 *A Total Systems Model of the Organization's Macro-Micro Elements.*

most relevant. We do not imply that the variables used represent a final or complete listing. Nevertheless, we believe that these variables are sufficient to demonstrate how a total systems model functions, and how the macro and micro levels can and should be integrated.

A more important issue in the operationalization of the present model is how to handle inconsistencies within and between categories, that is, when either dimensions within categories, or categories themselves, are opposite one another. Although considerable progress has been made in developing operational measures of the relevant situational and organizational variables, significant inconsistencies in research findings remain and there are criticisms of methodologies used. Further work is required in order to construct an operational taxonomy of relevant variables that effectively defines and measures these variables. If this occurs, it is possible that several dimensions utilized in the present model may collapse together empirically and lead toward a simplified model.

A simplified model could then be tested empirically. If the results are in conflict with the model's predictions, it will be necessary to consider whether the theory/model is incorrect, or whether the firms being studied have applied the model incorrectly. When considering the second possibility, it should be remembered that if a firm has achieved a satisfactory level of performance, applying the model incorrectly, higher levels of performance can be achieved if the model is applied correctly. However, if dimensions or categories are found to be opposite one another (negatively correlated), it would be necessary to treat each as a separate independent variable in making (and testing) predictions across levels.

*Finally*, the reader should not interpret the model to imply that all organizations possess a monolithic or homogeneous structure. Instead, the model should be viewed as one condition of a set of possible conditions which may exist within the organization. For example, organizational subsystems may face different environments or utilize different technologies. Given such internal differentiation it would be appropriate to construct a unique Figure 3-3 for each subsystem. This approach would be most applicable when confronted with a mixed organizational design (39). However, the discussion of such complexities is beyond the scope of this paper.

At this point, based upon existing contingency theory and research, it is possible to substitute specific environmental, technological, and size characteristics into the conceptual model (Figure 3-4). Because of the large number of variables listed, and the potentially large number of possible combinations, we describe only one particular situation. This will be sufficient to demonstrate the relevance of a total systems perspective that incorporates both

macro and micro levels and to illustrate possible implications for managers and researchers. We consider a situation in which the organization is large, the environment is uncertain, and the organization's technological base is continually changing. The relevant materials entering the organization's technological process are varied and complex (see Figure 3-4).

---

## An Example

The basic problems in this example are (a) obtaining congruence between size, technology, environmental uncertainty, and organization structure and (b) obtaining congruence between organization structure and dominant employee behavior. For congruence on the macro level, the internal structure would have to reflect the characteristics listed under "Internal Structure." The selection of these structural characteristics is based on the contingency models discussed above. Therefore, what remains is to determine what employee behaviors are congruent with existing structural, technological, and size characteristics. It is possible, for explanatory purposes, to select the appropriate employee behaviors from those listed in Figure 3-3.

*First*, as depicted in Figure 3-4, the internal situation can be described as dynamic and uncertain, with a complex and varied technology. In such a situation, only those individuals who are (a) active, (b) capable of behaving in many ways, and (c) capable of independent action can hope to effectively monitor and adjust to their surroundings. Because the internal situation is complex, changing, and uncertain, only employees who can deal with abstractions and are cognitively complex will be able to cope with the varied inputs likely to be received. Without this ability, effective decision making cannot occur within this type of environment.

*Second*, it can be argued that when the internal situation is dynamic and uncertain,

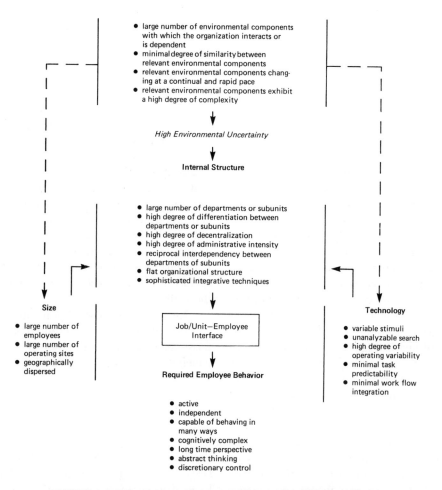

External Environment

- large number of environmental components with which the organization interacts or is dependent
- minimal degree of similarity between relevant environmental components
- relevant environmental components changing at a continual and rapid pace
- relevant environmental components exhibit a high degree of complexity

*High Environmental Uncertainty*

**Internal Structure**

- large number of departments or subunits
- high degree of differentiation between departments or subunits
- high degree of decentralization
- high degree of administrative intensity
- reciprocal interdependency between departments of subunits
- flat organizational structure
- sophisticated integrative techniques

**Size**

- large number of employees
- large number of operating sites
- geographically dispersed

Job/Unit—Employee Interface

**Technology**

- variable stimuli
- unanalyzable search
- high degree of operating variability
- minimal task predictability
- minimal work flow integration

**Required Employee Behavior**

- active
- independent
- capable of behaving in many ways
- cognitively complex
- long time perspective
- abstract thinking
- discretionary control

FIGURE 3-4 *A Contingency Example Utilizing a Total Systems Model.*

with a complex and varied technology, meaningful feedback will likely be both minimal and infrequent. If this is true, then what is needed are employees who have a long time perspective and as a result can deal effectively with such ambiguity.

*Third,* it is frequently argued that in an environment matching the one described in Figure 3-4, a satisfying approach to decision making is appropriate. This is because the organizational system by definition, is an open system and, as such, prevents individuals from

being completely aware of all relevant information or controlling all relevant variables. Therefore, it follows that what is needed are individuals who can engage in, and effectively carry out, decision-making strategies consistent with the satisficing requirements of the situation.

*Finally,* in a dynamic, uncertain internal situation in which a varied and complex technology is employed it is desirable to have decisions made at the point of richest information. Consequently, employees will frequently be called on to make on-the-spot decisions. Such a decentralized environment requires individuals capable of handling discretionary control.

## Congruence Must Exist

Congruence must exist between the characteristics of the internal situation and the dominant behaviors of the employees performing within that environment. Given the example presented in Figure 3-4, behaviors which fall to the right of the continua in Figure 3-3 would produce a congruent state, while behaviors on the left of the continua would produce an incongruent state. Incongruencies are likely to produce dysfunctional consequences for the organization.

Similar arguments could be developed with an internal situation characterized by stability and certainty, with a simple and unidimensional technology. However, with such a bureaucratic environment, behaviors to the left of the continua in Figure 3-3 would now produce a congruent state, while behaviors to the right would produce an incongruent state. Again, incongruencies will result in dysfunctional consequences for the organization.

We are suggesting congruence between three levels of the organization: (a) the environment, size, technology level; (b) the structural level; and (c) the work unit-employee level. Unfortunately, the macro contingency theorists focus on the congruence between the first two levels, while the micro theorists have concentrated on the unit level (individual, small group, and task). The understanding of organizational behavior will not advance if we are concerned exclusively with *one* of the following: (a) correlation of organization structure, technology, and so on, with gross organizational performance levels—thus negating the human element; or (b) correlation between the characteristics of the individual and task performance—thus negating the possible moderat-ing impact of organization structure, technology, and so on, on task performance.

We have attempted to specify a sample list of general behaviors that might be important in the linking of macro and micro orientations. What is really needed is a behavior taxonomy that specifies the individual-task component interaction behaviors required to perform a job. This goes along with a description of the structure ⟷ individual interactions that moderate the effectiveness of the same task behaviors in different organizational contexts. We contend that an individual may be perfectly capable of performing a task under a particular set of organizational conditions, but that the same individual's behavior patterns may not be successful in a second situation. The literature of both macro and micro theorists has failed to specify the dynamics of the interaction between these three levels.

Nevertheless, based upon the conceptual model and arguments presented above, it is possible to develop a number of propositions which can act as a guide to future research and theory development.

*Proposition 1.0*—Level of organizational success will depend on congruence between both the external environment and internal structure and internal structure and dominant employee behavior patterns.

*Proposition 1.1*—The greatest likelihood of desired levels of organizational success will occur when congruence exists on both the macro and micro levels.

Success refers to long-run organizational performance or growth measured in terms of some quantifiable variable, such as profits, number of new products introduced, market share, and so on. The actual variable used should be situationally based, a function of the industry, organization, or unit studied. Short-run, or static, performance would be an inappropriate measure because an organization may be capable of appearing successful in the short run by exploiting its environment, but such behavior will likely cause decreasing effectiveness as the impact of exploitation permeates the system. Also important is the fact that long-run performance will more accurately reflect the degree to which the desired balance has been achieved between (a) the goals sought by the organization's interrelated subsystems and total organizational goals, and (b) employee needs and organizational needs. We believe that long-run balance in both areas is critical to long-run performance.

Measured success represents some point on a continuous range of possible values, not a simple success-failure dichotomy. We argue that the highest levels of success will occur when there is congruence on both the macro and micro levels. Once the organization moves from this optimum state, the actual level of measured success decreases.

When attempting to utilize a long-run measure of success, one must study the longitudinal relationship between congruence and performance. This is necessary because (a) there is likely to be a lag between actual performance levels and the point at which congruence (or incongruence) was obtained; (b) the more consistently the state of congruence is maintained, the higher the levels of long-run performance; and (c) congruence, and therefore success, will reflect the organization's ability to alter macro-micro characteristics when adjusting to changes in its environment (that is, static to dynamic), the flow of new ideas which are necessary for continued growth, or increased levels of employee expertise.

*Proposition 2.0*—Individuals who are required to function within a dynamic, complex, and decentralized organizational situation should possess those dominant behaviors which fall to the right of the continua in Figure 3-3.

*Proposition 2.1*—Individuals who are required to function within a stable, simplistic, and centralized organizational situation should possess those dominant behaviors which fall to the left of the continua in Figure 3-3.

*Proposition 3.0*—Individuals who utilize a complex and varied technology as part of their task, or job responsibilities, should possess those dominant behaviors which fall to the right of the continua in Figure 3-3.

*Proposition 3.1*—Individuals who utilize a simplistic and unidimensional technology as part of their task, or job responsibilities, should possess those dominant behaviors which fall to the left of the continua in Figure 3-3.

We differentiate between structural characteristics and technology (task) characteristics because we believe that the interface between technology and dominant employee behaviors may be more direct than the interface between structural characteristics and dominant employee behaviors. In fact, they may both act independently. Therefore, it is possible for the technology utilized to mediate the impact of structure on the employee.

*Proposition 4.0*—Given an adequate source of potential employees, the most efficient means of achieving congruence on the micro level will be through the selection process.

*Proposition 4.1*—Given the lack of an adequate source of potential employees, the most efficient means of achieving congruence on the micro level will be through employee orientation and training programs.

*Proposition 4.2*—Where possible the organization can reorganize its internal structure to produce congruence on the micro level. However, the ability to obtain congruence on the micro level by altering structure is limited by the concomitant need to maintain congruence on the macro level.

*Proposition 5.0*—Given the underlying assumptions of contingency theory and the increased dynamics of the external environment, it will be necessary to periodically reassess the match on both the macro and micro levels.

## CONCLUSIONS

We cannot become preoccupied with simply designing organizations to match the demands of the environment. We must also match the design of the organization to the workers. The problem is how to achieve this congruence. Figure 3-3 lists possible behaviors that are to be matched with appropriate structural conditions in our model. Then the manager's job becomes one of either (a) selecting, training, and developing these appropriate behaviors, or (b) changing the structure of the organization. We believe there is a range of or limit to the degree of restructuring permissible before the structure becomes incongruent with the environment. Any changes to the structure should be made only if the fit with the environment is not affected.

The areas of selection and training seem to hold the greatest possibility for achieving a fit. If we are able to specify the behaviors that are effective in performing a task within a particular organizational context, then we can design a training program to modify employee behaviors. However, one might argue that the behaviors listed in Figure 3-3 are of the type most resistant to change, especially if one views them as dominant behavior patterns.

The greatest hope for the matching of individual, structure, and task lies in the area of selection. Unfortunately, personnel staffing specialists tend to select employees without giving macro variables much consideration (37). Traditional selection models have been concerned with establishing a relationship between some criterion of performance and a set of predictor variables. The set of predictor variables is selected either by chance or through an analysis of the tasks comprising the job. Little attention is given to how the structural variables might moderate the performance of the task.

The addition of structural variables in selection strategies would have the following potential effects: (1) Selection specialists would become more concerned with understanding why and how individual, task, and macro variables interact to determine levels of task performance. This should moderate the "prediction at all costs" emphasis of selection research. (2) The long-range benefits of understanding how and why certain behaviors are effective in certain situations and not in others would lead to a more comprehensive theory of organizations, and in the end the precision of our predictions about behavior will also increase. (3) We should be able to specify the structural conditions under which a particular individual's behavior would be effective. We would no longer be unable to explain why a valid selection device in one organization proved to be invalid in a second organization even though the tasks performed were identical.

More research is needed that incorporates both macro and micro variables to assess the interactive relationships between the two levels and how this interaction affects organizational performance. It would also be necessary for such studies to be longitudinal in order to more effectively assess what happens to these relationships over time. Arguments about which approach is more correct will not really bridge the gap between macro and micro theorists (14). Therefore, researchers must develop a total systems perspective that will specify those individual behaviors which are congruent with given structural, technological, and size characteristics, and which in turn are congruent with the complexity/dynamics of the external environment.

# REFERENCES

1. Aldrich, H. E. "Technology and Organizational Structure: A Reexamination of the Findings of the Aston Group," *Administrative Science Quarterly*, Vol. 17 (1972), 26–42.

2. Argyris, C. "Personality and Organizational Theory Revisited," *Administrative Science Quarterly*, Vol. 18 (1973), 141–167.

3. Brief, A., and R. Aldag. "Employee Reactions to Job Characteristics: A Constructive Replication," *Journal of Applied Psychology*, Vol. 60 (1975), 182–186.

4. Burns, T., and G. M. Stalker. *The Management of Innovation* (London: Tavistock, 1961).

5. Child, J. "Organization Structure and Strategies of Control: A Replication of the Aston Study," *Administrative Science Quarterly*, Vol. 17 (1972), 163–177.

6. Child, J. "Predicting and Understanding Organization Structure," *Administrative Science Quarterly*, Vol. 18 (1973), 168–185.

7. Coburn, D. "Job-Worker Incongruence: Consequences for Health," *Journal of Health and Social Behavior*, Vol. 16 (1975), 198–212.

8. Dill, W. R. "Environment as an Influence on Managerial Autonomy," *Administrative Science Quarterly*, Vol. 3 (1958), 409–443.

9. Duncan, R. "Characteristics of Organizational Environment and Perceived Environmental Uncertainty," *Administrative Science Quarterly*, Vol. 17 (1972), 313–327.

10. Filley, A. C., R. J. House, and S. Kerr. *Managerial Process and Organizational Behavior* (Glenview, Illinois: Scott, Foresman, 1976).

11. Ford, J. D., and J. W. Slocum. "Size, Technology, Environment and the Structure of Organizations," *Academy of Management Review*, Vol. 2 (1977), 561–575.

12. Gillespie, D. F., and D. S. Mileti. "Technology and the Study of Organizations: An Overview and Appraisal," *Academy of Management Review*, Vol. 2 (1977), 7–16.

13. Harrison, E. F. *The Managerial Decision-Making Process* (Boston: Houghton Mifflin, 1975).

14. Hunt, J. E., and L. L. Larson. *Leadership: The Cutting Edge* (London: Feffer and Simons, 1977).

15. Jelinek, M. "Technology, Organizations, and Contingency," *Academy of Management Review*, Vol. 2 (1977), 17–25.

16. Kast, F. E., and J. E. Rosenzweig. *Contingency Views of Organization and Management* (Chicago: Science Research Associates, 1973).

17. Katz, D., and R. L. Kahn. *The Social Psychology of Organizations* (New York: John Wiley, 1966).

18. Lawrence, P. R., and J. W. Lorsch. *Organization and Environment: Managing Differentiation and Integration* (Homewood, Illinois: Richard D. Irwin, 1967).

19. Luthans, F., and T. I. Stewart. "A General Contingency Theory of Management," *Academy of Management Review*, Vol. 2 (1977), 181–195.

20. March, J., and H. Simon. *Organizations* (New York: John Wiley, 1958).

21. Mealiea, L. W. "Learned Behavior: The Key to Understanding and Preventing Employee Resistance to Change," *Group and Organization Studies*, Vol. 3 (1978), 211–223.

22. Mealiea, L. W. "The Interaction Between Two Personality Types and Intraorganizational Differences in Structuredness and Its Effect on Individual Mobility, Satisfaction-Dissatisfaction, and Perception of Structuredness," *Dissertation Abstracts*, Vol. 33A, No. 9, March 1973, 4608A.

23. Mohr, L. B. "Organizational Technology and Organizational Structure," *Administrative Science Quarterly*, Vol. 16 (1971), 444–459.

24. Morse, J. J., and J. W. Lorsch. "Beyond Theory Y," *Harvard Business Review*, Vol. 48 (May–June 1970), 61–68.

25. Morse, J. J., and D. Young. "Personality Development and Task Choices: A Systems View," *Human Relations*, Vol. 26 (1973), 307–324.

26. Mullen, J. H. "Personality Polarization as an Equilibrium Force in a Large Organization," *Human Organization*, Vol. 25 (1966), 330–338.

27. O'Reilly, C. A. "Personality-Job Fit: Implications for Individual Attitudes and Performance," *Organizational Behavior and Human Performance,* Vol. 18 (1976), 36–46.

28. Perrow, C. *Organizational Analysis: A Sociological Perspective* (Belmont, California: Wadsworth, 1970).

29. Pheysey, D. C., et al. "Influence of Structure at Organizational and Group Levels," *Administrative Science Quarterly,* Vol. 16 (1971), 61–73.

30. Pugh, D., et al., "A Conceptual Scheme for Organizational Analysis," *Administrative Science Quarterly,* Vol. 8 (1963), 289–315.

31. Pugh, D., et al., "Dimensions of Organization Structure," *Administrative Science Quarterly,* Vol. 13 (1968), 65–105.

32. Pugh, D., et al., "The Context of Organizational Structure," *Administrative Science Quarterly,* Vol. 14 (1969), 91–144.

33. Pugh, D., et al , "An Empirical Taxonomy of Structures of Work Organizations," *Administrative Science Quarterly,* Vol. 14 (1969), 115–126.

34. Reimann, B. C. "On the Dimensions of Bureaucratic Structure: An Empirical Reappraisal," *Administrative Science Quarterly,* Vol. 18 (1973), 462–476.

35. Reimann, B. C. "Dimensions of Structure in Effective Organizations: Some Empirical Evidence," *Academy of Management Journal,* Vol. 17 (1974), 693–708.

36. Robey, D. "Task Design, Work Values, and Worker Response: An Empirical Test," *Organizational Behavior and Human Performance,* Vol. 12 (1974), 264–273.

37. Schneider, B. *Staffing Organizations* (Pacific Palisades, California: Goodyear, 1976).

38. Thompson, J. D. *Organizations in Action* (New York: McGraw-Hill, 1967).

39. Tosi, H. L., and S. J. Carrol. *Management Contingencies, Structure and Process* (Chicago, Illinois: St. Clair, 1976).

40. Tosi, H. L., et al. "On the Measurement of the Environment: An Assessment of the Lawrence and Lorsch Environment Uncertainty Questionnaire," *Administrative Science Quarterly,* Vol. 18 (1973), 27–36.

41. Van de Ven, A. H. "A Framework for Organization Assessment," *Academy of Management Review,* Vol. 1 (1976), 64–78.

42. Wanous, J. "Individual Differences and Reactions to Job Characteristics," *Journal of Applied Psychology,* Vol. 59 (1974), 616–622.

43. White, P. E. "Intra and Inter Organizational Studies: Do They Require Separate Conceptualizations?" *Administration and Society,* Vol. 6 (1974), 107–152.

44. Woodward, J. *Industrial Organization: Theory and Practice* (London: Oxford University Press, 1965).

For several decades American organizational psychologists have dreamed of and sought to create humanized organizations. While it is not clear exactly what a humanized organization is, various writers seem to agree that in humanized organizations members are: (a) treated as ends rather than as means; (b) engaged in meaningful, challenging work; (c) encouraged to develop their uniquely human abilities fully; (d) treated justly and with a dignity which places them well above the nonhuman aspects of organization; and (e) able to exercise substantial control in organizational decisions—particularly those decisions which affect them directly.

As writers have dreamed of organizations which would be characterized by at least some of these features, often they have appeared to assume that such organizations would be easy to develop. Optimists have come to see them as inevitable, whereas many of the pessimists see humanized organization as requiring only the enlightenment of managers. Recently these dreams seemed sound because organizations appeared to need these very characteristics if they were to be effective and to survive.

A number of things pointed towards the necessity for more humanized organizations. Bennis (4) noted some of these including: (a) the exponential growth of science; (b) turbulent environments; (c) a younger, more mobile, better educated work force; (d) a growth in the confluence between persons of knowledge and persons of power; (e) a change in managerial philosophy towards the emphasis on a new concept of humanity based on complex and shifting needs; (f) a new concept of power based on collaboration and reason; and (g) new organizational values based on humanistic-democratic ideals. As Bennis and Nord (4, 16) have observed, humanized organizations have been slow to develop.

Why have organizations been so resistant to humanization? There is no simple answer,

# 4

# Organizational Politics

*Dreams of Humanization and the Realities of Power*

WALTER R. NORD

but some valuable insights can be gained by exploring the role that power and political processes play in the dynamics of organizations.

The working definition of *power* used here is derived from the work of Adams (2) and Bachrach and Baratz (3). *Power is the ability to influence flows of the available energy and resources towards certain goals as opposed to other goals.* Power is assumed to be exercised only when these goals are at least partially in conflict with each other. Given this conceptualization, humanizing organizations can be accomplished by altering the flow of resources and energy so that at least some of the five aspects of humanization listed above are given increased emphasis.

The quest for humanized organizations can be broken in two parts. First, consider the design of systems in which the achievement of humanized goals and organizational success on traditional criteria of effectiveness are mutually supportive. Secondly, consider those cases where the two sets of outcomes are in conflict. It is this second set of cases where consideration of power provides insights into why organizations have remained so resistant to power sharing, to just and dignified treatment of individuals, and to the provision of challenging and growth-producing work. Examination of four postulates about power and organizations will help to focus on some of these constraints.

P1:  *Organizations are composed of coalitions which compete with one another for resources, energy, and influence.*

Organizations are a mixture of common goals, individual goals, and subgroup goals. Conflict among competing parties for resources and energies is seldom completely resolved, and the conflicting parties are often arrayed in a number of coalitions.

As Zaleznik (23) argued, competition to become a dominant coalition (or part of one) is an intense and an important feature of life in organizations. Moreover, competing coalitions are often engaged in what approach zero-sum games. If one coalition exercises dominant control over resources and the allocation process, other coalitions cannot. Sometimes these struggles are reflected in what appear to be the palace revolts which result in the ouster of top level corporate officials, but, as Zaleznik showed, the struggles are often more subtle and less spectacular. While more information about the magnitude and frequency of these conflicts is needed, the climates created by such struggles are not likely to be conducive to the achievement of humanized ends of justice, dignity, and so on.

The focus on organizations as coalitions highlights some other constraints upon humanization. In particular, we discover why turbulent environments have not had the straightforward effects of humanizing organizations which have often been assumed. Following the strategic contingencies theory of organizational power developed by Hickson et al. (10) and Hinnings et al. (11), it is clear that changes in the environment affect the balance of power among the various coalitions within the organization, because skills and/or resources which were highly valued become less important. Other skills and resources which were once unimportant become highly valued. Participants whose power is threatened are apt to respond defensively and/or aggressively; those who have gained power are apt to seek to consolidate their position. Consequently, the response of the total organization is not the rational adaptation of a harmonious system, but is the resultant vector of conflicting interests, distorted information, and struggle.

Contrary to the beliefs of some organizational behaviorists, because rapidly changing environments introduce power struggles within organizations, turbulent environments may be in conflict with humanizing organizations. The more turbulent the environment, the more pervasive and strong the resulting internal strife may be. There is little reason to expect that the warring parties will treat each other in humanized ways, and the scars, particularly when the resources and rights of one or more parties have been reduced or eliminated, are apt to be slow to heal.

> *Various coalitions will seek to protect their interests and positions of influence by moderating environmental pressures and their effects.*

It is typically assumed that rapidly changing environments humanize organizations because they induce deroutinization and, consequently, create the need for a large number of organizational participants to exercise greater discretion and to use a wide variety of their skills and talents. Thompson's (22) analysis suggests that, while increased discretion may occur, such increases will not be pervasive because members of the dominant coalition are often effective in routinizing the organization's core technology and protecting it from fluctuations in the environment. While there may be *an increase in size of the dominant coalition,* if the core technology is adequately buffered, the change in the environment may affect very few people.

For example, consider an automobile firm facing changes in materials, governmental regulations, and consumer preferences. The effects of these changes are frequently absorbed by engineering and other technical adjustments. There is, at best, a small chance that operatives on the assembly line will experience significantly more variety in their work or exercise more discretion. Members of dominant coalitions, operating under the norms of rationality, are motivated to limit the discretion of lower level participants in order to avoid disruptions in the operation of core technologies. Thus, while turbulent environments may force the dominant coalition to dilute its power slightly, there is no assurance that this dilution will humanize the work of all or even most people.

P3:  *The unequal distribution of power itself has nonhumanizing effects.*

The unequal distribution of power itself stimulates outcomes which are contrary to many of the characteristics of humanized organizations. Some of these outcomes stem from the influence of power inequalities on the powerful; others are due to the influence of power inequalities on the less powerful.

## THE POWERFUL

Thompson (22) noted that the dominant coalition frequently attempts to design structures which reduce the discretion of lower level participants. Often, the discretion of lower level participants is limited by explicit decisions made by those in authority. As political scientists such as Bachrach and Baratz (3) suggested, one of the most significant advantages the powerful have is the power of nondecision—the ability to suppress and/or thwart challenges by preventing an issue from being considered

subject to a decision. Movement towards humanized organizations frequently will require that issues handled by nondecision in the past are negotiated in the future. As the history of trade unionism documents, such a process is often bitter, and the humanized outcomes are by no means inevitable.

In addition to the effect of reducing the ability of individuals to control their own outcomes, various processes used to increase predictability often result in perceived injustice, threats to individual esteem and dignity, and other dehumanizing consequences. O'Day's (18) description of intimidation rituals and Swingle's (21) discussion of mechanisms of bureaucratic strangulation provide some interesting examples. A number of studies (12, 13) have shown how possession of power itself leads to nonhumanized treatment of lower level participants by the powerful. Kipnis concluded:

. . . the control of power triggers a chain of events, which, in theory, at least, goes like this: (a) with the control of power goes increased temptation (sic) to influence others' behavior, (b) as actual influence attempts increase, there arises the belief that the behavior of others is not self-controlled, that it is caused by the powerholder, (c) hence, a devaluation of their performance. In addition, with increased influence attempts, forces are generated with the more powerful to (d) increase psychological distance from the less powerful and view them as objects of manipulation.

Similarly, Zimbardo's (1) discussion of his mock prison and Rosenhan's (20) observations of how hospital personnel related to mental patients provide convincing evidence that the possession of power itself leads the powerful to treat the less powerful in a nonhumanized fashion.

Overall, it appears that the possession of power has important dehumanizing effects. Not only are many individuals deprived of the ability to control their own outcomes but, in McGregor's terms, there seems to be a tendency for powerful people to adopt Theory X assumptions about their subordinates.

## EFFECTS ON THE LESS POWERFUL

The unequal distribution of power has complementary, nonhumanizing effects on the less powerful. Examples are: Harrington's (9) description of "twisted spirit" of the American poor and the "culture of poverty"; Lefcourt's (14) work on the psychology of powerlessness; Gouldner's (8) observation of feelings of dependence that result in servile attitudes toward superiors; and Nemeth's (15) report that inequalities in power inhibit cooperative behavior; these studies reveal the dehumanizing consequences of "powerlessness". Similarly, Culbert's (5) work reveals how relatively powerless individuals become trapped by shared assumptions which make them vulnerable to excess influence and induce them to accept the status quo. Thus, it seems reasonable to hypothesize that humanized relationships will be more probable when there is relative equality in power among individuals than when gross discrepancies exist.

P4:    *The exercise of power within organizations is one very crucial aspect of the exercise of power within the larger social system.*

One of the most productive outcomes of assessing the relationship between power and humanized organizations may well be that such discussions direct us to the work of political scientists. Their ideas point to some important omissions in thinking about power and control of work organizations.

Dahl (6) provides a basis for exploring some of these considerations. He observed that in America we have made a strange ideological distinction about the exercise of power. Power exercised in political organizations ought to be public and democratic, but power *within* economic organizations need not be democratic and ought to be left in the hands of the owners or managers of the firm. In his words:

. . . the prevailing ideology prescribes "private" enterprise, that is, firms managed by officials who are legally, if not de facto responsible to private shareholders . . . It is widely taken for granted that the only appropriate form for managing economic enterprise is a privately owned firm . . . Ordinarily technical arguments in favor of an alternative must be of enormous weight to overcome the purely ideological bias in favor of the private firm (6, p. 117-18).

Dahl was more concerned with macro level analysis (that is, the fact that the given magnitude of many decisions made by General Motors, they cannot reasonably be considered private matters) than he was with democracy *in* the workplace.

Pateman (19) extended Dahl's ideas into the workplace. She suggested that since organizations are so important in the lives of people, a fully democratic society is possible only if democratic voting is extended to organizations. She maintained that unless such an extension is made, voting and representation are doomed to be largely formal matters. Pateman wrote:

The aim of organizational democracy is democracy. It is not primarily increased productivity, efficiency, or better industrial relations (even though these things may even result from organizational democracy); rather it is to further justice, equality, freedom, the rights of citizens, and the protection of interests of citizens, all familiar democratic aims.

It is only a radical, participatory approach to organizational democracy that is likely to foster the expertise, skills, and confidence, both in the daily work process and in the exercise of democratic citizenship within the enterprise, that are vital if members of the organization as a whole are to be equipped to meet the challenge of control that will come from the technostructure (19, p. 21).

This argument leads to a direct consideration of the right to exercise power within an organization in a democratic society. Inquiry into this question has potentially radical implications. When we start to discuss power in this way, we are beginning to ask as Ellerman (7) did, "Who is the firm?" We may come to inquire about the rights by which certain individuals or groups now exercise control and come to consider alternative bases of power as means of humanized organizations and to a more fully democratic society. We may discover that equal access to power (political democracy) is a necessary (but certainly not sufficient) condition for humanized social organization.

## CONCLUSION

The feelings which underlie this article can be summarized by a comparison of the two Golden Rules. First, many of us who seek to humanize organizations dream of organizations where the powerful people, either out of self interest or out of moral commitment, follow the first (or the normative) Golden Rule—"Do unto others as you would have them do unto you". By contrast, the second or the descriptive golden rule, which I first saw on the wall in a men's room at Washington University, states, "Them that has the gold makes the rules".

The distribution of power and resources in existing organizations supports humanized relationships only to a limited degree. Humanization of such systems is by no means inevitable, but instead may require considerable struggle. Analysis and facilitation of the process will be aided by greater emphasis on the role of power and the realization that organizations are political systems embedded in larger political systems.

## REFERENCES

1. "A Pirandellian Prison," *New York Times Magazine,* April 8, 1973, pp. 38–40, 49.

2. Adams, R. N. *Energy and Structure: A Theory of Social Power* (Austin, Texas: University of Texas Press, 1975).

3. Bachrach, P. and M. S. Baratz, *Power and Poverty: Theory and Practice* (New York: Oxford University Press, 1970).

4. Bennis, W. G. "A Funny Thing Happened on the Way to the Future," *American Psychologist* 25 (1970): 595–608.

5. Culbert, S. A. *The Organization Trap* (New York: Basic Books, 1974).

6. Dahl, R. A. *After the Revolution? Authority in a Good Society* (New Haven: Yale University Press, 1970).

7. Ellerman, D. "The Ownership of Firm Is a Myth," *Administration and Society,* 7 (1975): 27–42.

8. Gouldner, A. W. *The Coming Crisis of Western Sociology* (New York Basic Books, 1970).

9. Harrington, M. *The Other America* (Baltimore: Penguin Books, 1962).

10. Hickson, D. I., C. R. Hinnings, C. A. Lee, R. E. Schneck, and J. M. Pennings. "A Strategic Contingencies' Theory of Intraorganizational Power," *Administrative Science Quarterly,* 19 (1971): 216–229.

11. Hinnings, C. R., D. J. Hickson, J. M. Pennings, and R. E. Schneck. "Structural Conditions of Intraorganizational Power," *Administrative Science Quarterly* 19 (1974): 22–44.

12. Kipnis, D. "Does Power Corrupt?" *Journal of Personality and Social Psychology* 24 (1972): 33–41.

13. Kipnis, D., P. J. Castell, M. Gergen, and D. Mauch. "Metamorphic Effects of Power," *Journal of Applied Psychology,* 61 (1976): 127–135.

14. Lefcourt, H. M. "The Function of the Illusions of Control and Freedom," *American Psychologists* 28 (1973): 417–425.

15. Nemeth, C. "Bargaining and Reciprocity," *Psychological Bulletin* 74 (1970): 297–308.

16. Nord, W. R. "The Failure of Current Applied Behavioral Science: A Marxian Perspective," *Journal of Applied Behavioral Science,* 10 (1974): 557–578.

17. Nord, W. R. "Economic and Socio-Cultural Barriers to Humanizing Organizations," in H. Meltzer, and F. R. Wickert, *Humanizing Organizational Behavior* (Springfield, Illinois: Charles C Thomas, 1976), 175–193.

18. O'Day, R. "Intimidation Rituals: Reactions to Reform," *Journal of Applied Behavioral Science* 10 (1974): 373–386.

19. Pateman, C. "A Contribution to the Political Theory of Organizational Democracy," *Administration and Society* 7 (1975): 5–26.

20. Rosenhan, D. L. "On Being Sane in Insane Places," *Science* 179 (1973): 250–258.

21. Swingle, P. G. *The Management of Power* (Hillsdale, N.J.: Lawrence Erlbaum Associates, 1976).

22. Thompson, J. D. *Organizations in Action* (New York: McGraw-Hill, 1967).

23. Zaleznik, A. "Power and Politics in Organizational Life," *Harvard Business Review* 48 (1970): 47–60.

M anagement denotes the development of group and individual structures for formulating and executing policy through the integration of the functional activities of objective setting, planning, organizing, staffing, leading, and controlling; it also includes the development of a value system appropriate to the achievement of the goals of the organization. In brief, management is concerned with discovering how tasks should be performed and ensuring they are performed in the most economical way.

But management is more than structures, processes, and values; it is also concerned with people. One might describe management as the business of getting things done through others. Managing arises whenever work is specialized and is undertaken by two or more persons. As soon as specialization emerges, work must be coordinated, and there must be some understanding of what the objectives are, what is to be done, how it is to be done, who is to do it, how people are to be motivated, and whether it was done. To carry through these functions, managers are employed to make decisions and communicate to members of the organization.

*Objective setting* is primarily concerned with the definition of the mission, goals, and targets. *Planning* refers to the specific action of appropriate means to achieve these missions, goals, and targets. *Organizing* refers to the selection of appropriate organizational designs to translate plans into a structure of task and authority. Organizing is concerned with such issues as centralization versus decentralization and delegation of authority. *Staffing* ensures that the organizational structure is staffed by competent and highly motivated people. *Leading* means ensuring that organizational members give their best and that the mission of the firm is achieved. Evaluation and control describe those activities which ensure that actual outcomes are consistent with planned outcomes.

# III

# PROCESS VARIABLES

**Objective setting**    If a company is to be effective, one must ensure that set objectives are not only communicated to the top managers, but also understood and implemented. Objective setting is a delicate and difficult business that requires a subtle knowledge of planning and politics. One way of involving managers in this process is the concept of management by objectives, described and evaluated in Chapter 5 of this book.

**Planning**    The planning system is a systematic effort to decide what needs to be done and how it is going to be done. The need for planning emerges from the middle of the organization where middle level managers, uncertain how to proceed, ask top management for guidance and direction. While the objectives and strategies of a company may remain the same from year to year, it is nevertheless necessary that they be articulated and reviewed in the light of changing events. Plans are usually prepared on a three-to-five year time horizon.

While there is some debate between "top-down" and "bottom-up" objective setting, most companies use a combination of both in goal setting. Contrary to the widely believed notion that only the Japanese employ "bottom-up" planning, most North American companies make a systematic effort to get top and middle management to participate in the planning process.

A strategic plan cannot be developed unless a company makes a systematic effort to scan the environment to ascertain what changes are taking place that are likely to affect them. Since the company itself is continually changing, it is necessary for the executives to maintain a high level of vigilance to ensure that their plans are up-to-date and appropriate, and that their objectives and goals are articulated in an explicit and quantitative fashion. With quantitative goals, it is possible for the management to exercise some degree of control.

Most companies use a variety of planning techniques. Planning can be divided into three levels: long-range strategic planning, operational programming, and plans, and tactical planning.

Strategic planning is concerned with the company's basic mission, objectives, policies, and strategies that influence the acquisition, utilization, and disposal of resources. Operational or medium-range programming is the process and technique whereby functional plans are integrated to achieve long-range plans. This usually involves preparation of manuals of procedures and handbooks. Tactical or short-range planning emerges frequently as yearly operational budget summaries.

If planning is to be effective, does it have to be rational and contingent? Normally, it is assumed that planning in a stable environment requires a rational analytic process that specifies objectives and measurable goals. Planning in an unstructured situation, however, is likely to be more intuitive. Michael B. McCaskey in *Goals and Direction in Personal Planning* advises the individual facing an ambiguous environment and conflicting values to use intuition, judgment, and holistic sensing. McCaskey says that planning does not have to be goal-directed to be effective.

**Organizing**    Once plans have been developed, it is necessary to develop the organizational design which will help to get the plan implemented. Organizational design begins with the process of arranging groups of job roles into particular patterns. Formerly, it was traditional to arrange these patterns in the form of a pyramid, with roles and procedures precisely defined. Authority, influence, and information were arranged by levels with each successive level having more of each of these characteristics. The classical or mechanistic organization is ideal for structured tasks, and is highly suitable for people with low tolerance for ambiguity and a strong need for security. Organic organizations are highly suitable for innovation and for people who like a challenge. The choice between mechanistic and organic is contingent upon the task and the people involved. Basically, in organic design, it is necessary to engage in both differentiation and integration.

The most important thing to know about organizing is that different organizational forms are required for different problems.

**Staffing** Liam Hudson, the British psychologist, developed the idea that people can be divided into two types: convergers and divergers. The converger (a typical example would be a physical scientist) likes to think in algorithms; he works towards the answers "at the back of the book". The diverger (a typical example would be a social scientist) prefers heuristics, which opens up categories rather than pigeonhole ideas.

Thus it seems reasonable to believe that many people pick their roles according to a complicated set of rules. These rules recognize their unconscious needs, take into account their cognitive styles, and somehow offer them the opportunity to exploit their neurotic disabilities.

The staffing process also deals with how people are selected and socialized into the organization. Thus, the study of staffing is the bridge between the concepts of organizing and leading.

To be effective, staffing interviewers must carefully plan the selection process. They should first examine the job to understand what skills are required, what types of decisions must be made, and what are the physical conditions and the work environment.

The interviewer must develop a variety of listening skills. He must be good at "active listening", which requires a fundamental openness towards the interviewee and helps him feel he is part of the process.

Too often interviewers make the following mistakes: they ask leading questions; they make

their decisions too early in the interview; they allow themselves to be overwhelmed by particular stereotypes; they do more talking than they should; they fail to direct the interview; they do not know what they are looking for.

Many personnel managers use the assessment center as a means of selecting executives who are ready for promotion. A typical assessment center requires the applicant to take part in a series of exercises such as giving lectures or leading groups. Selectors meet afterwards to formulate a recommendation about the suitability of each candidate.

**Leadership** Leadership is the ability to recognize and exploit the drama of the moment, hold or steal the floor, and move events in their true historical direction to allow a people or a group to achieve their preordained destiny. Thomas Carlyle articulated the sentiments of the modern romantic movement: the history of an organization is but the curriculum vitae of great leaders, who show an informative capacity for turning the dross of everyday life into dramatic moments of fateful opportunity.

A leader is a person who is willing, indeed eager, to publicly accept the challenge of filling the principal role in the organizational drama even though some traditional or ritualistic denial of seeking greatness in nomination is required.

There is a necessary relationship between the leader and the led. The leader cannot lead unless he has followers who follow. The art of following is the technique for controlling leaders from below by the display of selective response patterns of behaviors and attitudes which serve to make the leader behave in a preferred way. Hence, the very simple but extremely useful definition of leadership as *the ability to influence others*. The calibre of leadership is probably the most important factor determining organizational outcomes. Even the most democratic organizations follow the iron law of oligarchy. Inevitably, charismatic leaders come to talk of organizations. Leaders seek power and, of course, power can be corrupting. Thus, leadership must be made responsible.

In a work group, everyone leads at least some of the time; interdependance becomes extremely important. Managers manage these interdependancies by emphasizing their vulnerability to the whims and caprices of the subordinates. To do all this effectively, the manager must have considerable political skills.

Control   To make sure the process subsystem conforms to the overall goals of the system, a control subsystem is required. To ensure that the system can learn and adapt from its successes and failures, a memory subsystem is needed to keep the score.

To understand how the system and its subsystem work together to achieve its goals, it is necessary to consider the role which information plays in the process. It is necessary to provide information in a timely and structured way to facilitate day-to-day decision making. Controllers in a company are responsible for integrating accounting, planning, and budgeting data to ensure that the right things are happening. Management must upgrade the data reporting system so the necessary information is available to keep the organization under control.

All complex systems incorporate some form of control. A business organization would just disintegrate without control. In short, organization means control. Modern research findings suggest that organizations require different kinds of differentiation and integration if they are to be successful.

Most executives use a thermostat model of control. But controls cannot function unless the thermostat has been set at some objective, and the system planned in some way so that execution and information-gathering are interlocked. These four elements—objective setting, planning, execution, and information-gathering—must be interlocked through feedback. In practice, standards are maintained through budget coherence which is measured through management information systems. Control is essentially concerned with ensuring the efficient and effective accomplishment of the organization's goals.

M BO—Management by Objectives—has achieved great recent popularity in management circles (1), not only in private industry but increasingly in hospitals, school districts and the like. General Mills, Minnesota Mining and Manufacturing, Honeywell, PPG, Kimberly-Clark, these are but a few of the companies which have experimented with this promising new technique (2). But there are numerous organizations which have tried it out and then abandoned it—and probably many more in which the program never really got off the ground or, after quick initial success, was gradually allowed to become moribund (3). Too many managers look upon MBO either as a gimmick or a cure-all, without giving careful thought to the objectives they want MBO to accomplish—or the adjustments which must be made if these objectives are to be achieved. In other words, there is too little MBO-type thinking to the concept of MBO itself. This failure to recognize the fuzziness in MBO's own objectives has contributed to the ambiguity of MBO's results.

MBO is too useful a concept to be accepted blindly. Its difficulties must be squarely faced if management is to take full advantage of its strengths. Let me start out with the question of objectives, then describe the major problems which arise from MBO in practice, and finally suggest the realistic limits to MBO's use.

## CONFUSION AS TO OBJECTIVES

MBO is an umbrella concept covering a multitude of objectives. For some it is a means of introducing a Theory-Y oriented form of autonomy in which managers are given freedom to set their own goals. Others approach it in terms of Theory-X—as a means of tightening

# 5

# Objective Setting

*Management By Objectives: A Critical View*

GEORGE STRAUSS

managerial control and getting subordinates to do exactly what management wants.

The personnel director of an industrial laboratory looked upon it as a form of individual performance appraisal; the lab manager hoped it would get "the lab moving together as a team"; but for the majority of managers it seemed merely an additional contribution of their paperwork. One man said, "MBO, I do that. That's management by exception. If a man gets out of line you straighten him out" (4).

What did the originators of the concept want MBO to accomplish? Here we find little real agreement either.

## PERFORMANCE APPRAISAL

As much as anyone, Douglas McGregor was responsible for the MBO concept, although he never used the term himself (5). McGregor was looking for a method of performance appraisal which was superior to the traditional rating system (6). Critics argued that the traditional system:

. . . stressed personality traits, which were subjective and difficult to measure or change;
. . . provided that ratings be determined in a unilateral fashion with the supervisor "playing God" and judging the subordinate's personal worth (as opposed to his performance);
. . . tended to emphasize past mistakes rather than future performance.

MBO sought to overcome all these problems by basing appraisal on (a) quantitative, measurable (or at least concrete) performance goals (b) set jointly by superior and subordinate. Thus the subordinate is judged by standards he helped determine.

## PLANNING AND CONTROL

Soon it became apparent that MBO was useful, not just as a personnel tool, but as a means of planning and control (7). MBO's new use was as an improved form of budgeting.

In too many companies, planning consists merely of adopting short-run cost budgets and setting sales targets. Global objectives may be set, but relatively little thought is given to how these goals are to be reached. And with the primary emphasis placed on *this* period's costs, profits and sales, there is a tendency to ignore other variables which may contribute to profits over longer periods, variables such as equipment maintenance, employee and product development, and customer relations.

MBO (at least when it works as it should) requires management to define exactly what it wants to accomplish and to specify all important objectives, especially those commonly ignored. It reduces the emphasis on short-run profits (8), increases the number of managerial goals and forces the explicit consideration of exactly what steps must be taken if these goals are to be fulfilled. In this way, it helps subordinates learn what is required of them, thus reducing their need for guesswork. As a result, it makes decision-making more rational, both for boss and subordinate. In sum, MBO can become a coordinated process of planning which involves every management level in determining both the goals which it will meet and the means by which they are to be met.

## A DECISION-MAKING TOOL

Some companies go even further. MBO is viewed as a tool to help top management reevaluate whether the organization's present activities contribute to the organization's real objectives. MBO here is looked upon not as a means of evaluating individuals or of communicating management priorities, but as a tough-minded approach to problem-solving. (It is in a sense analogous to PPBS at the governmental level.)

As I will argue below, the autonomy and self-direction implied by the first objective runs somewhat counter to the coordinated control inherent in the second, and neither are entirely congruent with the decision-making approach of the third. Unfortunately, these inconsistencies have been insufficiently recognized by those who would make MBO a multi-purpose remedy. Further, both literature and practice today seem to be giving greater emphasis to MBO-as-planning and playing down its role in evaluation (9). And yet the rhetoric inspired by the early emphasis of self-direction at times leads to false hopes that MBO will democratize the organization.

## SOME TYPICAL PROBLEMS

So much for objectives. What sorts of problems arise under MBO in practice? Here are some typical comments:

"There is a lot of paperwork in MBO. All sorts of goals are set and we talk big. But on a day-to-day basis, nothing changes. We are all too busy fighting fires for me to get involved in those extra things which I promised to do in MBO. And so is my boss."

"I could meet all my goals in training my men and developing new accounts, but in so doing I would lose $1,000,000 in bread-and-butter sales. MBO emphasizes fringes over the main objectives."

"MBO doesn't work where there is job rotation. My predecessor expected to be transferred soon. He accepted some unreasonable goals and I just don't feel bound by them."

"There is no follow up in my organization: They set goals with a big flourish, but no one pays any attention to them six months later."

"Things move so fast that by the time the review period comes around the goals are no longer relevant."

"If you don't meet goals in my company you can always find excuses. MBO just teaches you to lie better."

The above may imply only that the bosses of the managers who made these comments have failed to understand or accept the MBO philosophy. But more is involved. There are inherent conflicts between MBO and other management policies and, as suggested earlier, inconsistencies between the goals of MBO itself.

## SUBORDINATE PARTICIPATION IN GOAL SETTING

As long as the subordinate is judged in terms of how well he does in terms of goals he himself sets, there is a danger that he will set his goals just as low as he can so as to give himself greater leeway in case of trouble. After all, his apparent success is a function of initial goals. If his goals are modest, it is easy to look good. And so—where MBO is working poorly—the subordinate tries to set a low initial goal and sell his boss that the goal is really hard.

I suspect that only in a minority of cases do subordinates feel really free to set goals as they wish. MBO may work where the managers' everyday style of managment is participative and nondirective. But it is too much to expect the ordinary hard-bitten manager, who is directive and decisive, to transform himself suddenly into a participative manager when he engages in MBO (10). In any case, knowing that his boss is the one who hands out rewards, the typical subordinate may look anxiously for some indication of what the boss thinks are proper goals. Once these become clear, he will quickly adopt them with "enthusiasm." Indeed, some subordinates might prefer that their boss indicate his wishes frankly from the start, instead of putting them through guessing games.

Actually the freedom of the subordinate to set his own goals is highly restricted whenever any kind of common plan is required (11). It makes little sense for production to plan 15 percent more output if marketing plans only 10 percent more sales or for a plant manager to decide to rebuild a production bay if top management has decided to curb capital expenditures. Individual goals have to be consistent with organizational goals (12). Thus organizational demands may conflict with individual desires, raising problems which I will discuss later on.

## OBJECTIVE STANDARDS

MBO involves setting objective standards. Instead of telling a foreman he should exert more forceful leadership, he is setting the goal of increasing production by 17 percent or introducing a new line of equipment by November 1.

The trouble with such goals is they often force the subordinate to *look* good rather than *be* good and to emphasize the measurable rather than the unmeasurable. To be sure, some MBO systems make provision for unmeasurable goals, but exact numbers inevitably speak louder than vague descriptions. Production, which is measurable, is emphasized over employee development, which is not. Or, if employee development is to be measured, it is in terms of such superficial measures as the gross number of employees sent to training classes, not how this training changes behavior on the job (13). Creative work, such as research, personnel or advertising, is often difficult to evaluate, as indeed is most staff work. Because of this difficulty, quality may be sacrificed for sheer quantity.

A laboratory director set as his goal the enhancement of his laboratory's professional prestige, but since prestige is difficult to measure, he set as his performance target a certain number of papers to be read at professional meetings. And to fill this quota he "encouraged" individual subordinates to accept the writing of papers as goals for themselves. The result, as might be expected, was that the required number of papers were read, but that they were of such poor quality as to lower rather than raise the laboratory's prestige. (The story might have been less tragic, however, if the director's subordinates had felt really free to reject their assignments.)

Overemphasis on measurable data may also encourage the covering up of poor performance or the actual falsification of data. Long-run improvement may be slighted to look good during the current evaluation period. Since each individual is anxious to make himself look good, cooperation is discouraged. In addition, to the extent that a manager's overall performance is evaluated on the basis of a relatively few measures, there is always the danger that accidental factors outside of his control may distort the picture. A good manager with bad luck may look worse than a bad manager with good luck.

Unless an endless number of factors are measured, some significant items may be ignored or fall into the chinks between measured goals. And when one goal can be achieved only at the potential expense of another, the manager often has only imperfect standards for choice. He may easily emphasize side goals over the main show. ("I could meet all my goals in training my men and developing new accounts, but in so doing I would lose $1,000,000 in bread-and-butter sales.")

An important question relates to the assign-ing of responsibilities. For example, if a new product flops, who is held responsible: product development, for not doing its homework? manufacturing, for poor quality? or marketing, for insufficient sales effort? Some authors suggest that managers should be held responsible merely for factors under their direct control. Others argue for joint goals, with joint responsibility. Both approaches encourage buckpassing.

Staff effort is particularly difficult to measure, because staff, of course, has to achieve its results through others.

## ORGANIZATION REWARDS

How is MBO to be tied into the organizational reward system? There are those who say that MBO and salary appraisal should be two separate processes, but this is difficult to work in practice.

Of course, there are real problems in integrating the two systems. If a man's pay depends on how well he meets the goals he sets for himself, he has every incentive to set these goals low and to blame his failure on someone else. Certainly the greater the emphasis we place on MBO in terms of determining salaries, the more likely subordinates are to emphasize short-run measurable results over longer-run intangibles.

But in a money-oriented society, if MBO isn't tied into the reward system, why should anyone pay attention to MBO at all? If MBO sets one set of goals and compensation rewards another, we get nothing but confusion.

So the two have to be integrated. But this means not only that goals have to be accepted by the individual and be consistent with the overall organizational plan, but also that they must be fair and equitable, so that one manager is not setting a goal which is harder than another's. To satisfy all these conflicting objectives is far from easy.

Finally, and certainly complicating both MBO and reward systems, is the fact that the organization exists in a turbulent environment. A company's sales record may be more a function of what happens in Washington than the effectiveness of its individual sales managers.

## PARTICIPATION

MBO today has two primary objectives, individual performance appraisal and managerial planning and control (14). The first objective implies that each manager will participate in setting his own individual goal, the second that these individual goals will be consistent with those of the organization as a whole. If these two objectives are not to clash, individual managers must participate in setting not only their own goals but those of the organization generally. In theory this means that there is a great deal of consultation, crossing all managerial levels, until a master plan is developed which everyone *freely* accepts.

Followed to its logical conclusion, MBO is a means of introducing participative (Theory Y, System 4, Argyris's YB) management on an organization-wide basis. The revolutionary implication of this is that each individual manager will do more than determine the details of how to carry out organizational goals; he will participate in determining the goals themselves. If meant seriously, MBO could be an organization development technique more potent than, say, sensitivity training or the Grid. It would threaten the corporate power structure and transform the traditional hierarchical structure of decision-making into something closer to Likert's System 4 interlocking chain of highly participative work groups.

Whether such a drastic change would be desirable is beside the point. Corporate democracy is more than most managements bargained for when they agreed to accept MBO. Over the last 10 years, the MBO literature has played down and redefined the concept of subordinate goal setting, so that the idea today differs considerably from that originally proposed by McGregor. In practice, MBO today is often viewed as means of tightening, not loosening, top management controls. Despite some trimmings of participation, top management typically sets the *basic* goals. Subordinates may have some freedom to set secondary goals (with regards to housekeeping or training, for example, but not with regards to production levels or capital outlays), to voice objectives and to determine how to *carry out* basic goals. Essentially the freedom is one of means, not ends. At Minneapolis Mining and Manufacturing,

the process starts with the department manager sitting with each of his immediate subordinates to get across the general idea of what is to be required, based on objectives established at the top of the corporation . . . Then each of these men sits with his subordinates, until the lowest man involved has been brought into the picture. At this point, the process reverses direction and specific objectives come up from the bottom, along with detailed plans for attaining them. The objectives are so set that the requirements will be met; if not, they are changed. *A boss cannot accept a subordinate's requirements unless he knows that they will produce what is required (15).*

The trouble is that those who view MBO primarily as a means of increasing individual participation may raise expectations which are inconsistent with organizational realities.

To introduce a program of objectives may be to change the subordinate's expectations about participation and involvement . . . There seems to be a clear implication that he will have something to say about the factor or problem in which he is involved. The most serious human relations problems probably occur in organizations where there is an incongruity between the verbalized level and actual level of subordinate influence; that is, participation may be a stated policy, but in practice does not occur (16).

## A REALISTIC VIEW

If any arguments are valid, it would be wrong to view MBO either as an all-purpose cure for every management ill or as a Trojan Horse which can be used to insinuate full-fledged Theory Y concepts of management throughout the organization. MBO can play a useful role, even if it isn't the star of the show.

1. As suggested just above, it is misleading and unrealistic to suggest that MBO can permit subordinates to set goals just for themselves, except in secondary areas. MBO in fact requires more communications, perhaps more mutual influence, but probably less autonomy and individual freedom. Group participation may in-

crease, individual discretion may not. Where MBO is viewed as an exercise in subordinate motivation, the subordinate may "own" the goals, but the boss feels little commitment to them. The reverse may be true where the goals are imposed by the boss in conformance with a master plan. It is extremely difficult to develop joint ownership or commitment.

2. Hard-nosed as managers are supposed to be, many find it difficult to operationalize their goals—to be really specific as to what they want either their subordinates or themselves to obtain. The research studies to date suggest that it is the setting of clear, concrete goals which is important, not the sense of participation (17). Concrete goals direct performance, reduce uncertainty and serve as an instrument of communications—and do so whether the goals are introduced directively or participatively.

3. MBO may point out where greater coordination between managers is required. The goal setting process may be particularly useful in facilitating what has been called "bargaining" between boss and subordinate, line and staff, or departments tied together in the work flow (especially when such bargaining is confined to the details relating to goals set by higher levels). Department A may agree to cut scrap losses by 10 percent, but insists Department B must tighten tolerance by a given amount. Personnel must recruit better trained employees, and that the boss obtain a capital authorization to purchase two new machines by April 15. Where there is joint responsibility, individual inputs should be specified in advance. The process of hammering out agreements on matters such as this may be MBO's most valuable by-product (18).

4. Effective MBO may permit and even require structural changes. Cases have been reported where MBO has led to broader spans of control and the elimination of organizational levels. As various studies have shown rules and goals can serve as substitutes for close supervision (19).

5. Reasonable care should be taken to in-

sure that the right goals are set: the measures of success should measure what is really important to achieve, not trivia; the short run should not be emphasized over the long run, the measurable over the subjective, or the performance of single units at the expense of the organization as a whole. There is room for some experimentation with "contingency goals" (if Product X is released by April 15, we will raise sales level to 30,000 units by July 1) or "variable goals" (for every one percent increase in production, unit costs will be reduced by .2 percent). MBO can discourage flexible response to unexpected happenings; hopefully it can be designed to do the reverse.

6. Goals, however, can be overstressed. Ingenuity in solving problems is what counts, not ingenuity in measuring performance. It would be hopelessly unproductive to try to seek to develop a concrete goal for every aspect of performance. Goals may highlight special areas of emphasis. But managers should be rewarded on their overall performance, not just aspects specifically measured. Judgment and discretion are required in interpreting performance data. Results do not "speak for themselves."

7. MBO must solve the problem of its relationship to reward systems. I think salary appraisal should be a fairly explicit procedure in which individuals are (in most cases) told the basis for pay decisions. MBO results should perhaps be the major input into this process, but the reward system should take into account a broader set of variables than does MBO, including many nonmeasurable.

8. Individual contributions should not be overemphasized. Some companies now base their rewards not just on the individual's own performance but also on the performance of his department and the organization as a whole, and this would seem to be a desirable move.

9. To a considerable extent the effectiveness of an MBO program depends on how the superior reacts when a subordinate fails to meet his goals. If the superior acts in a punitive manner, the subordinate will fear to take risks in the future and will seek to be given only the

most conservative goals. Thus the boss must permit failure. On the other hand, if the boss completely ignores the failure, the subordinate may decide the entire MBO program is meaningless. Obviously the middle ground is preferable: the superior should use the failure as a springboard for a discussion of how performance in the affected area may be improved in the future.

## CONCLUSION

MBO has a number of attractive features. Its emphasis on specific goals makes performance appraisal more objective, and even limited subordinate involvement in goal-setting tends to make "goals more realistic and palatable to the individual . . . No small accomplishment" (20). MBO is a step toward a systems view of management, linking individual goals to those of the organization as a whole, strategies to objectives and facilitating coordination (bargaining) between departments. Ideally, it forces management at each level to specify exactly what it is seeking to accomplish, and it can be an effective means of communication, at least downward.

MBO's main limitations are of two sorts:

1. As the quotations previously presented illustrate, in many companies MBO is viewed as a gimmick or a slogan rather than as a method of management. Impractical goals are established without considering the likelihood of their being realized, and, once the going gets tough, they are forgotten.

2. MBO is not very realistic if looked upon entirely or primarily as a method of performance appraisal or subordinate goal-setting. Unless they deal with trivia, individual goals must mesh with those of the organization. At the most MBO can permit (a) greater individual control over how broader goals are met and (b) perhaps, within narrow limits, some greater influence regarding the level of these goals themselves.

Of the two fathers of the MBO concept, McGregor emphasized participation. Drucker goal-setting. The Drucker approach seems to be winning out. In many companies MBO is viewed chiefly as a means of communicating top management's goals. MBO is increasingly achievement rather than human relations-oriented.

Most companies which have experimented with MBO have treated it as a personnel technique (or even a gimmick), on the order of T-groups, brain storming, employee counseling or the case method approach to training. Given management's propensity to abandon old programs of this sort whenever a new fad comes along, I suspect that by 1980 the term MBO will be something of an anachronism. And yet, in a number of companies it will have left a legacy of more systematic planning, tighter, more realistic controls and better communications.

For those companies considering the adoption of MBO, I would say, "Try it. It is a fail-safe device which (compared, for example, to T-groups, which can do real harm) at worst will merely arouse false hopes."

## REFERENCES

1. See, for example, John P. Campbell and others, *Managerial Behavior, Performance, and Effectiveness*, McGraw-Hill, New York. 1970. pp. 62–67. In Britain, too, it is "the current management top fashion." *The Economist*, April 25, 1970, p. 60.

2. According to a 1964 survey, 23 percent of the 141 companies surveyed made "much use" of "appraisal against specific objectives." W. S. Wickstrom. *Developing Management Competence: Changing Concepts—Emerging Practices,* National Industrial Conference Board. Studies in Personnel Policy. No. 189. 1964, p. 26. A similar 1964 study reported but five percent of the companies responding utilized MBO. Bureau of National Affairs, *Managerial Appraisal Programs,* Personnel Practices Forum, Survey No. 74, September, 1964. It seems reasonably likely that the percentages are considerably higher today.

3. Recently I polled the participants in a management course of mine as to the experience of their companies with MBO. These managers came from a broad range of manufacturing firms. Of the approximately 25 percent who came from companies which had tried MBO, about one-third said the experience had been bad; in most of these companies MBO had been either formally dropped or, more commonly, it had just faded away. In another third, MBO was judged a success, and in the final third the experience was mixed. This is hardly my idea of rigorous research, but I suspect more careful studies would come to roughly the same conclusions.

4. I am indebted to Raymond Miles for this case. For other useful suggestions. I owe a debt to David Bowen, Joseph Robinson, Charles Snow, and John Sims—as well as to the Berkeley Organizational Behavior-Industrial Relations Ph.D. Seminar.

5. Perhaps equally responsible was Peter Drucker. See his *The Practice of Management,* Harpers, New York, 1954.

6. See Douglas McGregor, "An Uneasy Look at Performance Appraisal," *Harvard Business Review,* Vol. 35, No. 3, May–June 1957.

7. George Odiorne was to a large extent responsible for popularizing this approach to MBO. See his highly influential *Management by Objectives,* Pitman, New York, 1964.

8. In Likert's terms, MBO places emphasis on intervening as well as on end-results variables. Rensis Likert, *The Human Organization*

McGraw-Hill, New York, 1967. MBO can also take advantage of "human assets accounting."

9. The changing emphasis means that MBO is less the property of the personnel department (or individual managers at all levels) and more the property of top management.

10. According to one study, subordinate goal setting leads to higher goal achievement than does goal setting by the boss only when the boss's usual pattern of managment is participative. John R. P. French, Jr., Emanuel Kay, and Herbert H. Meyer, "Participation and the Appraisal System," *Human Relations,* Vol. 19, No. 1, 1966, p. 14.

11. According to one study of a single company, higher level managers feel greater freedom to set their own objectives in the MBO process than do those at lower levels; greater freedom is also felt by managers in areas, such as marketing, where top management control is relatively difficult and the need for close coordination with other departments relatively little. Henry L. Tosi, Jr., and Stephen J. Carroll, "Some Structural Factors Related to Goal Influence in the Management by Objectives Process," *MSU Business Topics,* Spring, 1969, pp. 45–50.

12. Some companies distinguish between *personnel development* and *performance* objectives. Such a personal development objective for a design engineer might be to spend more time with the marketing staff, so that his product design might better anticipate changes in consumer preferences—or to attend a leadership training program to improve his relations with subordinates. Individual managers have considerably greater freedom to set their personal objectives than their performance objectives. Indeed there is tie-in between freedom to set personal objectives and what has been called the "open system" approach to management development (10). Theodore M. Alford, "Checkers or Choice in Manpower Management, *Harvard Business Review,* Vol. 45, January-February, 1967. By and large personal goals are secondary to performance. And so, MBO permits substantial subordinate participation only in relatively unimportant areas.

13. In other words, where output variables cannot be measured, the tendency is to measure input.

14. The decision-making objective, as yet, is running a poor third, though it is rapidly closing the gap.

15. National Industrial Conference Board, *Managing By and With Objectives*, Studies in Personnel Policy, No. 212, 1968, p. 58.

16. Tosi and Carroll, pp. 50 and 45.

17. French, Kay, Meyer, *op. cit.*, and Stephen L. Carroll, Jr., and Henry Tossi, "Goal Characteristics and Personality Factors in a Management-by-Objectives Program," *Administrative Science Quarterly*, 15, (1970), pp. 295-305.

18. That bargaining of this sort is common among departments I have suggested elsewhere. George Strauss, "Tactics of Lateral Relationship," *Administrative Science Quarterly*, Vol. 7 (1962). MBO merely formalizes and legitimizes the process. This bargaining should not be confused with unrestricted autonomy. The bargaining within constraints provided by higher management.

19. Strauss, George, and Leonard R. Sayles, *Personnel*, 3rd ed., Prentice-Hall, Englewood Cliffs, N.J., (1972).

20. Rothstein, William G., "Executive Appraisal Programs," *ILR Research*, Vol. 8, (1962), p. 17.

---

## BIBLIOGRAPHY

Anthony, Robert N. "The Trouble with Profit Maximization." *Harvard Business Review* (November–December, 1960), pp. 126–134.

Argenti, John. "Defining Corporate Objectives." *Long Range Planning*, Vol. 1 (March, 1969), pp. 24–27.

Berger, M. "Management by Results." *Dun's Review*, Vol. 100, No. 5 (1972), pp. 111–113.

Branch, Ben. "Corporate Objectives and Market Performance." *Financial Management*, Vol. 2, No. 2 (1973), pp. 24–29.

Gross, Bertram. "What Are Your Organization's Objectives?" *Human Relations*, Vol. 18, No. 3 (1965), pp. 195–216.

Hayes, Douglas A. "Management Goals in a Crisis Society." *Michigan Business Review*, Vol. 22, No. 5 (November, 1970), pp. 7–11.

Houston, Charles Lukens, Jr. "Setting Corporate Objectives." *Targets for Management*, General Management Series No. 17. New York: American Management Association, Inc., 1955, pp. 3–14.

Howell, R. A. "A Fresh Look at Management by Objectives." *Business Horizons* (Fall, 1967).

Lasagna, J. "Make Your MBO Pragmatic." *Harvard Business Review* (November–December, 1971), pp. 64–69.

Mee, John F. "The Synergistic Effect." *Business Horizons*, Vol. 8, No. 2 (Summer, 1965), pp. 56–58.

McFarlane, Alexander N. "The Search for Purpose." *Conference Board Record*, Vol. 2, No. 2 (February, 1965), pp. 29–32.

Odiorne, George S. *Management by Objectives*. New York: Pitman Publishing Corporation, 1965.

O'Donnell, Cyril. "Planning Objectives." *California Management Review*, Vol. VI, No. 2 (Winter, 1963), pp. 3–10.

Rue, L. W. and T. B. Clark. "Dangers Inherent in Growth Objectives." *Managerial Planning* (May–June, 1975), pp. 24–28.

Sullivan, M. R. "Setting and Achieving Management Objectives." *Assuring the Company's Future Today*, General Management Series No. 175. New York: American Management Association, Inc., 1955, pp. 3–10.

Urwick, Lyndall F. "The Purpose of a Business." *Dun's Review and Modern Industry* (November, 1955), pp. 51, 52, 103–105.

Vroman, H. W. "Differentiating MBO-Appraisal Systems: A Contingency View." *Journal of Business Research*, Vol. 3, No. 1 (1975), pp. 53–58.

Wickens, J. D. "Management by Objectives: An Appraisal." *Journal of Management Studies*, Vol. 5 (October, 1968), pp. 365–379.

Wieland, G. F. "The Determinants of Clarity in Organization Goals." *Human Relations*, Vol. 22, No. 2 (1969), pp. 161–172.

Williams, Charles. "National and Corporate Goals." *Interfaces*, Vol. 1, No. 4 (June, 1971), pp. 1–9.

Personal planning involves imaging the future and deriving the consequences of that image for present patterns of behavior. People usually suppose that the future can only be imaged in terms of goals, but alternative modes for planning, such as domain and direction planning, do not involve goal setting. Planning does not have to be teleological to be directed.

---

In a basic reference on planning, Steiner (37) has called for better research and theory to understand the proper planning process for different people, different sized organizations, and different conditions. Other writers have stressed the need to fit the planning process to the situation (30, 32, 34). Contingency theorists, in particular, have begun to elaborate the major constraints and influences which affect the choice of a planning process. This work recognizes that there are at least several different modes of planning, and that a planning process should be chosen to fit the important features of a given situation. Contingency theorists have begun to identify important situational characteristics and corresponding planning processes.

According to several contingency theorists, planning for a well-defined problem, in a stable environment, is likely to be a rational, analytical process that specifies objective and measurable goals. Planning for an ill-defined problem in a rapidly changing, fuzzy environment is likely to be more intuitive and heuristic (9, 18, 24). While the first set of conditions calls for systems operating in a relatively closed and mechanistic fashion, the second set calls for systems which operate in a more open and organic fashion (6, 20, 21). Another major contingency affecting the mode of planning is the psychological type and predispositions of the individual. Investigators have proposed this as a major variable in the design of managment information systems (25, 26) and in policy formulation (17); clearly the impact of individual

# 6

# Moving from Strategic Objectives to Operation Goals

*Goals and Direction in Personal Planning*

MICHAEL B. MCCASKEY

personality should be considered in designing a system as heavily dependent upon information as a planning process.

There is a voluminous and useful literature for personal planning in relatively stable and well-defined situations. But it is less helpful for the individual who faces a fuzzy environment, or one involving conflicting personal values and a significant degree of uncertainty. How does an individual plan in a situation where the problem is identifying what the problem is (3, 8, 10, 14)?

One major alternative in the literature is "disjointed incrementalism" (23). For an administrator facing a complex environment which over-extends anyone's analytic capabilities and which often involves many conflicting interest groups, Lindblom (speaking about government administrators) proposes a system of making successive limited comparisons. Instead of trying to formulate a grand strategy, or rationally analyzing all the elements, the administrator improves at the margin, taking each day's problems and comparing them to recent and nearby alternatives (5, 23).

For some situations, for some time periods, this may be the only way to proceed. But to use disjointed incrementalism is to be essentially planless. This type of strategy offers no way to anticipate the future. Disjointed incrementalism leaves the individual passive toward what the next day brings, overlooking what could be done actively to seek out opportunities.

This article describes a middle ground between planning in terms of detailed and specific goals and being planless. In a sense it is planning without goals. Such a possibility may not seem contradictory if we take a closer look at what planning is.

Planning is imaging the future (4, 11) and deriving the consequences of that image for present behavior. Most people think that the future can only be, or is most appropriately, imaged in terms of goals. They then apply the advice given for "good" or "effective" goal-setting (to be specific, objective, factual, and measurable) to all planning situations. The possibility exists to image the future in terms other than goals, and this results in very different planning modes. To illustrate alternative modes of planning, this article presents one alternative: imaging the future in terms of symbols, and planning in terms of domain and direction.

This type of planning uses intuition and explicitly makes a place for judgment and holistic sensing of a situation. It follows the spirit of distinguished photographer Paul Strand's statement: "The young people often ask me how I choose the things I photograph. The answer is I don't. They choose me." (39, p. 90).

Many people do use intuition, judgment, and hunches in their planning; but they do so feeling that they are somehow violating the canons of good planning. Especially if they do not set specific, objective goals, they feel they are offending norms of behaving rationally. How goals and rationality are related is an important question for developing alternative modes of planning.

## GOALS AND RATIONALITY IN PLANNING

Many praise goal-setting, and yet few actually specify goals as part of planning for their personal lives. Soelberg's (36) study of career planning and decision making among a group of MBA and doctoral students at MIT illuminates the relationship of goals to personal planning.

From lengthy interviews and questionnaires over a three to five month period, Soelberg found that a decision-maker nearly always reduces job possibilities to two. Soelberg also found that one makes up one's mind before being aware of that fact and before admitting it to oneself or to others. Only *after* making an implicit choice does one assign numbers to alternatives and "add it all up" to *confirm* the choice already made. Soelberg theorized that the decision-maker needs time to distort information to favor the chosen alternative, and thereby reduce the pain of foregoing other alternatives. Benjamin Franklin, a wise observer of human nature, commented: "So convenient a thing it is to be a *reasonable* creature, since it enables one to find or make a reason for every thing one has a mind to do" (12, p. 33). Psychoanalysts have long realized how frequently people rationalize their actions.

Related to this point is the difference between the "context of discovery" (where we make our plans) and the "context of justification" (where we communicate those plans to someone else). We make plans in a hazy world of incomparables, some facts, conflicting emotions, and hard-to-nail-down intuitions. In discovering what our plans are, we often use a rough-but-ready calculus combining logic and intuition (2, 28). When explaining or announcing our plans to others we clear away much of the "unacceptable" debris. The world becomes less hazy, and the cobwebs of emotions and intuitions are cleared away when we reconstruct our line of thought and give reasons for doing what we do. In presenting our plans we want to seem rational. In fact, we feel so uncomfortable about planning without goals that even if, at the time of planning, we did not set specific goals, we invent them later to help justify our actions to others. But the switch to a context of justification should not obscure how the planning actually took place.

Our cultural training assumes that behavior is teleological, directed toward some "telos" or goal. Consider how pervasive these expectations of teleology are. We often ask children what they want to be when they grow up. If they give specific answers, we smile and reward them. But if they have no goal, not even a childish one, we are less sure how to respond. When someone behaves badly we ask, "Why did you do that?" as if human action always has a reason, involving a consciously chosen purpose. We commonly think of people as behaving rationally, and we assume that this entails their having a predetermined goal.

The common sense view that goals should precede action is harshly enforced as a norm. A student in a seminar on alternative modes of planning forcefully made this point from his own experience. He had decided to leave a successful business career to begin work toward a Ph.D. As he put it, "I never could articulate the reasons, so I sometimes thought I was crazy." He added that many of his coworkers responded as if there were something crazy about his making an important shift in career plans without being able to state the reasons why. Others in the seminar reported similar experiences. Most people feel they *should* choose their goals first and then plan their actions in light of these goals. The norm is that one should act and plan in light of predetermined, and preferably quite specific, goals. For many Americans the rational norm is so strong that we are puzzled and upset when this expectation is violated. This article argues that the rational norm holds for only *some* planning situations. Indeed, in many situations, we may discover our goals only by acting.

Although a goal is generally assumed to be an end-state, the terminal point of a planning process, underlying a goal is often a desire for a longer-term *process* rather than a desire for an *end-state* itself. Vickers (40) has noted that a person often expresses a personal goal as getting the job or getting married. But most people do not merely want to get the job or to get married. What they seek is a living relationship, rather than a terminal state. A person wants to live with someone or gain certain benefits from a job. Moving in a particular direction can be satisfying in itself, and journeying is often more important than the destination. As more people come to understand and value being in-process, they might find it less puzzling to acknowledge that not all behavior is teleological. And they might then begin to look for a broader definition of rationality.

The work of several thinkers is leading towards such a broader understanding (7). Leavitt (22) has surveyed supplements to analytic method—Zen, encounter groups, ESP, and creativity research. He tentatively concludes that the conventional definition of rationality has been overly narrow, and that we need to integrate analytic and alternative methods. The implications of split brain research seem headed in the same direction (31). It appears that (for most right handers) the left hemisphere of the brain handles logical, analytical, verbal, and numeric operations; the right

hemisphere of the brain seems to be more holistic, visual, spatial, artistic, and intuitive. In schooling and in running business and government, the western world has emphasized left hemisphere approaches, and yet both hemispheres represent valuable modes of dealing with reality. The limitations of a solely analytic approach are dramatically shown in Halberstam's (15) examination of the analysts and planners for the Vietnam war. Such findings lead to the question, "What would one gain by using both sides of the brain in planning?"

These appreciations can be brought into the planning sphere. We know that in dealing with the new, the novel, and the ill-defined, right hemisphere activities (holistic, intuitive) have marked advantages over left hemisphere operations. This should provide a clue in our search for alternative methods of planning. Planning must image the future. If one does not use goals to image the future, then what does one use?

## DOMAIN AND DIRECTION PLANNING

Planning begins with and results from the mutual interaction between an individual and the environment. By rewarding and punishing behaviors, elements in the environment influence the individual to behave in certain ways. Parents, schools, church, and government viewed in this light are all influences of socialization presenting differing, often conflicting, demands and opportunities. But while some processes and choices of life fall more under the influence of environmental forces, others are more controlled by the individual (2). For individuals also try to influence the environment to gain what they want. Their actions represent attempts to shape a personal living space within

the larger environment. An individual's environment is a shifting and chaotic field of conflicting values, opportunities, and obligations.

By planning, the individual attempts to establish order in the shifting field. He or she images the desired future and derives the consequences of that image for present patterns of behavior. Setting specific goals is not the only effective way to image the future. One alternative mode is to identify one's domain and direction.

*Domain* is the area in which one wants to operate, the arena of favored activity and personal commitment. Domain defines those aspects of the environment that concern the individual; domain also defines the criteria for assessing one's own performance (38). Creating and choosing a domain answers the questions, "What do you want to do? In the shifting field of choice and obligation, what territory do you want to mark out?" Just as an animal marks out its territory and warns other animals about intruding, a person's choice of a domain marks his or her boundaries for action and commitment.

*Direction* is a symbolic expression of who one wants to become. It is a choiceful unfolding of the self toward a particular set of possibilities. Determining direction is built upon self-examination and an individual's deep sense of who he or she is. Direction suggests orchestration, bringing together diverse interests and needs, creating personal rhythm and melody. Vickers has described life as a set of conflicts, stating that an individual's main activity is either to resolve or contain these conflicts (40). Setting and maintaining direction becomes the art of living, reconciling different obligations and developing a thrust of one's own.

An illustration from literature may help clarify what domain and direction are. In Kazantzakis's *Zorba the Greek* (19), one of the Boss's important domains is writing. Despite momentary regrets and self-doubts, he has a passion for writing—the one activity which seizes him and lifts him outside himself. At times, the Boss seems to have no choice but to write, no matter what sacrifices it costs. Writing is his most persistent answer to the question, "What do you want to do?" In trying to define the Boss's direction, we see how direction incorporates his style of doing and reflects the conflicts within himself. For the months that he works with Zorba, the Boss is trying out a new direction. Because he is dissatisfied with his cautious, bookish approach to life, he wants to immerse himself in business and practical affairs. During his partnership with Zorba, he

moves toward being more spontaneous, more physical, and more sensual. Operating the mine with Zorba becomes a symbol for trying out this new direction for himself.

As a symbol direction is an important yet slippery concept that should be elaborated further. One illustration of the power, and uneven unfolding, of a symbol is the history of the United States' self-definition as a democratic republic. As government by the poeple, "democracy" had a more limited meaning when the country was founded than it does today. Over the decades, people argued and fought about the meaning of democracy. The process was marked by discussion, debate, power struggles, and a civil war. As a result, unlanded people, then former slaves, and finally women gained the right to vote. The same contentious history also marks other concepts in our country's history, such as "equal opportunity" and "equal justice before the law".

On the individual level as well, a direction/symbol provides a preliminary and incomplete statement of purpose with which to face the protean future. In the present, even an incompletely understood symbol allows one to take action, to choose or reject alternatives. In the future, by virtue of its incompleteness, a symbol can take on new meanings. If a symbol continues to be important, one successively enlarges or shifts its meaning as one learns from actions more about one's direction. The process is uneven because it involves conflict of values and comparison of incomparables. In fact, conflict is absolutely necessary to sorting out what the symbol means. Because direction is a symbol it can provide both closure and openness. Direction/symbol provides definition which can be altered as the future becomes a somewhat different present from what was envisioned.

Although goal-directed planning is often intended to be a flexible and adaptive process, in practice people tend to over-emphasize the external end-state. Many imperatives for this type of planning seem designed to give goals a vivid objective reality, and sometimes individuals feel tyrannized by these external demands. But a person engaged in domain and direction planning (or directional planning) emphasizes the process of interaction between individual and environment, recognizing that neither is definable apart from the other. Domain and direction planning is intrinsically rather than extrinsically oriented, since planning begins by considering the individual's thrust.

Directional planning is interactive and requires heavy feedback loops from the environment. The individual and the environment mutually shape each other, and domain and direction are changed with the interaction. By acting, one becomes clearer about just what the domain and the direction are. In the same way that "democracy" became clearer through iteratively acting and dealing with consequences, individuals act, system-environment relationships are changed, and domain and direction are altered.

Two considerations further illuminate what planning is and how it can be used. First, planning should be a learning process. And second, the type of planning an individual prefers is connected to one's psychological type.

Both goal-directed planning and directional planning should be used as learning processes. Especially in turbulent environments, planners must be adaptive and learn from changing conditions. Even though our knowledge may be incomplete, we must still take action. What we learn as we go along will undoubtedly affect our plans. Why try to plan as if we could specify it all beforehand, as if the future could be blue-printed? Instead, we should view planning of all types as a continuing process in which we will have learned from acting in the previous period. Recent work elucidating the planning processes of organizations (33), communities (13), and societies (27), has stressed the learning character of planning. It is especially true on the individual level that planning is a set of approximations being revised in time as we learn more about ourselves and the environment.

To view planning as a learning process may lessen people's feeling that they should always be able to express their reasons before acting. Since we sometimes discover our reasons after acting, and yet must start planning before we can fully articulate our reasons, this learning should become part of the planning process itself.

Secondly, one's preference for a planning mode is strongly connected to one's psychological type. Some psychological types are drawn to, and most comfortable with, the specificity and analytic approach of goal-directed planning. With the Myers-Briggs (29) terms as one convenient typology, persons most likely to set specific goals are sensation-thinking types. They prefer to weigh and analyze large amounts of data. They tend to enter scientific and engineering occupations. For highly motivated people of this type, having specific goals is a great help in channeling their efforts. Though our culture is dominated by the sensation-thinker orientation, there are distinctly different types of people who also need to plan. In Myers-Briggs terms three other major personality types are prevalent. Especially for those using feeling and intuition to approach the world, setting specific goals is often an inadequate means to image the future. They need to deal with symbols, and domain and direction planning is one possibility for them.

The main point is that goal-directed planning is best suited for, and is urged upon others by, one psychological type. For other personality types, other planning modes are more likely to be appropriate. This should be kept in mind when evaluating the urgings of a boss, a friend, or an expert, to plan with specific goals. If goal-directed planning does not call forth one's best effort, one should understand why, and look for other modes in which to plan.

## AN EXERCISE FOR DOMAIN AND DIRECTION PLANNING

One exercise which illustrates planning in the new mode suggests the spirit of this type of planning. It also suggests how one might tap into the artistic, holistic, and intuitive dimensions of life for planning purposes. The exercise originated with Shepard (35), and has been successfully adapted by Clark, Krone, and McWhinney in open systems planning.

In a group of four or five people, each constructs a collage. Magazines, old calendars, and other printed materials with a wide variety of pictures are piled in the center of the group. Individuals select pictures that appeal to them and that somehow represent who they are and what domains they are interested in. They also clip any words or phrases that "select themselves" as they skim through the publications. Each person then arranges his or her pictures and words on a large sheet of paper, adding any felt pen embellishments that seem necessary.

Each person shows his or her collage to the other members in the group. People try to view each collage holistically and comment on what they see—the themes, the elements, the "feel", the response the collage evokes from them. Individuals then discuss their collages at whatever level and in as much detail as they wish. To close the interaction, each person selects a phrase or a symbol that characterizes who he or she is and what domains interest him or her.

Participating in the exercise often evokes strong emotions. People cry, laugh, and become exhilarated as they create and discuss their collages. The process always seems to turn out positively, perhaps because the ambiguity of the symbols puts control in the hands of the individual, and perhaps because people who are in the group are willing to help. The exercise represents a different way of discovering and communicating who one is and what one's interests are. Symbols can represent much more, and can be more clearly tied to a person's emotions than a carefully worded exposition on the same subject. The exercise taps into artistic and nonlinear modes of appreciation (in Vickers' sense of the word) which release a powerful sense of energy. The exercise is a good illustration of what is to be gained by exploring modes other than a strictly logical, analytical approach to planning.

Many other techniques could be described. Keeping a dream journal, writing one's own obituary, listing characters in movies and novels that one identifies with, writing ten answers to the question, "Who am I?", and drawing a subjective life line are some of the possibilities. These are ways to image the future and to help determine domain and direction by tapping into fantasy and into the playful and artistic side of ourselves.

The planning exercises most effectively take place with two or more poeple. Something important happens in the effort to express feelings and ideas to someone else. In the process of making feelings and thoughts clear to another, they often become clearer to oneself. Friends respond from different perspectives, identifying themes and seeing patterns that one might be unaware of. Furthermore, despite the frontier emphasis on rugged individualism, one's planning often involves other people's lives. The planning process is enriched by disclosing one's self to them and letting them participate in the planning.

## SUMMARY

Planning involves imaging the future and deriving the consequences of that image for present patterns of behavior. Images of the future may be more or less well-defined. People usually suppose that the future can only be imaged in terms of goals, and "good planning" has come to mean setting specific, objective, and measurable goals. However, alternative modes for planning, such as domain and direction planning, do not involve goal setting. A key argument of this article is that planning does not have to be teleological in order to be directed.

Imaging efforts that use left hemisphere operations (logical, analytical, verbal) end with specific, objective, and measurable goals. Such efforts seem appropriate to problem-solving which comes after the problem has been "found" and defined. Imaging efforts that use right hemisphere operations (fantasy, intuition, symbolizing) head toward visuals or slogans which are symbols for the future. This mode of imaging the future seems appropriate to a problem-finding stage. This article has elaborated upon right hemisphere planning modes because they are at present inadequately understood and yet stand to be useful.

We have discussed several important points about the planning process on the individual level, including:

1. Goals are often used to rationalize previously made decisions. They help justify a planned course of action to others, but the rationalization and justification processes should not blind us to the role of intuition and fantasy in the actual planning process.

2. Alternative planning modes use symbols instead of goals to image the future. Symbolizing uses a wholly different way of appreciating reality that is in part playful, in part artistic and intuitive. These operations have powerful emotional components that can evoke strong commitment.

3. Alternative planning is intrinsic and inprocess. The planning is revised as one goes along and as both individual and environment change. Heavy feedback loops are needed to increase the learning.

4. One can plan alone, but the process gains when it is done with someone else. Externalization, obtaining a different perspective, sharing power, and working in the context of discovery rather than justification contribute to the planning process.

5. A person using goal-directed planning aims to be specific about what he or she hopes to accomplish. I have argued for additional modes of imaging the future which are symbolic, and therefore more appropriate and powerful ways to plan in some situations.

## REFERENCES

1. Angyal, Andras. *Foundations for a Science of Personality* (New York: Viking Press, 1969).

2. Argyris, Chris. "Management Information Systems: The Challenge to Rationality and Emotion," *Management Science*, Vol. 17 (1971), B-275 - B-292.

3. Bonge, John W. "Problem Recognition and Diagnosis: Basic Inputs to Business Policy," *Journal of Business Policy*, Vol. 2 (1972), 45–53.

4. Boulding, Elsie. "Learning to Image the Future," in W. G. Bennis, K. D. Benne, R. Chin, K. E. Corey (Eds.), *The Planning of Change*, 3rd ed. (New York: Holt, Rinehart, and Winston, 1976), pp. 431–444.

5. Braybrooke, David, and Charles E. Lindblom. *A Strategy of Decision* (New York: Free Press, 1963).

6. Burns, Tom, and G. M. Stalker. *The Man-*

*agement of Innovation* (London: Tavistock, 1961).

7. Christenson, Charles. "The Power of Negative Thinking," *Working Paper* 72–41 (Boston: Harvard Business School, December 1972).

8. Delbecq, André L., and Andrew H. Van de Ven, "A Group Process Model for Problem Identification and Program Planning," *Journal of Applied Behavioral Science*, Vol. 7, No. 4 (1971), 466–492.

9. Dessler, Gary. *Organization and Managment: A Contingency Approach* (Englewood Cliffs, N.J.: Prentice-Hall, 1976).

10. Drucker, Peter F. *The Practice of Management* (New York: Harper and Row, 1954).

11. Fox, Robert S., Ronald Lippitt, and Eva Schindler-Rainman. *Towards A Humane Society* (Fairfax, Va.: NTL Learning Resources Corp., 1973).

12. Franklin, Benjamin. *Autobiography* (New York: Dulton, 1964).

13. Friedman, John. Retracking America: *A Theory of Transactive Planning* (New York: Anchor/Doubleday, 1973).

14. Golde, Roger A. *Muddling Through* (New York: AMACOM, 1976).

15. Halberstam, David. *The Best and the Brightest* (New York: Random House, 1972).

16. Jayaram, G. K. "Open Systems Planning," in W. G. Bennis, K. D. Benne, R. Chin, and K. E. Corey (Eds.), *The Planning of Change*, 3rd ed. (New York: Holt, Rinehart and Winston, 1976), pp. 275–283.

17. Kakar, Sudhir. "Rationality and Irrationality in Business Leadership," *Journal of Business Policy*, Vol. 1 (1971–72), 39–44.

18. Kast, Fremont E., and James E. Rosenzweig. *Contingency Views of Organization and Management* (Chicago: Science Research Associates, 1973).

19. Kazantzakis, Nikos. *Zorba the Greek* (New York: Simon and Schuster, 1952).

20. Klapp, Orrin E. "Opening and Closing in Open Systems," *Behavioral Science*, Vol. 20 (July 1975), 251–257.

21. Lawrence, Paul R., and Jay W. Lorsch. *Or-*

*ganization and Environment* (Boston: Division of Research, Graduate School of Business Administration, Harvard University, 1967).

22. Leavitt, Harold J. "Beyond the Analytic Manager," *California Management Review*, Vol. 17 (1975), 5–12, 11–21.

23. Lindblom, Charles E. "The Science of 'Muddling Through,' " *Public Administration Review*, Vol. 19, No. 2 (1959), 78–88.

24. McCaskey, Michael B. "A Contingency Approach to Planning: Planning with Goals and Planning without Goals," *Academy of Management Journal*, Vol. 17 (1974), 281–291.

25. McKenney, James L., and Peter G. W. Keen. "How Managers' Minds Work," *Harvard Business Review*, Vol. 52 (May–June 1974), 79–90.

26. Mason, Richard O., and Ian I. Mitroff, "A Program for Research on Management Information Systems," *Management Science*, Vol. 19, No. 5 (1973), 475–487.

27. Michael, Donald N. *On Learning to Plan—And Planning to Learn* (San Francisco: Jossey-Bass, 1973).

28. William T. "Intuition and Relevance," *Management Science*, Vol. 11 (1967), B157–B165.

29. Myers, Isabel Briggs. *The Myers-Briggs Type Indicator* (Princeton, N.J.: Educational Testing Service, 1962).

30. Newman, William H. "Strategy and Management Structure," *Journal of Business Policy*, Vol. 2, No. 1 (Winter 1971/72), 56–66.

31. Ornstein, Robert E. *The Psychology of Consciousness* (San Francisco: Freeman, 1972).

32. Sayles, Leonard. "Technological Innovation and the Planning Process," *Organizational Dynamics*, Vol. 2 (Summer 1973), 68–80.

33. Schon, Donald A. *Beyond the Stable State* (New York: Random House, 1971).

34. Shank, John K., Edward G. Niblock, and William T. Sandalls, Jr. "Balance 'Creativity' and 'Practicality' in Formal Planning," *Harvard Business Review*, Vol. 51 (January–February 1973), 87–95.

35. Shepard, Herbert A. "Life Planning," in K.

Benne, L. Bradford, J. Gibb, and R. Lippitt (Eds.), *Laboratory Method of Changing and Learning* (Palo Alto, Calif.: Science and Behavior Books, 1975).

36. Soelberg, Peer O. "Unprogrammed Decision Making," *Industrial Managment Review*, Vol. 8 (1967), 19–29.

37. Steiner, George A. *Top Management Planning* (New York: MacMillan, 1969).

38. Thompson, James D. *Organizations in Action* (New York: McGraw-Hill, 1967).

39. Tomkins, Calvin. "Profiles: Look to the Things Around You," *New Yorker*, Vol. 50 (Sept. 16, 1974), 44–48 ff.

40. Vickers, Geoffrey. "Motivation Theory—A Cybernetic Contribution," *Behavioral Sciences* Vol. 18 (1973), 242–249.

Many observers are concerned these days about the quality of work life in organizations, about organizational productivity, and about possible changes in the work ethic of people in contemporary Western society. Indeed, there has been a clamor in the popular press of late that we are in the midst of a major "work ethic crisis" that has its roots in work that is designed more for robots than for mature, adult human beings. Even the very idea of work has taken on negative connotations for some commentators. Studs Terkel begins his work *Working*, in which the thoughts and feelings of workers from many occupations are reflected, as follows:

This book, being about work, is, by its very nature, about violence—to the spirit as well as to the body. It is about ulcers as well as accidents, about shouting matches as well as fist fights, about nervous breakdowns as well as kicking the dog around. It is, above all (or beneath all), about daily humiliations. To survive the day is triumph enough for the walking wounded among the great many of us. . . .

## IS THERE A CRISIS?

Those who perceive that we are in the midst of a crisis in the world of work tend to argue that no less than a revolution in the way productive work is done has occurred in the United States in this century. Organizations have steadily increased the use of technology and automation in attaining organizational objectives. Consistent with this trend (and with the dictates of the "scientific management" approach to work design, as espoused by F. W. Taylor at the turn of the century), work has become dramatically more specialized, simplified, standardized, and

# 7

# Selecting a Managerial Design

*The Design of Work in the 1980s*
J. RICHARD HACKMAN

routinized. Moreover, organizations themselves have become larger in size and more bureaucratic in function. Partly as a consequence of the increase in organizational size, managerial and statistical controls are used more and more to direct and enforce the day-to-day activities of organization members.

The efficiencies of advanced technology, the economies of scale, and the benefits of increased managerial control have generated substantial increases in the productive efficiency of organizations and substantial economic benefits for both the owners of organizations and society as a whole. These economic benefits, in turn, have contributed to a general increase in the affluence, education, and personal level of aspiration of individuals in American society. As a result, people today want jobs that allow them to use their education, that provide "intrinsic" work satisfactions, and that meet their expectations that work should be personally meaningful. No longer will people accept routine and monotonous work as their legitimate lot in life.

According to this line of thinking, we have arrived at a point where the way most organizations function is in direct conflict with the talents and aspirations of the people who work in them. Such conflict manifests itself in increased personal alienation from work and in decreased organizational effectiveness. What worked for Taylor early in this century, it is argued, simply cannot work now because the people who populate organizations, especially well-educated younger workers, will not tolerate it.

Other observers hold a contrary view. Reports of worker discontent and demands for fulfilling work activities, they suggest, have been greatly exaggerated in the popular press and in behavioral science journals. The work ethic "crisis" may be more manufactured than real, they say, and probably represents a serious misapprehension of the actual needs and aspirations of people at work.

Considerable evidence can be marshaled in support of this contention. Perhaps most widely publicized is a project sponsored by the Ford Foundation to test how satisfied U.S. automobile workers would be working on highly "enriched" team assembly jobs in a Swedish automobile plant. Six Detroit auto workers were flown to Sweden and spent a month working as engine assemblers in a Saab plant. At the end of the month, five of the six workers reported that they preferred the traditional U.S. assembly line. As one put it: "If I've got to bust my ass to be meaningful, forget it; I'd rather be monotonous." Arthur Weinberg, a Cornell labor relations expert who accompanied the six workers to Sweden, summarized their negative reactions:

. . . They felt it was a deprivation of their freedom and it was a more burdensome task which required more effort which was more tedious and stressful. They preferred the freedom the assembly line allowed them, the ability to think their own thoughts, to talk to other workers, sing or dance on the assembly line, which you can't do at Saab. There is a freedom allowed on the assembly line not possible in more complex work. The simplified task allows a different kind of freedom. The American workers generally reacted negatively to doing more than one task. They were not accustomed to it and they didn't like it.

Other studies support the results of this transatlantic experiment and cast doubt on the popular notion that people who work on routine and repetitive tasks invariably experience psychological and emotional distress as a consequence.* Perhaps most supportive of the "no crisis" view are the data reported by Robert P. Quinn, Graham L. Staines, and Margaret R. McCollough in a 1974 Department of Labor

*See, for example, George Strauss's "Is There a Blue-Collar Revolt against Work?" (in *Work and the Quality of Life*, edited by James O'Toole, MIT Press, 1974) or "Loneliness and Dissatisfaction in a Blue-Collar Population," by Iradj Siassi, Guido Crocetti, and Herzl P. Spiro (*Archives of General Psychiatry*, 1974, 30: 261–65).

monograph titled *Job Satisfaction: Is There a Trend?* These researchers examined findings from national surveys of job satisfaction from 1958 to 1973 and found no decline in job satisfaction over the past two decades. The present level of employee satisfaction is, as it has been, quite high: Better than 80 percent of the work force consistently report being "satisfied" with their jobs.

The findings do show that younger workers are more dissatisfied with work than older workers. Yet younger workers also were more dissatisfied than their older colleagues 25 years ago, casting doubt on the hypothesis that contemporary young workers are at the cutting edge of a trend toward increasing job alienation and dissatisfaction. A crisis in job satisfaction? No. Data such as those summarized above suggest that the "crisis" may lie more in the minds of journalists and behavioral scientists than in the hearts of people who perform the work in contemporary organizations.

## ARGUMENTS ON BOTH SIDES

Both the argument for and argument against a crisis in job satisfaction can be persuasive, and both sides of the question can be argued forcefully and with ample supportive data. How can we come to terms with this seeming conflict in the evidence as we attempt to generate some predictions about how work will be designed and managed in the 1980s? My own resolution of the issue takes the form of two complementary conclusions. Each of the conclusions strikes me as valid and as consistent with existing evidence about the state of work and workers in contemporary society. Yet, as will be seen, the conclusions provide quite different bases for decisions about how to proceed with the design of work in the decades to come.

Conclusion One: *Many individuals are presently underutilized and underchallenged at work.* It seems to me indisputable that numerous jobs have become increasingly simplified and routinized in the last several decades, even as members of the U.S. work force have become better educated and more ambitious in their expectations about what life will hold for them. The result is a poor fit between large numbers of people and their work. These people, whom James O'Toole calls "the reserve army of the underemployed," have more to offer their employers than those employers seek, and they have personal needs and aspirations that cannot be satisfied by the work they do.

It also is indisputable that many people do *not* seek challenge and meaning in their work but instead aspire to a secure job and a level of income that permits them to pursue personal interests and satisfactions off the job. Do the underutilized and underchallenged workers comprise three quarters of the work force or only one quarter?

We cannot say for sure. What we can say—and this statement may be much more important—is that for some unknown millions of people work is neither a challenge nor a personally fulfilling part of life. And the organizations that employ them are obtaining only a portion of the contribution that these people could be making.

Conclusion Two: *People are much more adaptable than we often assume.* When they must, people show an enormous capability to adapt to their environments. Through almost whatever happens to them, people survive and make do: gradually going blind, winning the lottery, losing one's home to fire or flood, gaining a spouse and children—or losing them. The same is true for work. Some of us adjust to challenging, exciting jobs; others of us to a pretty routine and dull state of affairs. But we adapt. Not to do so would open us up to constant feelings of distress and dissatisfaction, noxious states that we are well motivated to avoid.

This plasticity often goes unrecognized by those who argue loudly on one or the other side of the "work ethic" debate. Part of the reason is that it is very hard to see adaptation taking place, except when the environment changes dramatically and suddenly. When change is gradual, as it is when a young person adjusts to his or her job, it can be almost invisible. We tend, in our studies of work and workers, to catch people after they have adapted to their work situation or before they have done so rather than right in the middle of the adaptation. It is tough to figure out what is happening (or has happened) to a person at work if you look only once.

Precisely because we do adapt to our work environment, it is dangerous to take at face value self-reports of how "satisfied" people are with their work. Consider the case of Ralph Chattick, a 44-year-old worker in a metal fabrication shop on the outskirts of a large midwestern city. Ralph (not his real name) has worked in the same department of his company since graduating from high school and is being interviewed about his job.

*Are you satisfied with your work?*

Yes, I guess so.

*Would you keep working if you won a million dollars in the lottery?*

Sure.

*Why?*

Well, you have to do something to fill the day, don't you? I don't know what I'd do if I didn't work.

*Do you work hard on your job?*

I do my job. You can ask them if I work hard enough.

*Is it important to you to do a good job?*

Like I said, I do my job.

*But is it important to you personally?*

Look, I earn what I'm paid, okay? Some here don't, but I do. They pay me to cut metal, and I cut it. If they don't like the way I do it, they can tell me and I'll change. But it's their ball game, not mine.

Ralph is telling us that he is basically satisfied with his work. But how are we to interpret that? Take it at face value and conclude that he is a "satisfied worker"? No, there are some signs in this interview excerpt that all is not well with Ralph. Yet it also would be inappropriate to take a "yes" such as that provided by Ralph and routinely assume that he *really* isn't satisfied. Ralph is not lying to us. He is satisfied, as he understands what we are asking.

The phenomenon of job satisfaction becomes clearer, and the diagnostic task more difficult, when we put ourselves in Ralph's place and consider the alternatives he has in responding. In fact, things are not awful, which is part of the reason for responding affirmatively. Moreover, Ralph has made numerous small choices over the years (such as deciding not to change jobs or to quit work and attend school) that have increased his personal commitment to his job. To answer other than affirmatively would raise for Ralph the specter that perhaps these choices were poor ones, that in fact he has done a bad job in managing his career: "If I'm dissatisfied with this job, then what the hell have I been doing here all these years? Why haven't I done something about it?" That is an anxiety-arousing issue to face and one that most of us would prefer to ignore. So the easiest response, and one that represents Ralph's present feelings about his work situation fairly, is, "Sure, I guess I'm satisfied with my job."

Because, like Ralph, most people do adapt to their work, responses to questions about job satisfaction can be misleading, especially among people who have considerable tenure. For the same reason, self-reports of satisfaction or lack of satisfaction do not provide a sturdy enough basis on which to erect plans for organizational change—let alone national policy about quality of work life issues.

## CHOICES FOR THE 1980s

The conclusions drawn above cast doubt on the usefulness of trying to decide whether or not we are now in the midst of a work ethic "crisis." They also highlight two quite different routes that can be taken as choices are made about how to design and manage work in the next decade and beyond. One route, which derives from the conclusion that many people are underutilized by the work they do, leads to increases in the level of challenge that is built into jobs and in the degree of control jobholders have in managing their own work. In effect, we would attempt to change jobs to make them better fits for the people who do them.

The other route derives from the second conclusion; namely, that people gradually adapt and adjust to almost any work situation, even one that initially seems to underutilize their talents greatly. This route leads to greater control of work procedures and closer monitoring of work outcomes by management to increase the productive efficiency of the work force. Technological and motivational devices would be used to attempt to change the behavior of people to fit the demands of well-engineered jobs. The expectation is that in a carefully designed work environment employees gradually will adjust to having little personal control of their work, and the efficiencies gained by using sophisticated managerial controls of work and workers will more than compensate for any temporary dissatisfactions the workers may experience.

### Route One: Fitting Jobs to People

The core idea of Route One is to build increased challenge and autonomy into the work for the people who perform it. By creating job conditions that motivate employees *internally*, gains might be realized both in the productive effectiveness of the organization and in the personal satisfaction and well-being of the work force.

Specifically, the aspiration would be to design work so that employees experience the work as inherently meaningful, feel personal responsibility for the outcomes of the work, and receive, on a regular basis, trustworthy knowledge about the results of their work activities. Research by Greg Oldham and myself suggests that when all three of these conditions are met, most people are internally motivated to do a good job—that is, they get a positive internal "kick" when they do well, and feel bad when they do poorly. Such feelings provide an incentive for trying to perform well and, when performance is excellent, lead to feelings of satisfaction with the work and with one's self.

How might jobs be designed to create these conditions? Consider the assembly of a small electrical applicance, such as a toaster. Following traditional dictates of engineering efficiency, such devices usually are manufactured on some form of production line: One individual attaches the heating element to the chassis, another solders on the line cord, a third attaches the mechanical apparatus for handling the bread to be toasted, another inspects the assembled product, and so on.

An alternative design would be to make each employee, in effect, an autonomous toaster manufacturer. All necessary parts would be available at the employee's work station, and he or she would be skilled in all aspects of toaster assembly, inspection, and repair. The employee would perform the entire assembly task, would inspect his or her own work, and then (when satisfied that the apparatus was in perfect working order) would place a sticker on the bottom of the toaster. The sticker would say something along these lines:

This toaster was made by Andrew Whittier, an employee at the San Diego plant of General Toasters, Inc. I believe that it is in perfect condition and will give you years of reliable service. If, however, your toaster should malfunction in any way, please call me at my toll-free number, (800) 555-1217. We will see if we can clear up your problem over the telephone. If not, I will authorize you to send the toaster to me, and I will either repair it or send you a replacement, under the terms of the limited warranty that I packed in the box with the toaster.

What would such a design achieve? Meaningful work? Yes, I'm making a useful household appliance all on my own. Personal responsibility for the work outcomes? Yes, I am personally accountable for the performance of any toaster I release for shipping; there is no one to blame but myself if I ship a bad product. Knowledge of results? Yes, in two ways. First, I do my own inspection and testing before shipping, which means I can self-correct any assembly problems. Second, I obtain direct and personal feedback from customers about any problems they have with my work (not to mention the embarrassment of having it announced on the shop loudspeaker that "Andy, you have another call on the 800 line . . . !").

Surely such a design would lead to a high internal motivation to perform effectively and, for able employees who value the internal rewards that can be obtained from doing a demanding job well, high satisfaction with the work. The quality of work should improve also. However, there might be some decrease in the *quantity* of work done by a given worker on a given day, as compared with the work done on the more technically efficient production line.

The hypothetical design for toaster manufacturing described above has much in common with many "job enrichment" experiments carried out in numerous organizations in the last decade. Although the changes made in such projects inevitably involve alterations, not just of the task itself, but of many aspects of the work organization, the focus clearly is on the work done by individual employees.

A different approach, but one that has many objectives in common with individual job enrichment, is to design work so that it is done by a more or less autonomous *group* of employees. Use of the work group as a design device requires simultaneous attention to the technical and social aspects of the work system, which often is advantageous. Indeed, the group may be the *only* feasible design alternative for creating a whole and meaningful piece of work in some cases. For example, the assembly of automobile transmissions requires coordinated activity among several individuals because of the weight of the materials and the complexity of the assembly.

Probably the best-known application of group work design in a U.S. organization is in the Topeka pet food plant of General Foods, where an entire new manufacturing organization was designed around the concept of the semiautonomous work group. Each work team at Topeka (consisting of seven to fourteen members) was given responsibility for a significant organizational task. In addition to doing the work required to complete the task, team members performed many activities traditionally reserved for management—such as coping with manufacturing problems, distributing individual tasks among team members, screening and selecting new team members, and participating in organizational decision making. Moreover, employees on each team were encouraged to broaden their skills on a continuous basis so that employees and their teams would become able to handle even more responsibility for carrying out the work of the organization. Early reports from Topeka indicate that the innovative project has generated numerous beneficial outcomes, both for the organization and for the people who do the work.

Autonomous work teams and job-enrichment interventions have been used successfully in many organizations. Yet we still have much to learn about how to design, install, and diffuse such innovations most effectively—and about when they do (and do not) generate beneficial outcomes for people and for organizations.*

If we can find most of the answers during the next few years, the shape of work in the next decade could turn out to be quite different from what it is today. Assuming that we follow Route One, and do so competently and successfully, here are some speculations about the design and management of work in the mid-1980s.

1. Responsibility for work will be pegged clearly at the organizational level at which the work is done. No longer will employees experience themselves as people who merely execute activities that "belong" to someone else (such as a line manager). Instead, they will feel, legitimately, that they are both responsible and accountable for the outcomes of their own work. Moreover, the resources and the information needed to carry out the work (including feedback about how well the work is being done) will be provided directly to employees, without being filtered first through line and staff managers. As a result, we will see an increase in the personal motivation of employees to perform well and a concomitant increase in the quality of work being done.

2. Explicit consideration will be given to questions of employee motivation and satisfaction when new technologies and work practices are invented and engineered, on a par with the consideration now given to the employee's in-

*An informative summary and interpretation of what is known about the effects of Route One innovations (and what remains doubtful or ambiguous about their consequences) is provided by Raymond A. Katzell, David Yankelovich, and their colleagues in the monograph *Work, Productivity, and Job Satisfaction* (Psychological Corp., 1975).

tellectual and motor capabilities. No longer will equipment and work systems be designed solely to optimize technological or engineering efficiency, and motivational problems left in the laps of managers and personnel consultants after work systems are put in place.

Moreover, there will be no single "right answer" about how best to design work and work systems. Sometimes tasks will be arranged to be performed by individuals working more or less alone; other times they will be designed to be performed by interacting teams of employees. Choices among such design options will take into account the character of the work itself (such as any technological imperatives that may exist), the nature of the organization, and the needs, goals, and talents of the employees. In many cases work will be "individualized" to improve the fit between the characteristics of an employee and the tasks he or she performs. Standard managerial practices that apply equally well to all individuals in a work unit will no longer be appropriate. Instead, managers will have to become as adept at adjusting jobs to people as they now are at adjusting people to fit the demands and requirements of fixed jobs.

3. Organizations will be leaner, with fewer hierarchical levels and fewer managerial and staff personnel whose jobs are primarily documentation, supervision, and inspection of work done by others. A new way of managing people at work will be needed, giving rise to new kinds of managerial problems. For example, to the extent that significant motivational gains are realized by enriched work in individualized organizations, managers will no longer have the problem of "how to get these lazy incompetents to put in a decent day's work." Instead, the more pressing problem may be what to do *next* to keep people challenged and interested in their work.

As people become accustomed to personal growth and learning at their work, what was once a challenge eventually becomes routine—and even more challenge may be required to keep frustration and boredom from setting in. How to manage an organization so that growth opportunities are continuously available may become a difficult challenge—especially if, as predicted, the number of managerial slots into which employees can be promoted shrinks.

4. Last, if the previous predictions are correct, eventually a good deal of pressure will be brought to bear on the broader political and economic system to find ways to make effective use of the human resources that are no longer needed to populate work organizations. Imagine that organizations eventually do become leaner and more effective and, at the same time, that the rate of growth of society as a whole is reduced to near zero. Under such circumstances, a number of people will be "free" for meaningful employment outside traditional private and public work organizations. To expand welfare services and compensate these people for not working would be inconsistent with the overall thrust of Route One toward meaningful, productive work. So would wholesale reductions of the workweek, unless useful "leisure" tasks could be created at the same time.

What, then, is to be done with the surplus of people and of time? Can we imagine groups of public philosophers, artists and poets, compensated by society for helping create an enriched intellectual and aesthetic environment for the populace? An interesting possibility, surely, but one that would require radical rethinking of public decision making about the goals of society and the way shared resources should be allocated to achieve these goals.

## Route Two: Fitting People to Jobs

If we take Route Two, the idea is to design and engineer work for maximum economic and technological efficiency and then do whatever must be done to help people adapt and adjust in personally acceptable ways to their work experiences. No great flight of imagination is required to guess what work will be like in the 1980s if we follow Route Two; the sprouts of this approach are visible now. Work is designed and managed in a way that clearly subordinates the needs and goals of people to the demands and requirements of fixed jobs. External controls are employed to ensure that individuals do in fact behave appropriately on the job. These include close and directive supervision, financial incentives for correct performance, tasks that are engineered to minimize the possibility of human mistakes, and information and control systems that allow management to monitor the performance of the work system as closely and continuously as possible. And, throughout, productivity and efficiency tend to dominate quality and service as the primary criteria for assessing organizational performance.

If we continue down Route Two, what might we predict about the design and management of work in the 1980s? Here are my guesses:

1. Technological and engineering considerations will dominate decision making about the design of jobs. Technology is becoming increasingly central to many work activities, and that trend will accelerate. Also, major advances will be achieved in techniques for engineering work systems to make them ever more efficient. Together, these developments will greatly boost the productivity of individual workers and, in many cases, result in tasks that are nearly "people proof" (that is, work that is arranged virtually to eliminate the possibility of error because of faulty judgment, lapses of attention, or misdirected motivation). Large numbers of relatively mindless tasks, including many kinds of inspection operations, will be automated out of existence. The change from person to machine will both increase efficiency and eliminate many problems that arise from

human frailties, as suggested by B. M. Oliver in a 1977 essay in *Scientific American* on the future of automated instrumentation and control:

Automatic test systems do not fudge the data or make mistakes in recording it or get tired or omit tests or do any of the dozens of troublesome things human beings are apt to do. Whatever tests the program specifies will be made regardless of the time of day or the day of the week; no front office pressure to ship goods by a certain date can compromise the computer's inspection.

Accompanying these technological advances will be a further increase in the capability of industrial psychologists to analyze and specify in advance the knowledge and skills that will enable a person to perform almost any task that can be designed satisfactorily. Sophisticated employee assessment and placement procedures will be used to select people and assign them to tasks, and only rarely will an individual be put into a job for which he or she is not fully qualified.

The result of all these developments will be a quantum improvement in the efficiency of most work systems, especially those that process physical materials or paper. And while employees will receive more pay for less work, they will also experience substantially less discretion and challenge in their work activities.

2. Work performance and organizational productivity will be closely monitored and controlled by managers using highly sophisticated information systems. Integrated circuit microprocessors will provide the hardware needed to gather and summarize performance data for work processes that presently defy cost-efficient measurement. Software will be developed to provide managers with data about work performance and costs that are far more reliable, more valid, and more current than is possible with existing information systems. Managers increasingly will come to depend on these data for decision making and will use

them to control production processes vigorously and continuously.

Because managerial control of work will increase substantially, responsibility for work outcomes will lie squarely in the laps of managers, and the gap between those who do the work and those who control it will grow. There will be accelerated movement toward a two-class society of people who work in organizations, with the challenge and intrinsic interest of managerial and professional jobs increasing even as the work of rank-and-file employees becomes more controlled and less involving.

3. Desired on-the-job behavior will be elicited and maintained by extensive and sophisticated use of extrinsic rewards. Since (if my first prediction is correct) work in the 1980s will be engineered for clarity and simplicity, there will be little question about what each employee should (and should not) do on the job. Moreover (if my second prediction is correct), management will have data readily at hand to monitor the results of each employee's work on a more or less continuous basis. All that will be required then, are devices to ensure that the person actually does what he or she is *supposed* to do.

Because many jobs will be routinized, standardized, and closely controlled by management, it is doubtful that employee motivation to perform appropriately can be created and maintained from intrinsic rewards (people working hard and effectively because they enjoy the tasks or because they obtain internal reinforcement from doing them well). So management will have to use extrinsic rewards (such as pay or supervisory praise) to motivate employees, providing such rewards for behavior that is in accord with the wishes of management.

In recent years the fine old principle of contingent rewards has been dressed up in the rather elaborate and worldly clothes of "behavior modification," as espoused by B. F. Skinner. Research evidence shows that in many circumstances contingent rewards do have a powerful effect on individual behavior. If we follow Route Two, I predict that behavior modification programs will be among the standard motivational techniques used in work organizations in the 1980s.

4. Most organizations will sponsor programs to aid employees in adapting to life at work under Route Two conditions, including systematic "attitude development" programs to foster high job satisfaction and organizational commitment. Sophisticated procedures for helping employees and their families deal with alcohol, drug abuse, and domestic problems also will be offered by many organizations. These latter programs will become much more prevalent (and necessary) than they are at present, I believe, because of some unintended spin-offs of the movement toward the productive efficiencies of Route Two.

Consider, for example, a person working in an organization in the mid-1970s whose work is undemanding, repetitive, and routine. It might be someone who matches checks and invoices and then clips them together to be processed by another employee. Imagine that we asked that individual the following question: "What happens to you, what are the outcomes, when you try to work especially hard and effectively on your job?" The answers are likely to be far from inspiring. Probably they will have more to do with headaches and feelings of robothood than with any sense of meaningful personal accomplishment from high on-the-job effort. Clearly, such perceived outcomes reveal a lack of any positive internal motivation to work hard and effectively.

Now let us transport that employee via time machine to the mid-1980s and place him or her in a very similar job under full-fledged Route Two conditions. The work is just as routine and undemanding as it was before. The differences are that now there is greater management control over hour-by-hour operations and valued external rewards are available—but the rewards are there only when the employee behaves in close accord with explicit management specifications. How will our hypothetical employee react to that state of affairs?

At first, he is likely to feel even more like a small cog in a large wheel than he did before. Before the new management controls were introduced, he could get away with some personal games or fantasies on the job. Now that is much harder to do. Moreover, the problem is exacerbated, not relieved, by the addition of the performance-contingent rewards. The negative intrinsic outcomes of hard work in the 1970s are still felt—but they have been supplemented (not replaced) by a set of new and positive *extrinsic* outcomes. So the employee is faced with contingencies that specify, "The harder I work, the more negative I feel about myself and what I'm doing, the more likely I am to be tired and headachy on the job, and the more likely I am to get praise from my supervisor and significant financial bonuses."

That state of affairs is precisely what we might devise if we wished deliberately to drive someone insane—that is, having the work and its rewards arranged so that strong positive and strong negative outcomes are *simultaneously contingent on the same behavior* (in this case, working hard). Some of the problems of drug usage, alcoholism, and industrial sabotage that are found in work organizations appear to derive from this kind of no-win state of affairs. And if we move vigorously down Route Two, we can predict with some confidence that signs of employee "craziness" will increase.

Only a small proportion of the work force will exhibit severely maladaptive behaviors, however, even under full-fleged Route Two conditions. As suggested earlier, people have a good deal of resilience and usually can adjust and adapt to almost any work situation if given enough time and latitude to do so. So although we can predict that many people will suffer from tension and stress in adjusting to work in the 1980s and will find their aspirations for personal growth and development at work significantly dampened, we don't think that major overt problems will be observed with any frequency.

Yet because *any* "crazy" employee behavior is anathema to management (and clearly dysfunctional for organizational effectiveness), managers will attempt to head off such behaviors before they occur. When they do occur, management will deal with them as promptly and as helpfully as possible. So we should see in the 1980s a substantial elaboration of organizational programs to help people adapt in healthy ways to their work situations and to minimize the personal and organizational costs of maladaptive responses to the work. All will applaud such programs, because they will benefit both individual human beings and their employing organizations. Few will understand that the need for such programs came about, in large part, as a result of designing work and managing organizations according to the technological and motivational efficiencies of Route Two.

## AT THE FORK IN THE ROAD

Which will it be in the 1980s—Route One or Route Two? There will be no occasion for making an explicit choice between the two. Instead, seemingly insignificant decisions about immediate questions such as how to design the next generation of a certain technology, how to motivate employees and increase their commitment to their present jobs, and how best to use the information technologies that are becoming available will determine what road we follow.

My view, based on the choices that are being made even now, is that we are moving with some vigor down Route Two. That direction, moreover, is unlikely to change in the years to come, for at least two reasons.

First, we know how to operate according to Route Two rules, and we're fumbling at best when we try to design a work unit in accord with Route One. Present theory about how to design enriched jobs and autonomous work groups is still primitive and is depressingly uninformative about how the properties of people, jobs, and organizational units *interact* in determining the consequences of a given innovative design for work. Also, we are only just beginning to develop procedures for assessing the economic costs and benefits of innovative work designs and for reconciling the dual criteria of efficiency and quality of work life in designing work systems.

Although it is not surprising, given the paucity of theory and research on work redesign, it is significant that no trained, competent cadre of managers and behavioral scientists primed to create innovative work systems in contemporary organizations exists. We do have a substantial and growing set of case studies describing successful work redesign projects, but little *systematic* knowledge about how to proceed with such work redesign activities has emerged from these studies. Moreover, there are very few instances in which even a highly successful program has been diffused throughout the larger organization in which it was developed—let alone from organization to organization—with the same success. Even the much-touted Topeka experiment has not had much of an impact on the broader General Foods organization, and it is now being viewed with a good deal of skepticism by some commentators (see, for example, "Stonewalling Plant Democracy," *Business Week*, 28 March 1977, pp. 78–82).

Second, even if we *did* know how to design and manage work according to Route One dictates, my guess is that we would decide not to do so. There are many reasons. One is that Route One solutions, if they are to prosper, require major changes in how organizations themselves are designed and managed; Route Two solutions fit nicely with traditional hierarchical organizational models and managerial practices. Another is that Route One depends heavily on behavioral science knowledge and techniques, whereas Route Two depends more on "hard" engineering technology and traditional economic models of organizational efficiency. If behavioral science has ever won out over an amalgam of engineering and economics, the case has not come to my attention. Also, the kinds of organizational changes made under Route One are likely to impoverish some managerial jobs, at least temporarily, in favor of enriched rank-and-file jobs. Route Two solutions enrich managerial jobs and make them more interesting. Given who makes the choices about how organizations are to be run, it doesn't seem to be much of a contest.

But perhaps most telling is the fact that Route Two is much more consistent with the behavioral styles and values of both employees and managers in contemporary organizations. Experienced employees know how to adapt and survive in relatively routine, unchallenging jobs. Would these people, most of whom are comfortable and secure in their work lives, leap at the chance for a wholly different kind of work experience? Some would, to be sure, especially some of the younger and more adventurous members of the work force; but I suspect that many would not. Learning how to function within a Route One organization would be a long and unpleasant process for a lot of people, and it is unclear how many would be willing to tolerate the upset and the anxiety of the change process long enough to gain a sense of what work in a Route One organization might have to offer.

Managers, too, have good reasons to be skeptical about Route One and its implications. The whole idea flies in the face of beliefs and values about people and organizations that have become very well learned and well accepted by managers of traditional organizations. Among those beliefs are that organizations are supposed to be run from the top down, not from the bottom up; that many employees have neither the competence nor the commitment to take real responsibility for carrying out the work of the organization on their own; that organizational effectiveness should be measured primarily, if not exclusively, in terms of the economic efficiency of the enterprise; and that more management control of employee behavior is better management.

Am I being too pessimistic? Perhaps. There are documented instances of employees and managers alike responding with enthusiasm to work redesign projects that had many of the trappings of the Route One approach. Yet it is troublesome to note that few of these experiments have persisted or diffused widely throughout the organizations in which they took place. Why? An optimistic view is that we do not have enough knowledge and skill yet to maintain and diffuse innovations in organizations, but that with additional research we will soon be able to create the conditions necessary for Route One innovations to catch on and spread. The pessimistic view is that, without being fully aware of the fact, we have already progressed so far down Route Two that it may be nearly impossible to turn back.

As should be apparent from my remarks, I am in favor of the ideas and aspirations of Route One. But as may also be apparent, I suspect that the pessimistic outlook may have validity, that it may be too late to change directions, and that my description of Route Two will turn out to be a good characterization of what work will be like in the 1980s and beyond.

## SELECTED BIBLIOGRAPHY

Two books frequently cited to make the case that there is a work ethic crisis are Studs Terkel's *Working* (Pantheon, 1974), in which workers' own thoughts and feelings about what they do are reported, and *Work in America* (MIT Press, 1973), the report of a special task force appointed by the secretary of health, education and welfare.

Contrary views are taken by Mitchell Fein in "The Real Needs and Goals of Blue-Collar Workers" (*The Conference Board Record,* February 1972, pp. 26–33) and by William Gomberg in "Job Satisfaction: Sorting Out the Nonsense" (*AFL-CIO Federationist,* June 1973).

Several articles in the monograph *Improving Life at Work*, edited by J. Lloyd Suttle and myself (Goodyear, 1977), provide approaches to organizational change that are consistent with Route One guidelines. Included in the volume is a chapter on work design, in which I summarize the theory of individual job design developed by Greg Oldham and myself and describe the process by which changes in individual jobs are made. The classic work on individual job design has been done by Frederick Herzberg and is summarized in his new monograph, *The Managerial Choice* (Dow Jones-Irwin, 1976).

The well-known Topeka project, in which a new General Foods pet food plant was designed using autonomous work groups as the basic organizational unit, is described in Richard Walton's "How to Counter Alienation in the Plant" (*Harvard Business Review,* November–December 1972, pp. 70–81). A recent analysis of that experiment is provided by Walton in "Work Innovations at Topeka: After Six Years" (*Journal of Applied Behavioral Science,* Summer 1977, pp. 422–33).

A review of the theory and application of behavior modification in organizations, which was suggested as a motivational technique central to Route Two approaches, is provided in Craig E. Schneier's "Behavior Modification in Management: A Review and Critique" (*Academy of Management Journal,* September 1974, pp. 528–48).

Problems in maintaining and diffusing Route One innovations are described and analyzed in Walton's "The Diffusion of New Work Structures: Explaining Why Success Didn't Take" (*Organizational Dynamics,* Winter 1975, pp. 3–22). Some ideas for attempting to reconcile Route One and Route Two approaches are provided by Tom Lupton in "Efficiency and the Quality of Worklife: The Technology of Reconciliation" (*Organizational Dynamics,* Autumn 1975, pp. 68–80). Last, the likely relationships among work, education, and the national economy in the future are thoughtfully probed in James O'Toole's recent book *Work, Learning, and the American Future* (Jossey-Bass, 1977).

Personnel selection is emerging as a key issue in human resource management and as a major determinant of organizational effectiveness. This article focuses upon two key issues in human resource management: the selection process, and the emerging of the assessment center method in personal selection. The author concludes that the assessment center method is the best answer to the question of early identification of career potential.

## THE SELECTION PROCESS

Personnel selection is the process by which the organization screens and makes a decision concerning the acceptance or rejection of a potential candidate for a specific job opening. Organizations have been giving greater attention recently to the selection process because they recognize that it is the first step toward building and developing their human resources.

In the selection process, we try to match individual skills and potentials to job requirements. Let us first talk about job requirements, or what I call here Job Information Process (JIP).

### Job Information Process

Hiring an employee without an adequate analysis of the future work load, may lead to conflict between members of the department, or with other departments who may resent the slack caused by the newcomer. It is also costly. Therefore, an intensive analysis of work load should be the starting point for a concerned manager; the personnel officer should be a close liasion. Budget information can help forecast staffing needs based on sales or work load expectations.

# 8

# Staffing: Hiring, Firing, and Evaluating Executives

*Toward A Paradigm*
*Shift In Selection:*
*The Assessment Center*

A. BAKR IBRAHAM

The immediate supervisor is probably the best person to identify the skills and qualifications needed for the job opening. Job requirements can be identified in three steps.

- Job analysis
- Job description
- Job specification

Job analysis is the process of gathering and studying information about the job. Job description is a statement of the responsibilities and duties connected with the job. Job specification identifies the individual skills and qualities needed to perform a specific job. Job specification is the last step in JIP and the starting point of the selection procedure.

Let us now turn to the second phase: the selection process, or what I call here Applicant Information Process (AIP).

## Applicant Information Process (AIP)

The Applicant Information Process consists of the following steps:

- Application form
- Reference check
- Interview
- Tests
- Physical examination

**Application form**   After the initial screening to eliminate undesirable job applicants (candidates who do not meet the basic requirements for the job), potential candidates are then given an application form to fill out. The application form is similar in most organizations; it asks for basic information about the candidate. The application form is a short summary of the job applicant's career history.

**Reference check**   The next step is to verify the information given on the application form. A reference check is usually made to the applicants' immediate supervisor in her present job or possibly to her college or credit refer-

ence. The applicant's past success is a good indicator of future performance.

**Interview**   Although highly subjective, the interview is still the most universal and indispensable technique used to assess potential candidates, particularly in managerial jobs. The main objective of the employment interview is to gather and extract the significant information about the candidate. However, much of the success of the employment interview depends on the interviewer's observation skills.

**Tests**   Some organizations attach great importance to tests, partly because of their objectivity. Tests assess the qualities necessary for a particular job and can frequently predict future performance. A good test should be valid, reliable, and unbiased. Psychological tests that measure clerical, mechanical and vocational interests are widely used in personnel selection. However, personnel testing in recent years is facing strong opposition.

**Physical examination**   The physical examination is the final step in the AIP phase. The main reasons for preemployment medical examination are: (1) to assure the physical fitness of the applicant for a particular job, and (2) to establish a record for the candidate's medical condition before the job, for comparison purposes in case of later compensation claims.

## The Final Hiring Decision

To complete the selection process, a final hiring decision is made based on both the JIP and the AIP. We advise close coordination at all times of the personnel staff and the line manager (See Figure 8-1).

## Appraising the Selection Process

Although the function of selecting a potential employee is a key issue in human resource management, the use of a single technique, such as an interview, casts doubts on the predictive power of the traditional selection method described earlier to predict future performance, particularly in managerial jobs.

## A PARADIGM SHIFT IN SELECTION

In the last decade or so, there has been a major shift in the manner of personnel selection, specifically due to the introduction of the assessment center in large organizations. Unlike the selection method described previously, the assessment center has demonstrated a high predictive power of later job performance.

## An Assessment Center

An assessment center is a standardized selection method that uses a variety of different techniques, including tests, interviews, and case studies to evaluate a potential candidate.

The hallmark of the assessment center approach is its emphasis on behavior rather than on a set of traits.

The use of assessment centers can be traced back to the military. The first assessment center was set up in the United States Office of Strategic Service (OSS) (1) in 1943, during World War II. It was similar to the one set up by the War Office Selection Boards in Great Britain. The main purpose of the assessment center was to select and train OSS personel (2).

Interestingly, the exercises used in the OSS assessment center to select spies bears a close resemblance to the ones used now to select managers.

## The Management Progress Study

The first application of the assessment center approach in industry goes back to the longitudinal study known as the Management Progress Study, undertaken by the American Telephone and Telegraph Company (AT&T) under the supervision of Dr. Douglas Bray (1964) to study the development of young managers. The study results played a major role in establishing the validity of the assessment center method to predict future performance (3). Encouraged by AT&T's results, the assessment center spread to Standard Oil of Ohio, IBM, General Electric, Sears, and other companies in the United States.

## The Assessment Center Process

The assessment center process can be summarized in the following steps.

- Identification of job dimensions
- Selection and design of the instruments of measurement
- Observation and reporting

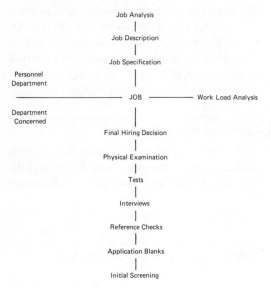

FIGURE 8-1 *Information Flow Diagram of Selection Procedures.*

- Evaluation
- Feedback

Let us now discuss each of these steps in order.

**Identification of job dimensions**   The first step requires the translation of job requirements into measurable dimensions relevant to success in the job. Following is a list that identifies and describes the different qualities necessary in a typical managerial position:

1.  Leadership: Effectiveness in bringing a group to accomplish a task and in getting ideas accepted, and building team spirit.
2.  Persuasion: Ability to organize and present material in a convincing manner.
3.  Flexibility: Ability to modify style and approach to reach a goal.
4.  Decisiveness: Readiness to make decisions and take action.
5.  Stress tolerance: Stability of performance when faced with ambiguity, time pressures, opposition, frustration, and new situation.
6.  Formal oral presentation skills: Ability to make a persuasive, clear presentation of ideas or facts in individual or group situation.
7.  Initiative: Ability to exert active efforts to influence events rather than react to them passively. Acts according to ones own convictions.
8.  Problem Analysis: Effectiveness in seeking out pertinent data; determining the source of the problem; recognizing patterns and trends.
9.  Planning, Organizing, and Controlling: Effectiveness in planning and organizing own activities and those of a group; ordering, scheduling employees, and realistic budgeting.
10. Use of Delegation: Ability to effectively and appropriately use subordinates and to understand where a decision can best be made.
11. Judgement: Ability to reach logical conclusions based on the evidence at hand; ability to evaluate people; entrepreneurial ability; and ability to make money from a business.
12. Intelligence: Ability to adapt, to solve problems, to learn quickly, and to sensibly understand an environment.
13. Financial Ability: Ability to understand financial data, and make correct decisions based on financial data, appreciation of how a business operates.
14. Motivation: The importance of work in deriving personal satisfaction and the desire to achieve at work.
15. Written Communication Skills: Ability to express ideas clearly in writing in good grammatical form.

**Selection and design of the instruments of measurement**   After identification and definition of the behavioral variables relevant to the job opening, the second step is to select and construct the measurement instruments needed, such as the pressure interview, the irate customer role-play, or the leaderless group situation. Each of these instruments is designed to measure certain behavioral characteristics. We will discuss briefly some of the exercises commonly used (See Figure 8-2).

The background interview is designed to extract information from the potential candidates. It could range in time from five minutes to two hours and is conducted by the assessment staff (assessors). The purpose of the background interview is to measure such qualities as oral communication skills, personal impact, energy, personal philosophy towards management process and so on. The potential candidates are usually asked to fill-out a background information sheet prior to the interview.

A pressure interview is a simulated exercise; where the potential candidate is placed in the target role. The candidate might face a committee on unethical practice, or she may deal with a disgruntled client. The purpose of this experience is to measure such qualities as stress tolerance, self-confidence, flexibility, personal impact, and convictions.

The leaderless group exercise is commonly used in assessment centers. This exercise also involves role playing; all potential candidates

```
┌─────────────────────────────────────────────────────────────┐
│                                                              │
│   EXERCISE:  Interview - Stress    CANDIDATE: _____     │
│   INTERVIEWER: _____      DATE: _____       │
│   EVALUATOR: _____      TIME: _____ : _____     │
│                                                              │
│                                                              │
│   ORAL COMMUNICATION SKILLS        1    2    3    4    5       │
│                                                              │
│   FLEXIBILITY                      1    2    3    4    5       │
│                                                              │
│   CONVICTIONS                      1    2    3    4    5       │
│                                                              │
│   PERSONAL IMPACT                  1    2    3    4    5       │
│                                                              │
│   ENERGY                           1    2    3    4    5       │
│                                                              │
│   STRESS TOLERANCE                 1    2    3    4    5       │
│                                                              │
│   SELF CONFIDENCE                  1    2    3    4    5       │
│                                                              │
│                                                              │
│                                                              │
│   OTHER OBSERVATIONAL BEHAVIOUR                               │
│                                                              │
│                                                              │
│                                                              │
│                                                              │
└─────────────────────────────────────────────────────────────┘
```

FIGURE 8-2 *Assessment Center Evaluation Form.*

are assigned different roles for participation in a group discussion concerning a specific issue. The candidates are asked to come to a group decision at the end of the meeting. This exercise is designed to measure qualities such as judgment, problem analysis, oral communication skills, decisiveness, initiative, leadership, conviction, impact, stress tolerance, planning and organizing skills, and energy.

Role playing with an irate customer and similar exercises, are particularly relevant when the candidate must spend a considerable amount of time interacting with others, for example, a sales job, a public relations job, or a management trainee. In these simulations, the assessee is placed in a particular role where, for example, she has to deal with an irate customer. These exercises present the assessor with an opportunity to observe a number of behavioral variables such as stress tolerance, persuasion, problem analysis, sensitivity (customer relations), judgment, decisiveness, flexibility, convictions, and oral communication skills.

TABLE 8.1  A Typical 3 Days Assessment Center Agenda

| Time | Activity | Hour |
|------|----------|------|
| Monday Morning | Registration and General Briefing Session | 9:00–12:00 |
|  | Welcome & Lunch | 1:00–3:00 |
| Evening | Leaderless Group Discussion-Cases | 3:00–5:00 |
| Tuesday Morning | Background Interviews | 9–11:30 |
|  | Free | 11:30–12:00 |
|  | Lunch | 12:00–1:00 |
|  | In-Basket Exercise | 1:00–4:00 |
|  | Free | 4:00–5:00 |
| Evening | Group Discussion Theory X & Y | 5:00–6:00 |
|  | Dinner | 6:00–8:00 |
|  | Pressure Interviews | 8:00–9:30 |
| Wednesday Morning | Irate Customer | 9:00–10:30 |
|  | Coffee | 10:30–11:00 |
|  | Lecturatte | 11:00–12:00 |
|  | Lunch & Free | 12:00–2:00 |
|  | Role Play-Case | 2:00–4:00 |
|  | Candidate Critique | 4:00–5:00 |

The above techniques are commonly used in assessment programs. However other types of exercises could be utilized to assess specific behavioral variables. For example, a lecturette exercise could be used for managerial positions to assess ingenuity and creativity, personal impact, energy, planning and organization skills, and oral communication skills. In this simulation, the assessee is asked to give a five or ten minute presentation on a topic selected by the assessment staff.

Writing exercises may be helpful in some cases as well.

**Observation and reporting**  The usual assessment center occupies three days of the assessee's time. In a typical center, participants are assessed in groups of six or twelve after being nominated by their immediate supervisors. While at the center candidates may play a business game, undergo an extensive interview, or participate in a group discussion or interview simulations (role playing). During these exercises, the assessment staff observes and judges the candidates' behavior and take notes on special assessment forms (see Figure 8-2).

**The evaluation process**  After the assessees have returned to their original jobs, the assessment staff meets to review, discuss, and evaluate the performance on each participant during the assessment exercise. Usually assessors match and discuss their own observations which they have formulated during the assessment program.

**Feedback**  Following the comprehensive evaluation of each participant, a final recommendation report is developed on each candidate, outlining potential training needs and placement. Candidates are then informed of the assessment results in individual meetings with the personnel officer in charge of the assessment center.

## METHODOLOGICAL ISSUES IN SELECTION

We have discussed, so far, the selection process and the use of the assessment center in personnel selection. In both issues, we mentioned two important methodological concepts: reliability and validity. In this section, we discuss both concepts as they relate to personnel selection.

### Reliability

Reliability refers to the consistency of the data obtained. Any selection device—test, interview, or other assessment techniques—should provide consistent readings. For example, if we use a personality inventory test to measure certain behavioral dimensions, we expect consistent and stable readings or repeatability, in measuring and remeasuring the same candidate.

### Validity

Validity is the degree to which a selection device or technique measures what it claims to measure. There are different types of validity: content validity, face validity, concurrent validity, and predictive validity. Content validity is the representativeness of the selection device content to the job content. Predictive validity is when, for example, the job applicant performance in a selection device highly correlates with future behavior. Concurrent validity is the content to which test scores are related to the requirements of the job. Finally, face validity is simply when a selection device or test *appears* adequate to measure what it claims to measure; it is mainly a matter of common sense and experience.

## CONCLUSION

The assessment center method seems the best answer to the question of early identification of managerial potential. Using this multiple method, an organization can observe and objectively evaluate a promising candidate in terms of her managerial skills and potential.

## REFERENCES

1. "A Good Man Is Hard to Find," *Fortune*, March, 1946.
2. Office of Strategic Services Assessment Staff, *Assessment of Men*, (New York: Rinehart and Company, Inc., 1948).
3. Bray, Douglas, D. L. Grant, and R. J. Campbell, "Formative Years in Business: AT & T's Long Term Study of Managerial Lives" (New York: Interscience Publishers, a division of John Wiley's Sons, Inc., 1974.)

*Every model of lower-level-participant power, grounded in a strategic contingencies theory of intraorganizational power, provides the conceptual basis for deriving a series of hypotheses concerning lower-level-participant power. Organizational power is related to access (to persons, information, instrumentalities), expertise, and effort. Generally speaking, the more contingencies that can be controlled by the lower-level participant (LP), the more power the LP has within the organization.*

Power and its impact in organizations has interested scholars since Machiavelli offered *The Prince* as a prescriptive treatment of power and its uses. However, recent authors have abandoned prescription in favor of description, attempting to understand and explain how organizational power is acquired, how it is used, and how it affects the organization. Much of the conceptual and empirical work concerning power in organizations has addressed the concept from either an individual perspective (What are the bases of individual power?) or from an inter/intraorganizational perspective (Why are some organizations or subunits more powerful than others?).

Early work on power was devoted to the first perspective (French & Raven, 1959; Martin & Sims, 1956; Mechanic, 1962.) The French and Raven piece is clearly reflective of this approach. Their bases of power (reward, coercive, expert, legitimate, and referent) specified in a limited way the situational nature of interpersonal power relationships. That is, the appropriate basis of power to be used by the individual in an organization will depend to a great degree on the situation.

Despite the fact that the French and Raven taxonomy of power bases dominated this literature for more than a decade, their efforts provided only implicit answers to such questions as "How does an individual amass power initially?" or "How does an individual add to current levels of power?" Simplistic responses such as acquiring *more* legitimate, expert, re-

# 9

# Executive Leadership

*Lower Participant Power:
Toward a Conceptual Integration*
RICHARD S. BLACKBURN

ward, coercive, or referent power provide the individual with little direction for accomplishing this. In fact, many of the responses to these and similar questions have resulted in what Salancik and Pfeffer alliteratively call "popularized palliatives for acquiring and exercising influence" [1977, p. 21].

A second approach to the study of power elevated the level of analysis from the individual to the organizational subunit. One of the earliest conceptual pieces on the power of organizational subunits was written by Hickson, Hinings, Lee, Schneck, and Pennings [1971]. Their research, subsequently supplied with empirical support [Hinings, Hickson, Pennings, & Schneck, 1974; Salancik & Pfeffer, 1974], postulated that while a "vertical-personalized" concept of power existed in organizations, so did a concept of power that spanned organizational subunits.

In particular, their strategic contingencies theory proposed that subunit power would be a function of (1) the ability of the subunit to cope with environmental uncertainties confronting the organization (coping ability); (2) the uniqueness of the efforts of that subunit in reducing uncertainty (substitutability); and (3) the centrality of the uncertainty-reduction efforts to organizational goals (centrality). The extent to which these variables enable a subunit to control the strategic contingencies of other subunits is reflected in the level of power attributable to the subunit of interest. The contingency theory provides a dynamic approach to the understanding of how power is amassed within organizational units by specifying the factors that influence levels of power.

In ignoring the role of the individual, however, these authors may have done themselves a disservice. As Schein contends:

Analyses of intra-organizational power will be deficient and possibly misleading unless the intentions of the individual powerholder within the organizational context are taken into account. . . .

Deemphasizing personal power should not mean discounting the person [1977, pp. 68–69].

While the individual perspective suffers from a tendency to be overprescriptive, the organizational perspective fails to consider the importance of the individual.

A third concern with the power literature is equally applicable to both approaches. There is an implicit assumption in this literature regarding the location of power and the powerful in most organizations. Such an assumption may well be valid in many instances. However, more than a few researchers have realized that this assumption may be too narrow, arguing that power and the powerful can also exist at lower organizational levels. In fact, it is likely that the reader can attest to this reality by recalling any recent encounter with lower-level participants in bureaucratic organizations.

Perhaps the most intriguing article in this literature is an early work by Mechanic [1962]. Mechanic's discussion of the sources of lower-participant power in complex organizations is a unique conceptual piece. Mechanic argued (nearly a decade before Hickson et al.) that the power of lower-level participants arises from (1) the individual's access to persons, information, and organizational instrumentalities; (2) the unique expertise of the individual; and (3) the individual's effort.

The discerning reader may have noted that the first two factors identified by Mechanic as sources of lower participant power (access and expertise) are similar to those factors suggested by Hickson et al. as sources of subunit power (centrality, coping ability, and substitutability). Thus, it appears that with minor changes a revised version of the Hickson et al. model could be developed with respect to lower-level participant power. The model could be called a "strategic contingencies model of lower-participant power." If such an integration of perspectives could be accomplished, then it might be possible to go beyond Mechanic's tentative conclusion regarding his development of the construct of lower-participant power: "It *appears* that these variables help to account *in part* for the power exercised by lower participants in organizations" [p. 364; emphasis added]. In fact, this model could provide a firm conceptual foundation for the further systematic study of lower-participant power in complex organizations.

## A MODEL

In developing a model underlying a contingency approach to lower-participant power, it should be noted that "lower participant" need not refer exclusively to operatives in an organization. Rather, the term will be used, as by Mechanic, to denote positions relative to higher-ranking participants. Thus, clerks and secretaries would be included in this classification as would all employees who find themselves subordinate to other organizational participants.

The model to be developed is presented in Figure 9-1. It synthesizes the elements contained in Mechanic's discussion of lower-participant power and the basic contingency approach of Hickson et al. viewed from an individual perspective. To facilitate the remainder of this discussion, a lower participant will be identified as an LP and a higher participant as an HP.

### Access

In his first hypothesis, Mechanic suggested that "organizational power is related to access to persons, information, and instrumentalities" [p. 353]. The inferred relationship in this hypothesis is, of course, a positive one, such that increased access would imply increased levels of organizational power for an LP. Mechanic further hypothesizes that tenure, attractiveness, and location or position will also be positively related to gaining this access.

Certainly, one cannot gain power at any

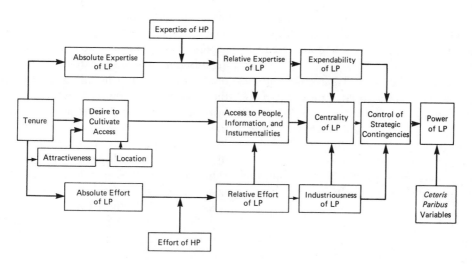

FIGURE 9-1 *Strategic Contingencies Model of Lower-Level-Participant Power.*

level within an organization unless one is a member of that organization. Hence, organizational membership of some duration will be the starting point in the proposed model. This is not to deny that an individual may gain power "over" an organization while not actually a member of it. However, this model considers only that power accruing to actual organizational participants.

Similarly, the more attractive one is the more likely one can gain or be granted access to instrumentalities of power. Mechanic originally equated an individual's attractiveness with personality. The concept is broadened here to represent both attractiveness of personality and professional attractiveness (general competence as opposed to unique expertise).

Finally, Mechanic proposed that location would affect access to instrumentalities of power. To the extent that an individual is in a position that provides for increased visibility and interaction with those at upper levels in the organization, that individual's power should increase. I believe that physical attractiveness as well as professional/personal attractiveness will be positively related to one's chances of being placed in such positions. Both physical attractiveness and professional/personal attractiveness are important determinants of location early in a career; the latter characteristic is probably the more important determinant as tenure increases.

Mechanic hypothesized that tenure, attractiveness, and location would improve the probability that an LP will gain access to important organizational persons, information, and instrumentalities. However, the model suggests that mere access to such resources does not improve one's power position in an organization unless one is willing to cultivate such opportunities.

The desire to cultivate access to power and the powerful is similar to what Schein (1977) recently called "intent of the powerholder." She classified these intentions as either con-

gruent or incongruent with the intent of the organization. That is, congruent intentions result in organizationally functional behaviors and incongruent intentions will likely result in dysfunctional behaviors.

The determinants of such behaviors are at present uncertain. One could speculate, however, that these determinants might include an individual's need for achievement or power, and other motivational needs such as need for esteem and social affiliation. Tenure, for example, could affect intentions or desires in contradictory ways: exposure to power and the powerful could either whet one's appetite for the rewards of power or nauseate one at the perceived abuses of power by the HP's. Given the preceding discussion, it appears that Mechanic's proposed relationships between tenure, attractiveness, and location, and power are not as straightforward as originally hypothesized.

## Expertise

In his third, fourth, and fifth hypotheses, Mechanic considers the role of expertise in the acquisition of power by lower participants. In particular, he suggests that power will accrue to the LP to the extent that the LP has expertise unavailable to the HP. To the extent that this expertise is in an area of importance to the organization, and to the extent that this expertise is so unusual as to not be easily replaceable, the LP gains more power. That the expertise be in a crucial area is important, for as Salancik and Pfeffer note, "power is . . . limited by the need for one's capacities in a social system" [1977, p. 9]. Much like the Hickson team's concept of substitutability, the expendability of an LP will be a function of the absolute levels of expertise possessed by both the LP and the HP.

The expertise of the HP will mediate the relationship between the LP's *absolute* expertise in an area and the LP's *relative* expertise as viewed by the organization. The extent to which the HP desires to maintain a relative expertise advantage over subordinates will be a function of (1) the absolute ability that is recognized in the LP and the extent to which it is allowed to be increased; (2) the perceived threat to the HP's job security; (3) the importance attached to the area(s) of expertise by the HP; and (4) the extent to which the HP may need a scapegoat in the event a wrong decision is made in the LP's area of expertise. This relationship between absolute and relative expertise will likely vary as a function of the HP's perceptions, self-esteem, and self-confidence. The allowed level of LP expertise and the extent to which this level can be or is manipulated by HP access to expert sources internal or external to the organization influences the expendability of the LP.

## Effort

Finally, Mechanic proposes in hypotheses six and seven that the willingness of an LP to exert effort in a particular area of importance to the organization can influence the power available to the LP. As with expertise, the amount of power to be realized as the result of the LP's effort will depend in part on the effort that the HP is willing to make in the same area. Hence, the model reflects the potential mediating effect of effort by the HP. Regardless of expertise levels, the relative effort of the LP will yield perceptions of industriousness by individuals in the organization.

## Summary of the Model

The propsed model indicates that the ability to gain access to important organizational resources will be a function of an LP's (1) desire to gain and cultivate that access; (2) relative expertise in areas of interest to the HP; and (3) willingness to make an effort in areas where the HP will not. The model suggests that unique expertise and industriousness might prompt holders

of organizational power to seek out such LPs and provide them with resources so that their expertise and effort work to benefit the organization. Acquisition and control of scarce resources is an indication of organizational power [Salancik & Pfeffer, 1977].

To the extent that an LP can cultivate access and enhance control over certain organizational resources of importance to key individuals, the LP can achieve a position central to either the core technology of the organization or the major organizational communication network. The extent to which one can achieve this central position will also be influenced by one's expendability and industriousness in areas of organizational importance.

Hickson et al contend that subunit power will accrue to that entity which controls the strategic contingencies of the organization through uncertainty reduction, non-substitutability, and centrality. Mechanic and this model suggest that power will accrue to that LP who can control organizational contingencies through unique expertise, centrality of position, and industriousness of effort in areas ignored by the HP.

From an individual perspective, Salancik and Pfeffer offer an intriguing summary comment about the nature of LP power in organizations: "Power adheres to those who can cope with critical problems of the organization. As such, power is not a dirty secret, but the secret of success" [1974, p. 3]. Given the implications of this model and in the spirit of Salancik and Pfeffer and Hickson et al., I propose a final hypothesis concerning LP power:

*Ceteris paribus,* the more contingencies that can be controlled by the LP, the greater the LP's power in the organization.

Throughout the model it has been assumed that other organizational variables have remained constant. Mechanic admonishes that one should:

strive for clarification by attempting to oversimplify organizational processes; the goal is to set up a number of hypothetical statements of the relationship between variables . . . "all other factors assumed to remain constant" (1962, p. 352).

The inclusion of *ceteris paribus* variables in this model may not be realistic, but it does simplify the discussion. Those factors which might be assumed to remain constant could include other LP-HP relationships and the extent of congruence between individual and organizational goals.

## IMPLICATIONS AND SUGGESTIONS

This model of lower participant power integrates the strategic contingencies theory of intraorganizational power of the Hickson group and Mechanic's sources of power for lower-level participants. It postulates that the power of lower participants is a function of their ability to control strategic organizational contingencies. Such contingencies could best be controlled by reducing one's expendability, by acquiring levels of expertise not available elsewhere, by increasing one's industriousness beyond levels adopted by higher-level participants, and by centralizing one's location near critical organizational channels.

If the sources of lower participant power are important theoretical and practical considerations, then empirical consideration of this model and the hypotheses proposed by Mechanic is apparently required. Such a task requires that the variables in the model be defined more accurately and operationalized more completely. An even more demanding task is prescribed by Hickson et al. These authors contend that what must be done is the difficult work of identifying those combinations of the independent variables which allow the foregoing final hypothesis to hold. To do this, however, empirical analyses utilizing more sophisticated multivariate approaches will likely be needed. The model offered here is an initial conceptual step in such an investigation.

## REFERENCES

Dahl, R. A. The concept of power. *Behavioral Science*, 1957, 2, 201–215.

French, J. R. P.; & Raven, B. Bases of social power. In D. Cartwright (Ed.), *Studies in social power*. Ann Arbor: University of Michigan Press, 1959.

Hickson, D. J.; Hinings, C. R.; Lee, C. A.; Schneck, R. E.; & Pennings, J. M. A strategic contingencies theory of intraorganizational power. *Administrative Science Quarterly*, 1971, 16, 216–229.

Hinings, C. R.; Hickson, D. J.; Pennings, J. M.; & Schneck, R. E. Structural conditions of intraorganizational power, *Administrative Science Quarterly*, 1974, 19, 22–44.

Martin, N. H.; & Sims, J. M. Power tactics. *Harvard Business Review*, 1956, 34, 25–29.

Mechanic, D. Sources of power of lower participants in complex organizations. *Administrative Science Quarterly*, 1962, 7, 249–264.

Pfeffer, J.; & Salancik, G. R. Organizational decision making as a political process: The case of a university budget. *Administrative Science Quarterly*, 1974, 19, 135–151.

Salancik, G. R.; & Pfeffer, J. The bases and uses of power in organizational decision making: The case of a university. *Administrative Science Quarterly*, 1974, 19, 453–473.

Salancik, G. R.; & Pfeffer, J. Who gets power—and how they hold it: A strategic contingency model of power. *Organizational Dynamics*, 1977, 5, 3–21.

Schein, V. E. Individual power and political behaviors in organizations: An inadequately explored reality. *Academy of Management Review*, 1977, 2, 64–72.

*The ineffectiveness of many management control systems is attributed to the cybernetic philosophy on which they are based. A distinction is made between routine industrial-type processes, for which a homeostatic paradigm is more suitable, and nonroutine, non-industrial-type processes, for which a political paradigm is recommended. Attempts at enforcing a cybernetic paradigm on the latter processes, like Program-Planning-Budgeting System and Management-By-Objectives, are bound to fail.*

Anthony and Vancil (1. p. 5) define Management Control as "the process by which managers assure that resources are obtained and used effectively and efficiently in the accomplishment of the organization's objectives." Others narrow this definition down and distinguish "planning" (the setting of goals) from "control" (living up to the goals that were set). Whether we use the wider or the more limited definition, management control is the domain

*par excellence* of formalized systems in organizations, and these systems tend to be designed according to a cybernetic philosophy.

By "cybernetic" is meant a process which uses the negative feedback loop represented by: setting goals, measuring achievement, comparing achievement to goals, feeding back information about unwanted variances into the process to be controlled, and correcting the process. This is a much narrower use of the term "cybernetic" than that advocated by Wiener who coined it to deal with the transfer of messages in the widest sense (17), but it corresponds more closely to its present use in practice. In spite of (or maybe owing to) its simplicity, the cybernetic-in-the-narrow-sense feedback loop has attained the status of a proper paradigm in a wide area of systems theory including, but not limited to the management sciences (15). A review of nearly 100 books and articles on management control theory issued between 1900 and 1972 (4) reflects entirely the cybernetic paradigm.

# 10

# Managing Information for Control and Evaluation

## *The Poverty of Management Control Philosophy*

GEERT HOFSTEDE

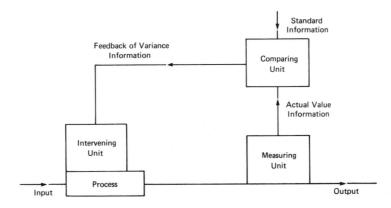

FIGURE 10-1 *Technical Control Model of an Organizational Control System*.
SOURCE: G. Hofstede, *The Game of Budget Control* (Assen. Van Gorcum, and London: Tavistock, 1967), p. 84.

In the cybernetic view, a management control process in its most simplified form is similar to a technical control process, for example, control of the heat of a room by a thermostat (see figure 10-1.

The model in Figure 1 uses only first-order feedback. More sophisticated models for which technical analogues also can be found use higher order feedbacks to control the lower order controllers. Another possible control model used in technical devices is "feed-forward", sometimes presented as an alternative for management control. Feed-forward, however, assumes that interventions are programmable in advance as a known function of environmental disturbances—a condition unlikely to be fulfilled in most management control situations.

All cybernetic models of control have to assume that:

1. There is a standard, corresponding to effective and efficient accomplishment of the organization's objectives.
2. Actual accomplishment can be measured. In Figure 1, the "measuring unit" is connected to the output of the process, but the measuring may include data about the input, or about the ratio between output and input. For example, in an industrial production process, the quantity of var-

ious inputs (labor, materials, energy) for a given quantity of output may be measured.
3. When standard and measurement are compared and variance information is fed back, this information can be used to intervene in the process so as to eliminate unwanted differences between measurement and standard for the next round.

There is no doubt that the cybernetic model of control has been eminently successful in the design of machines, electronic circuits, or similar technical systems, but management control in an organization is a social process in a social, or maybe socio-technical system. The "units" (see Figure 1) in this case are people, or even groups of people. This subjects the use of the cybernetic model to severe limitations because:

1. In many organizational situations, one or more of the three above-mentioned basic assumptions necessary for the validity of the cybernetic model are not justified: standards do not exist, accomplishment is not measurable, feedback information cannot be used. This is particularly the case for indirect (service) activities in industrial organizations and for all non-industrial organizations, such as schools, hospitals, and public bodies. I became painfully aware of this when discussing classical industrial-type management control (12) with a group of experienced man-

agement consultants working in non-industrial settings. After finding out that the cybernetic paradigm did not apply to these consultants' daily practice, we even started to wonder to what extent it *really* applies in many industrial settings.

2. The three assumptions of the presence of a standard, the measurability of accomplishment, and the usability of feedback are most justified for routine, industrial-type processes: industrial production and sales: the supplying of routine services to clients. But even these relatively machine-like processes are in reality social: the cybernetic control process as pictured by the model is only one of many interpersonal processes going on among the same people at the same time. Other processes—some of them by-products of the control system—may interfere with the control process, and sometimes may even lead to an outcome which is the opposite of what was intended by the designers of the system (6).

One remarkable fact about control processes in organizations which has become associated with the cybernetic paradigm is that they are usually tied to a division of labor—different units in the model correspond to different people who are specialized in their tasks. Measuring and comparing are often done by "staff" personnel of a controller's department, standards are set by higher "line" management, intervening is the task of lower line management, while the actual process to be controlled is carried out by operating personnel (workers). In the last resort, it is usually these workers' response to the control process which determines whether the control has been effective.

Proper functioning of the control process presupposes *communication* (17): the necessary messages should be sent and correctly received between the various specialized actors; it also presupposes that all will feel *motivated* to act according to the model (6). Already the proper sending and receiving of the necessary mes-

sages poses many problems, as the various persons involved have different types of education, work experience, and hold different values. The latter also affects their motivation pattern.

A difference in values between people in controllers' departments and line management is evident to anyone familiar with organizational folklore; moreover, it is illustrated by research. For example (6, p. 236), controllers' department personnel in five Dutch companies felt more than line managers that working does not come naturally to most people and that people therefore need to be controlled and prodded (a "Theory X" point of view); they also showed themselves more concerned with the method of measuring performances than with the content of what was measured. In another study of an international group of middle management personnel (8), those in accounting and control departments, compared to others, showed low concern for the efficiency and effectiveness of their actions but high concern with orderliness, following a systematic approach, and doing things according to a schedule. Both studies quoted suggest that people in control departments would tend to stress *form* where those in line roles would rather stress *content*.

In most cases, the controller's department is responsible not only for measuring and comparing, but also for design of the entire control system. An excessive stress on form rather than content explains why, at close scrutiny, many management control systems do *not* supply real control, but only "pseudo-control". Pseudo-control is a state of affairs in which a system is under control on paper (the figures look right) but not in reality. There are several ways to achieve pseudo-control, for example, by correcting the standards (rather than the process) whenever an important variance occurs, by choosing one's measures of performance so as to reflect the desired result (there are many ways to bend the figures without actually cheating), or by adjusting one element in the process at the expense of another which does not show up in the figures (reducing cost at the expense of quality).

The value differences between controller's department personnel and line management are just one type of social communication barriers in the system. We can also think of the way in which rank-and-file workers, with their particular education, work experience, and value systems, tend to react to control measures. We all know these are often met with considerable suspicion and resistance, going counter to the desired motivation, but control systems de-signers have been extremely slow to take account of these facts. As far back as 1953, Jonas (11, p. 188) signalled the tendency among cyberneticians to apply two kinds of doctrine—one to the people in their models, who are taken as robots, and another one to themselves: "he (the cybernetician) considers behavior, except his own; purposiveness, except his own; thinking, except his own." People usually dislike being taken as robots, and they will resist an organization built on such a double doctrine.

## AN ALTERNATIVE PARADIGM: HOMEOSTASIS

While the cybernetic paradigm, by distinguishing various "units" in the control process, has undoubtedly contributed to the division of labor in control process tasks, there can be cybernetic control without division of labor. Division of labor in control of production tasks may have been a productive innovation in the days of F. W. Taylor who advocated ". . . taking the control of the machine shop out of the hands of the many workmen, and placing it completely in the hands of the management, thus superseding 'rule of thumb' by scientific control" ("On The Art of Cutting Metals", 1906, p. 39; 4). It is recognized now that the separation of tasks and specialization which Taylor defended can go too far. What, among other factors, has changed since Taylor's days, at least in developed countries, is the worker. Today's worker is better educated, and to escape from starvation is no longer his or her primary work motive, but he or she can afford to look for a task with some intrinsic reward to it. Entrusting measuring, comparing, and intervening to specialized staff and line personnel implies an assumption that the operating personnel themselves cannot or do not want to adequately perform these tasks. This assumption, which is reinforced by the "Theory X" attitude found among certain people in controlling roles, may no longer be justified in many cases.

A fully documented example is available from a typewriter assembly workshop in Amsterdam (7). Up to 1969, assembly took place in long lines of 60–70 operators each. The process was controlled by specialists in various ways. Engineers calculated time standards and divided the total assembly job into individual tasks of as equal as possible duration. For control purposes, the lines were further divided into five sections of 12–14 operators. Each section had its quality inspector to check the section's production; quality inspectors produced computerized defect lists for the line manager, and specialized repair men repaired the defects. Five foremen, each assisted by a charge hand, supervised the five sections of two parallel assembly lines, so that each foreman was specialized in the supervision of one particular part of the assembly process. Foremen allocated workers to places, gave instructions, and watched over presence and absence; another computerized list showed the production and the various kinds of unproductive time for each worker. Specialized "dispatchers" provided the assembly operators with the parts they needed.

After extensive experiments, the department was reorganized in 1971 into semi-autonomous groups of 20 operators each. Operators divided the total assembly task among themselves according to each person's real capacities rather than based on a general standard. Quality defects were reported verbally within the group and corrected immediately; repair men became superfluous and switched to production. Operators started ordering their own parts instead of waiting for the dispatcher. The foreman's task changed drastically; it now demanded less technical, more social leadership, representing the group to the rest of the organization. Operators arranged among themselves replacement for temporary absences, and the production recording was reduced to counting the number of finished machines at the end of the day. The various computer lists were discontinued. Productivity increased by 18 percent in two months and continued improving: in the two-and-a-half years followed the reorganization the total gain was 46 percent, and quality improved.

The new situation also posed new problems. At the worker level, training time for new operators increased. As groups rather than individuals had become the basic elements in the production system, stability of group composition became much more of an issue than before. For these reasons, rapid extension, change and reduction of production programs and levels posed more problems under the new system. The number of constraints for planning had increased, the process had become less flexible. An explosive production volume increase in 1974 led to severe productivity and quality problems in 1975. Another difficulty was that the new structure was limited to the worker level and was not reinforced by corresponding changes in structure and philosophy at higher levels in the hierarchy and in staff departments. People at the interface between the classical and the re-structured part of the organization, such as supervisors found their roles extremely difficult. As a result, the organization of the department moved back to more classical management control procedures in later years, although the small working groups with their aspect of job enlargement (work cycles of about ten minutes instead of three minutes in 1969) were retained.

The case shows that, under favorable circumstances, semi-autonomous groups were created and took over most of the management control roles previously fulfilled by superiors and specialists. All tasks within the classical cybernetic control loop—measuring, comparing, feedback, intervening—were carried out within the group itself. Its links to the organization's needs were mainly established through the *standards* set by others in the organization for the group's tasks. Quality standards were given by the quality control department based on sales and customer service requirements; delivery programs by the production control department; productivity standards were present in the form of past production records. Rather than cybernetic, I would call such a control process *homeostatic*. Its analogy is not a technical device like a thermostat but a biological element represented by a *living cell*, which is equipped with internal processes capable of maintaining an equilibrium in a changing environment, provided that the environmental conditions do not become too unfavorable.

Like the word "cybernetic", "homeostatic" can be used to mean different things; the term is used here because of its predominantly biological connotation. Homeostatic processes are composed of cybernetic elements, but without the division of labor between controlling and controlled units; control is exercised within the system itself. We could also call these processes "self-regulating" (14).

The switch from a technical to a biological paradigm also explains one other aspect of homeostatic control processes which was illustrated in the typewriter assembly case: whereas a technical control device can quickly be put together and can be repaired if it breaks down, a cell must grow (which takes time), and it can die. Homeostatic control processes, therefore, are more vulnerable than cybernetic processes.

The transfer from cybernetic to homeostatic management control systems will demand a drastically changed control philosophy, especially with regard to the traditional division of labor tied to the cybernetic model. Those in controllers' departments involved in the design and introduction of control systems will have to widen their outlook to include a broad view of the socio-psychological processes going on between people in an organization. The homeostatic approach needs a new type of controllers. It may also need a new type of information systems. Considerable efforts are put today into developing and improving management information systems, but here again the designers' basic assumptions about socio-psychological processes are often remarkably simplistic and shallow.

## NONCYBERNETIC PROCESSES

So far, we have dealt with control situations for which the three main conditions of the cybernetic model were fulfilled: a standard exists, accomplishment is measurable, feedback can be used for corrective intervention. If we consider the full range of human organizations in which control processes occur, those that satisfy the conditions for the cybernetic model tend to be the more structured ones, those which more or less fit a machine analogue. In a criticism of the cybernetic paradigm in system theory in general, Sutherland (15) makes applicability of cybernetic control dependent on the determinedness of a system. If phenomena are completely determined, cybernetic control is obviously superfluous. It becomes useful for moderately stochastic phenomena. When phenomena are severely stochastic, cybernetic control becomes either technically or economically unfeasible. When phenomena are completely undetermined, cybernetic control has become meaningless. Translated in terms of everyday organization activities, Sutherland's moderately stochastic phenomena are the more structured ones: the routine industrial-type processes referred to before. In many other organizational situations (indirect departments in industrial companies, public bodies, schools, hospitals, voluntary associations), we are in Sutherland's area of severely stochastic or even completely undetermined phenomena, and we meet with great problems in applying the cybernetic model. What we notice in practice when we try to follow a cybernetic approach is: (a) Objectives may be missing, unclear, or shifting; (b) Accomplishment may not be measurable; and/or (c) Feedback information may not be usable. Each of these three conditions is illustrated below.

1. *Objectives are missing, unclear, or shifting*—If there is to be a standard, there should be objectives from which this standard is derived. Setting of standards presupposes clarity about the organization's objectives. Now social scientists have often stressed that to speak of "an organization's objectives" is unallowable; organizations cannot have objectives, only people can. We can speak of an organization's objectives only to the extent that there is either virtually complete consensus between all organization members about what should be done (for example, in a voluntary fire brigade); or a dominant coalition of persons within the organization with sufficient power to impose their objectives on all others, and with consensus among themselves (as in many business enterprises); or a single power-holder

whose objectives count as the organization's objectives (as in a small owner-controlled business firm).

Many organizations do not satisfy any of these three conditions, and their objectives are therefore ambiguous. Examples are:

• Democratic institutions such as the city governments in most Western countries—In this case, power is deliberately distributed among several persons or coalitions who hold different objectives for the entire organization; moreover, power is partly held by elected representatives, partly by permanent civil servants; the two groups differ considerably in their involvement with and expectations from the organization.

• Universities—Perhaps the extreme case of organizations in which power is widely distributed and different power groups hold very divergent views about objectives.

• Business organizations or parts of business organizations in which dominant coalitions are not unanimous about objectives—Business employees know that objectives may shift from one day to another, depending on who has the upper hand. This becomes even more likely where societal changes, such as attempts at establishing industrial democracy, bring new coalitions of orization members into the objective setting process.

In such cases, decisions, if they are consciously taken at all, are based on processes of negotiation and struggle and cannot be derived from any prior organizational objective. Objectives may forever remain unclear. This may even be true if someone in the organization publishes eloquent espoused objectives for public relations purposes—like those sometimes expressed in company charters. The objectives in use in the real-life situation of the organization's members are not necessarily the same as the published ones.

2. *Accomplishment is not measurable* — Even in cases where objectives are clear to all involved, it is often not possible to translate them into unambiguous, quantitative output standards against which performance can be measured. How should we measure the output of a police department? One of its final objectives is definitely to prevent crime, so we might consider the decrease of crime rates as an output measure. This assumes that other influences on crime rates can be neglected (which is not true) and that crime rates themselves can be measured objectively (whereas in fact they are partly derived from police reports; low reported crime rates could also mean administrative incompetence of police personnel to adequately register crimes). In such cases, organizations often resort to *surrogate* measures of performance (2), measures which are less directly tied to the organization's objectives but which are more easily measurable. In the case of the police department, the number of people arrested or the amount of fines levied could be such surrogate measures.

For many organizations or activities within organizations, outputs can only be defined in qualitative and vague terms; the only thing really measurable about such activities is their inputs—how much money and other resources will be allotted to them. These include most management and indirect activities in industrial organizations, like advertising, personnel departments, control activities in headquarters, research; most public bodies, like municipal and government services; most activities in schools, universities, hospitals and voluntary associations. In all these cases, the sole control of management exists at the time of resource allocation, but the criteria for resource allocation to this and not to that activity are judgmental. The essence of the process is negotiation, a political process in which many arguments other than the effective and efficient use of resources usually play a role—status of the negotiator, amount of support among influential persons which he/she might mobilize, personal relationship between negotiators, and sometimes nepotism.

One frequently used control device is whether similar funds allocated last year were really spent; its main effect is the spending of unnecessary funds. Skillful negotiators have many "ploys" at their disposal, and skillful resource allocators have many counter-ploys (2, p. 249). This is a part of the game of management control which has little to do with either effectiveness or efficiency of the organization—not because of anybody's evil intentions but simply because nobody is able to predict what resource allocation corresponds to maximum effectiveness.

3. *Feedback information is not usable*— The cybernetic model presupposes a recurring cycle of events: variance information is used to correct the present state of affairs to eliminate unwanted variances for the future. The model basically does not apply to one-time projects, like most investment projects, whether in private or in public organizations. As the project in its present form never returns, even large differences between planned and actual cost and performance have no effect on future projects.

It is remarkable that many organizations do not even attempt to do any project cost accounting to check whether predictions at the time of proposal were really fulfilled, and this can hardly be justified solely on the technical grounds that the benefits of one single project are difficult to disentangle. Once a proposal is accepted, the resources allocated to it become "sunk costs" and it is good management practice not to bother about such costs. However, this state of affairs stresses the negotiation element in the allocation of resources to in-vestment projects even more. It is often hardly important whether the project's forecasted costs and performances are realistic—it is important that they "look good" to the person or persons who decide about the allocation. Once the decision is taken, few people worry about real outcomes. This leads to deliberate underestimation of costs. A common practice in the game of investment budgeting is, for example, to budget for the price of a machine but not for its installation costs, auxiliary tools, or spare parts; once the machine is bought, the organization is forced to spend on these other items to get it going.

A few organizations do use regular evaluation studies of past investment projects; Hägg (5) studied these investment reviews and claims as one of their potential effects a "symbolic use". There is no change impact as far as planning of future projects is concerned. But managers use the review procedure by, for example, referring to it as a sign of progressive management. They can do this when asked questions about capital investment activities by researchers or superiors. The review procedure can also be looked upon as "institutionalized", as part of a tradition or a myth in the organization (5, pp. 58–59). Of course, it is also possible that reviews do have a change impact, or that they have no impact at all, not even a symbolic one. Hägg notes a general lack of interest by managers in the reviews; in cases where reviews could reveal outright failures in investment decisions, we could expect them to be unpopular among those who proposed and took these decisions.

## ENFORCING A CYBERNETIC MODEL

With all its weaknesses, management control in situations which do meet the three basic conditions for applying the cybernetic model (presence of standards, measurable accom-plishment, usable feedback) has still had a fair amount of success. In the developed countries of our world, an increasing part of the national income is spent on activities which do not meet these conditions—indirect departments in private organizations and all kinds of public activities, including education and health care.

Responsible managers have attempted to find ways to control the considerable resources spent on such activities. The success of the cybernetic model in other situations has led them to try to enforce a cybernetic approach for indirect and public activities, as well. In practice, this has been done by calling successful industrial consultants (McKinsey!) to propose reorganizations for non-industrial organizations—reorganizations which rarely have been carried out and even more rarely been successful. The transfer of Robert McNamara from the Ford Corporation to the Secretary of Defense in the sixties began a movement in U.S. public agencies towards a "Planning/Programming/ Budgeting System" which became widely known as PPBS or (PPB). PPBS has a number of objectives, but among these is control which it tries to execute by enforcing the cybernetic model, and in its most ambitious form it claims to apply to any organization. Reactions and experiences have been mixed. In 1967, C. L. Schultze, former Director, U.S. Bureau of the Budget, before a U.S. Senate Subcommittee, stated:

I look forward to substantial improvements next year in terms of schedule, understanding of the role and desired character of the Program Memoranda, and, perhaps more important, in terms of their analytic content. Analytic staffs have been assembled and have had a chance to shake down; a number of data collection efforts and long term study efforts should reach fruition; and we are learning how to state program issues in a way that facilitates analysis and comparison. We have not yet by any means achieved my expectations for the system. That is partly because I have such high expectations for it. Ultimately I expect we will realize these expectations (1, p. 702).

However, Wildavsky noted:

PPBS has failed everywhere and at all times. Nowhere has PPBS (1) been established and (2) influenced governmental decisions (3) according to its own principles. The program structures do not make sense to anyone. They are not, in fact, used to make decisions of any importance. Such products of PPBS as do exist are not noticeably superior in analytic quality or social desirability to whatever was done before (18, pp. 363–364).

The fundamental problem of an approach like PPBS—which has spread to other countries in spite of its ambiguous results in the U.S.A.—may be precisely that it extrapolates a cybernetic philosophy derived from industrial production and sales situations to organizations of a very different nature and that it never asked the basic question whether and when this extrapolation is justified. Within the public system there are activities which meet the criteria for a cybernetic control approach, such as quantifiable public services: garbage collection, public transport, the Post Office. Other activities miss one or more of the fundamental conditions for the cybernetic model, and no amount of trying harder, setting up analytic staffs (with all the value conflicts involved), and data collection will overcome this.

There is a certain parallel between PPBS in public administration and another popular technique of the sixties mainly used in private organizations: *Management By Objectives* (MBO). MBO is also based on a cybernetic philosophy (15): objective setting (jointly between the employee, who is often himself a manager, and his superior), performance review, and corrective action. Not unlike PPBS, MBO is supported by believers but also heavily attacked. Levinson calls it "one of the greatest management illusions" and "industrial engineering with a new name" (13). Few cases of successful implementation of MBO have been reported—that is, cases in which others than the one responsible for the implementation claim it has been successful in improving performance. Ivancevich (9), besides reviewing the rare literature on research about MBO, reports on a 3-year longitudinal study on the introduction of MBO in two out of three plants of one U.S. manufacturing company. The results were mixed, with one plant showing significant long-term improvement in performance, and the other not. His study dealt with production workers and salesmen, organization members whose accomplishment is to some extent measurable. In these cases enforcement of a cybernetic control model by MBO may not be too difficult and, if the program is well managed, it may lead to performance improvement. However, MBO is also advocated, and applied, for indirect jobs, in medical institutions, school systems and government agencies. In these cases, accomplishment is much less measurable, and it is rare to find surrogates acceptable to both parties. If a commonly agreed measurement of accomplishment is lacking, the cybernetic model again does not apply, and MBO is simply bound to fail. A second reason why MBO may fail, even if the cybernetic model does apply, is that MBO is based on simplistic and mechanistic assumptions about the relationships among the people involved: it uses a reward-punishment psychology (13). There is more going on between people than cybernetic objective setting and feedback alone.

## POLITICAL CONTROL

Blanket application of a cybernetic philosophy to non-cybernetic organization processes can only do more harm than good. This does not mean that the advantages of the cybernetic approach *to those cases where it applies* have to be dropped. Within most organizations, even indirect and public ones, there are activities which *can* be controlled in a cybernetic way: those which are mechanized so that individuals play no role in them; those where individuals play a role, but where there is consensus about what this role should be; but it is necessary that performance be measurable so that standards can be set. In these cases, a cybernetic control philosophy—or preferably even a homeostatic philosophy—can make a real contribution. But often these cybernetic cases will be the exception. The more typically human and less mechanistic an activity, the less the chance that the conditions for a cybernetic approach will be met.

The essence of the non-cybernetic situations is that they are *political;* decisions are based on negotiation and judgment (as an employee of a Dutch city government expressed it: on enlightenment by the Holy Spirit). Decisions often deal with *policies.* There is a well-known slogan: "There is no reason for it. It's just our policy." What this means is that policy is not merely composed of rational elements; its main ingredients are *values,* which may differ from person to person, and *norms,* which are shared within groups in society but vary over time and from group to group (16). It makes little sense to speak of control processes here, at least in the formal sense in which such processes are described in cybernetic situations. It does make sense to speak of a control *structure,* taking into account the power positions of the various parties in the negotiations. Within this structure, we may study the control *games* played by the various actors (3). Once resources are allocated, there is no automatic feedback on the effectiveness of their use; the only controls possible are whether the resources were really spent and if no funds were embezzled. Beyond that, it is a matter of trust in those in charge of carrying out the programs; the real control takes place through the appointing of a person to a task. Activities once decided upon will tend to perpetuate themselves; corrective actions in the case of ineffective or inefficient activities are not automatically produced by the control system but ask for a specific evaluation study; deciding upon such a study is in itself a political act which may upset an established balance of power.

As an example of a control aid that is still feasible in such a situation, Wildavsky (18, Ch. 19) describes the Public Expenditure Survey Committee (PESC) in the U.K. The PESC is an interdepartmental group which establishes a yearly report, showing the future cost of existing government policies, if these policies remain unchanged, over the next five years. The product of PESC is not planning or management control as such; it does not try to measure or evaluate outputs. It only presents an educated forecast of already committed inputs, as a base line for governmental planning and policy making. PESC does not assume any cybernetic model.

## CONCLUSION: THE USE OF MODELS

In thinking about organizations, we cannot escape from using models. To see why this is so, I find it helpful to refer to the General Hierarchy of Systems which was first formulated in different ways by Von Bertalanffy and Boulding (10, pp. 7–9). In the General Hierarchy of Systems, nine levels of complexity of systems are distinguished:

1. Static frameworks,
2. Dynamic systems with predetermined motions,
3. Closed-loop control or cybernetic systems,
4. Homeostatic systems like the biological cell,
5. The living plant,
6. The animal,
7. Man,
8. Human organizations, and
9. Transcendental systems.

Every next level adds a dimension of complexity to the previous one.

So we find organizations at Level 8, where the complexity is overwhelming. As the individual is at Level 7, it is fundamentally impossible for the human brain to grasp what goes on at Level 8. In order to think about organizations, we have to simplify: we use lower-level systems which we can understand as models for what we cannot understand. Early thinkers about organizations focussed on the organization chart, a first-level model. Scientific management was often concerned with procedures, second-level models. The cybernetic control process is already a more complex, third-level model, and the homeostatic "cell" model is found at the fourth level.

One consequence of the use of lower-level systems as models for organizations is that we automatically consider the people in the system (at least all except ourselves—see the quote from Jonas above), as if they were things—as means to be used; the goals are supposed to be given. But in fact, all organization goals derive from people: in the hierarchy of systems, the source of organization goals is at Level 7, with the individual. In an organization, the individual is *both goal and means;* but the use of lower level models implies dealing with people as means. We may do this only when there is consensus over goals, or goals can be imposed—so we see these are not just conditions for the applicability of the cybernetic model, but for any lower-level model, including biological ones.

In political situations, there is no consensus

about goals, and replacing the organizational reality by a model which treats people as means is no longer allowed. Using a cybernetic model—such as PPBS—in such a case means a covering up of the real issues and will be perceived rightly by most people involved as an attempt by a technocratic coalition to impose their implicit goals on all others.

## REFERENCES

1. Anthony, R. N., J. Dearden, and R. F. Vancil. *Management Control Systems: Text, Cases and Readings,* rev. ed. (Homewood, Ill.: R. D. Irwin, 1972).

2. Anthony, R. N., and R. Herzlinger. *Management Control in Nonprofit Organizations* (Homewood, Ill.: R. D. Irwin, 1975).

3. Crozier, M. "Comparing Structures and Comparing Games," in G. Hofstede and M. S. Kassem (Eds.), *European Contributions to Organization Theory* (Assen: Van Gorcum, 1976), pp. 193–207.

4. Giglioni, G. B. and A. G. Bedeian. "A Conspectus of Management Control Theory: 1900–1972," *Academy of Management Journal,* Vol. 17 (1974), 292–305.

5. Hägg, I. Reviews of Capital Investments," in S. Asztely (Ed.), *Budgeting och Redovisning som Instrument for Styrning* (Stockholm: P. A. Norstedt, 1974), pp. 53–68.

6. Hofstede, G. *The Game of Budget Control* (Assen, Van Gorcum, and London: Tavistock Publications, 1967).

7. Hofstede, G. "Deux Cas de Changement," in H. C. de Bettignies (Ed.), *Maitriser le Changement dans l'Entreprise* (Paris: Les Editions d'Organisation, 1975), pp. 175–199.

8. Hofstede, G. "Nationality and Espoused Values of Managers," *Journal of Applied Psychology,* Vol. 61, No. 2 (1976), 148–155.

9. Ivancevich, J. M. "Changes in Performance in a Management by Objectives Program," *Administrative Science Quarterly,* Vol. 19 (1974), 563–577.

10. Johnson, R. A., F. E. Kast, and J. E. Rosenzweig. *The Theory of Management of Systems* (New York: McGraw-Hill, 1963).

11. Jonas, H. "A Critique of Cybernetics," *Social Research,* Vol. 20 (1953), 172–192.

12. Juran, J. M. *Managerial Breakthrough: A New Concept of the Manager's Job* (New York: McGraw-Hill, 1964).

13. Levinson, H. "Management by Whose Objectives?" *Harvard Business Review,* Vol. 48, No. 4 (1970), 125–134.

14. Sandkull, B. "The Discontinuity of Modern Industry: A Quest for an Alternative Principle of Organizational Control," *Research Report No. 31* (Linkoping: Department of Management and Economics, Linkoping University, 1975).

15. Sutherland, J. W. "System Theoretical Limits on the Cybernetic Paradigm," *Behavioral Science,* Vol. 20 (1975), 191–200.

16. Vickers, G. *Making Institutions Work* (London: Associated Business Programmes, 1973).

17. Wiener, N. *The Human Use of Human Beings: Cybernetics and Society.* 2nd rev. ed. (Garden City, N.Y.: Doubleday, 1954).

18. Wildavsky, A. *Budgeting: A Comparative Analysis of the Budgetary Process.* (Boston: Little, Brown, 1975).

The corporate executive often is proud of the quality and sophistication of his or her decision-making. Increasingly uncertain, complex, and turbulent external environments cause a premium to be placed on the effectiveness with which problems can be identified, alternatives structured and proposed, choices made, and programs implemented.

Sophistication is required to cope with the environment and its impact, which in turn creates the need for specialized planning or other staff groups; full-time professionals with advanced skills are often assigned the task of investigating a problem and recommending solutions to the overloaded line executive (3). Staff analysis is heavily relied upon, for practical reasons of executive time and technical skill limitations; such analysis may possess influence which surpasses that which is warranted, from the effect of the authority of (staff) expertise. Even expert-client confrontation to resolve differences of opinion can result in movement of initial client positions to become identical with those originally made by the experts (12). Analytical breakdowns and insufficiencies (11), improper assumptions (7), or uncertainty absorption (6) are often covered up by the intricacies of the techniques applied to the problem (7). All this can operate to increase the executive's blind acceptance of, and implicit reliance on, the analytical process.

## REVIEW AND DISSENT

Because of potential dangers in approving an inadequate or erroneous analysis, substantial decisions are usually reviewed by the Executive Committee, the Finance Committee, or the Board of Directors. Less formally, one's superior may try to pick apart the analysis and

# 11

# Decision Making

*Improving Executive Decisions*
*by Formalizing Dissent:*
*The Corporate Devil's Advocate*
THEODORE T. HERBERT and RALPH W. ESTES

recommendations in order to be assured that assumptions and analytical procedures are sound.

While they are steps in the right direction, the qualifications of the review person or panel members are hardly likely to be specialized enough to allow detailed assessment of the analytical trail followed, to raise issues of alternatives not considered, or to question underlying and implicit value judgments.

The executive decision-making process can be only as effective as the analytical phase allows; yet time and expertise are not normally applied to managing the analytical process. Some assurances of objectivity and control for completeness can enhance the executive's confidence in the proposals submitted and in decisions based on the analyses. The executive is typically a generalist rather than a specialist; he or she relies on the expertise of another, assuming—or hoping—that the analytical intricacies hidden within the submitted proposal and recommendations are thorough, objective, realistic, and correct.

## FORMALIZED DISSENT

There are scattered examples of techniques by which control over the decision process is exercised by the executive. Although the techniques differ widely in specifics, they have in common the careful structuring of independent reviews, to balance and test the adequacy of an analytical endeavor. Formal dissenting roles are played by persons investigating the position or proposal of another, bringing to light biases or inadequacies, and generating counter-proposals.

One of the oldest examples of the formalized dissent role occurs within the Roman Catholic Church; the "Devil's Advocate" (formally termed "promoter of the faith") has been a continuing office since the early 1500s, with the prescribed function of thoroughly investigating proposals for canonization and beatification (10). The Devil's Advocate must bring to light any information which might cast doubt upon the qualifications of the candidate for sainthood. The bestowing of sainthood is not taken lightly. Since it represents extensions of the doctrinal fabric of the Church and affects the lives of congregation members, the negative side of the proposal for sainthood must be thoroughly and rigorously investigated. *Separation of the functions of promoter and*

*dissenter* ensures that both sides of the question will be thoroughly analyzed and presented, since the roles are not subject to intrapersonal conflict by residing in the same person (9). The very existence of a formal adversary may pressure the promoter to be much more thorough than if only the positive side were presented. (A review of the literature unfortunately reveals no evidence on the effectiveness of the techniques as used in the Catholic Church.)

The same dissenting function appears in the Anglo-Saxon legal system. The jury and judge ("executive") examine the merits of the proposal (the prosecution's mustering of all available evidence to show the defendant's guilt) and counter-proposal (the defense's presentation of all available evidence to show the defendant's innocence). Carefully structured is the process whereby prosecution and defense attempt to show the fallacies and omissions in the other's presentation to an impartial jury. The system allows complete airing of positive and negative sides of a single question. The verdict ("decision") may then be reached with the benefit of the best possible evidence ("data").

Corporate internal auditors provide a check on investment decisions or other proposals, by questioning basic issues of "afford-ability", helping to ensure that all relevant questions of cost or finance have been ad-dressed by those proposing the investments. Manufacturing firms which operate at the lead-ing edge of technological applications routinely employ outside consulting firms to appraise internally-developed product development ef-forts.

The British Parliamentary system, with its "loyal opposition", balances the unilateral pro-grams of the party in power, questioning almost routinely the government's proposals. The United States governmental system builds in a similar dissenting role for those opposed to a proposal ("bill") placed before the legislature, with hearings and debate on the floor of the legislative house.

The efforts of Ralph Nader and consumers' advocate groups also present negative informa-tion to the consuming public, balancing what they consider to be one-sided advertising claims. The dissenting role thereby provides more complete information to decision-makers who have neither the time nor expertise to gather and analyze data pro *and* con for house-hold consumption decisions.

Academics or learned societies incorporate a formalized dissent procedure to ensure rigor-ous treatment of the substance of research or theoretical papers. A "discussant" (usually an eager assistant professor), assigned to a paper presented before the society, may gleefully rake over the coals the presenter of an ill-prepared paper.

## SPECIFIC APPLICATIONS OF FORMALIZED DISSENT

Thornton (14) described a 1971 case in which the Civil Aeronautics Board (CAB) analyzed the effects of a proposed merger on two airlines and concluded that the merged airline's unit costs would increase over its predecessors'. An inde-pendent analysis refuted the conclusion, based on statistical techniques more valid than those used by the CAB.

In a field study/experiment, Mason (7) found that providing for reanalysis of and counter-plans for strategic plans yielded more effective, synergistic strategies by executives involved. Underlying assumptions were ex-posed, new alternative plans emerged, and creativity was enhanced.

In 1972, James Earl Carter (then Governor of Georgia) authorized an independent analysis of Corps of Engineers' environmental impact and cost/benefit studies of a proposed federal dam on the Flint River. The independent study found that major costs had been omitted, bene-fits inflated, feasible alternatives neglected, and significant negative impacts on environ-mental quality ignored (8).

One of the authors, in serving as internal consultant to a Federal Agency, was assigned the task of investigating positive recommen-dations previously made (and extensively documented) by a consulting firm on the economic feasibility and cost/benefits of a major program proposal. He was told to air *negative* aspects that had been "swept under the rug", so that they might be effectively rebutted with analyses done *before* they were raised by the project's opponents. In the process of retracing the cost/benefit computations upon which the recommendation for the program was based, several questionable assumptions were brought to light. These included choice of time-horizon, distribution of costs and benefits over the time horizon, discount rate, and program capacity utilization. Recomputation with changed assumptions yielded a shift from large benefits in relation to cost, to costs being moderately larger than projected benefits.

In short, the re-examination of a plan or proposal can bring to light inadequate or one-sided analyses. An independent expert person or group can help overcome the line executive's limitation on effective decision-making, the tendency to rely on unverified analyses and recommendations for action.

## THE CORPORATE DEVIL'S ADVOCATE

The essence of these techniques can be distilled and formalized for use in corporate decision processes. If volunteering criticism of another's work can be taken as a personal attack, constructive criticism may be withheld. Since the decision process needs valid analytical input to operate as effectively as possible, the assumption cannot be made that discussion and probing questions will control for quality. Contributing one's insights and criticisms does not necessarily follow from the opportunity to contribute; people may choose to withhold their involvement for personal or group-related reasons (1). Institutionalizing the dissent function may help depersonalize the conflict generated by criticism. A critical review by a specialist as technically competent as the staff proposers can help ensure that the analysis is adequate in all major aspects (2).

One benefit which may *not* be readily measurable is the improvement in quality of decision-making input by staff analysts. The analyst's trail to the recommendations, his or her judgments and decisions, are to be traced by another specialist, the Corporate Devil's Advocate; knowledge of such control or follow-up could ensure that controversial, subjective, or value-ridden elements will be minimized. For a process to be effective, it should be measured, evaluated, and rewarded appropriately—and the critical process is no different (4). Much of what has been said implies that the critical review process can be most appropriately applied to major strategic or other one-time propositions, as opposed to re-

curring or routine operational matters. But turbulent external environmental conditions, highly technical analytical procedures, subjective or value-laden criteria, or alternatives which embody some risk (as in the re-appraisal and reformulation of a firm's strategy in a stable industry) are other conditions in which the process may be of benefit.

The Devil's Advocate starts with the analyst's final copy of the proposal. The Devil's Advocate becomes immersed in the analyst's report only after having conducted an independent audit of the problem situation, to verify that the problem identified or assumed is the real problem. Reconstruction of the analyst's logic and data gives the Devil's Advocate an in-depth trace. Should inconsistencies appear, potential alternatives be omitted from consideration, irrelevant criteria be established, or window-dressing be added to impress the executive, the fallacies or inaccuracies must be listed, together with their impacts upon the recommendation. If the proposal is determined to be unsound, a reanalysis of the problem situation should be presented, complete with recommendation and justification.

As soon as the report of the Devil's Advocate is completed, a special confrontation session is held. Proposing analyst and Devil's Advocate each present their own efforts to the decision maker and whatever other executives are appropriate to the session. After formal critique of the proposal, the analyst and Devil's Advocate rationally rebut each others' reports. In the best of all possible worlds, this process may result in a new proposal which eliminates the fallacious parts of both recommendations and is comprised of the soundest elements of each. Failing this synergistic new recommendation, the decision maker must then turn to the task of deciding which—if either— recommendation to accept. The major differ-

ence is that shortcomings are now known.

The corporate Devil's Advocate may be an organizational member, an office within the firm, or a group composed of external and independent elements. The approach will vary with the firm, as well as with the nature of the problem and its associated proposal.

## THE INSIDE DEVIL'S ADVOCATE

Devil's Advocates who are organizational members may be established in temporary development positions or in permanent career slots. The Devil's Advocate position could be assigned to almost any promising member. Although background, training, and skills would not have to perfectly match the nature of the proposal, a match would probably prove helpful.

Such a position, as a management development device, could be rotated among junior executives with upper management potential. But the Devil's Advocate should not be exposed to status or rank differentials in the assignment; the analyst whose proposal is critiqued should always be at the same hierarchical level as the Devil's Advocate, to avoid pressure or other repercussions. For practical purposes, the Devil's Advocate might report directly to the president of the firm.

The concept *must* be enthusiastically understood and accepted to be workable. Acceptance by the chief executive and other executives will permit the Devil's Advocate to undertake the role freely, without fear of reprisal or recrimination. Privately, he or she may completely agree with the position of the promoter, but officially he or she *must* oppose and raise doubts about that position. The organization will thus ensure that no project is steamrollered through the decision-making process without full consideration of at least the major disadvantages and alternatives.

A pragmatic disadvantage associated with any specialized unit is the tendency to become differentiated from other organizational units in perspectives on goals, time, and interpersonal orientations (5). Rotating the assignment may help overcome this tendency toward goal displacement.

## THE EXTERNAL DEVIL'S ADVOCATE

Another general approach to the device is the external, completely independent Corporate Devil's Advocate. This may be a consulting firm contracted to evaluate the proposal and recommendations of an internal analyst group or of another external consulting group. Arm's-length treatment would be relatively assured,

even though difficulty might be experienced in recreating the processes through which the conclusions of an internal analyst were derived. Fresh looks at old problems could result in alternatives not previously considered.

Almost any important problem situation could benefit from an independent analysis of the problem definition, nature, and scope. Alternatives presented, or modifications thereof, can offer new insights and controls upon that

most difficult, yet critical, process—executive decision making.

## SUMMARY AND CONCLUSIONS

To ensure valid decision-making inputs, the device of the Corporate Devil's Advocate is proposed. Creating an offical "Nay-sayer", charged with the responsibility of dissenting with recommendations, aids in pointing out logical flaws and other fallacies or inaccuracies in major one-sided proposals.

Since major decisions today are crucial to long-run success in a competitive and volatile market place, the quality of these decisions must be optimized. An important approach is to

increase the overall validity of the complete decision-making process, from definition of the problem through to presentation of recommendations deriving from the analysis, and hence to implementation of the decision. An official dissenter can heighten the probability that decisions will be thoroughly researched and proposed solutions soundly based in reality. The Corporate Devil's Advocate also can do much to make sure that marginal or unwise decisions are not made at all.

## REFERENCES

1. Carr, David F., Thad B. Green, and Thomas W. Hinckle. "Exploring Nominal Grouping from a Social Facilitation Context," in Dennis F. Ray and Thad B. Green (Eds.), *Expanding Dimensions of Management Thought and Action* (Mississippi State, Miss.: Southern Management Association, 1976), pp. 69–81.

2. French, John R. P., Jr., and Bertram Raven. "The Bases of Social Power," in Dorwin Cartwright and Alvin Zander (Eds.), *Group Dynamics: Research and Theory*, 3rd ed. (New York: Harper and Row, 1968), pp. 259–269.

3. Herbert, Theodore T. "Assumptions and Limitations in Business Policy Educational Technology: Models for Analysis and Innovation," *Journal of Economics and Business*, Vol. 28, No. 3 (1976), 209–218.

4. Kerr, Steven. "On the Folly of Rewarding A, While Hoping for B," *Academy of Management Journal*, Vol. 18, No. 4 (1975), 769–783.

5. Lawrence, Paul R., and Jay W. Lorsch. *Organization and Environment: Managing Dif-*

*ferentiation and Integration* (Homewood, Ill.: Irwin, 1969).

6. March, James G., and Herbert A. Simon. *Organizations* (New York: Wiley, 1958).

7. Mason, Richard O. "A Dialectical Approach to Strategic Planning," *Management Science*, Vol. 15, No. 8 (1969), B-403–B-414.

8. Methvin, Eugene H. "The Fight to Save the Flint," *Readers Digest*, August 1974, pp. 17–22, 26.

9. Meyer, Herbert H., Emanuel Kay, and John R. P. French, Jr. "Split Roles in Performance Appraisal," *Harvard Business Review* (May–June 1965), 123–129.

10. *New Catholic Encyclopedia*, "Devil's Advocate," Vol. 4 (New York: McGraw-Hill, 1967), pp. 829–830.

11. Newman, William H., Charles E. Sumner, and E. Kirby Warren. *The Process of Management: Concepts, Behavior, and Practice*, 3rd ed. (Englewood Cliffs, N.J.: Prentice-Hall, 1972).

12. Nutt, Paul C. "The Merits of Using Experts or

Consumers as Members of Planning Groups: A Field Experiment in Health Planning," *Academy of Management Journal*, Vol. 19, No. 3 (1976), 378–394.

13. Thompson, James D. *Organizations in Action:* *Social Science Bases of Administrative Theory* (New York: McGraw-Hill, 1967).

14. Thornton, Robert L. "Controlling the Technician: The Adversary Approach," *MSU Business Topics* (Summer 1974), 5–10.

A value is a set of beliefs of what is desirable. Values are needed to help managers and employees make choices among competing objectives. Classical values, which emphasize rationality, causality, integrity, independence, deferred consumption, and hard work, are now under attack. Discussion of bureaucracy usually focuses on structural matters, such as hierarchy, promotion on merit, and guidance by precedent. The most important value underlying bureaucracy is a deep, pervasive belief in rationality and perfectability.

Currently, bureaucracy is under attack because of the emergence of new technologies and their value systems. Their rate of technological change is so rapid and pervasive that many people suffer from future shock, the stress and disorientation experienced when people are exposed to too much change too rapidly. This corporate growth has been bought at a terrible moral cost; people feel neglected and powerless.

The modern executive faces the value conflict of being an efficient profit-conscious, performance-oriented manager or an ethical person. Surveys have found that relationships with superiors are the primary source of ethical conflict. In addition, scarcely a day goes by without further allegation of corporate bribes, payoffs, and kickbacks. This activity is not generally perceived by executives as necessarily immoral. Nevertheless, many corporate leaders have expressed their concern about this erosion of business ethics.

Blame for corporate lawbreaking is increasingly placed on the executive. Any discussion of an executive's values and ethics leads to the conclusion that managers are and will be held morally responsible for their actions. Even though the modern view of organizational decision making argues for consensus formation and risk syndication in decision making, the reality of the matter is that while decision making is decentralized, responsibility is centralized.

Because the modern manager faces such value conflicts, it becomes imperative that he or

# IV

# VALUE VARIABLES

she be exposed to a deeper understanding of values in general and managerial values and organizational ideologies in particular. Values, in general terms, are the social glue that holds a structure in position and allows the process to run on track. Values are essential because structure and process cannot be precisely defined to meet every operational contingency that may emerge. Values are needed in the organization to help managers and other employees make choices among competing objectives. Everybody has values. Managers, like everybody else, need moral frames of reference within which they can exercise choices and thus commit themselves to a course of action with some underlying moral rationale. A value is a set of beliefs about what is desirable or "good".

The article by Harry Abravenal addresses itself to the issue defining what ideology is and developing a method of analyzing the prevailing ideologies in organizations. In this paper, Abravenal views ideology as a system with rational connections among values, facts, and commitments. Since ideology influences structure, process, goals, and performance, an analysis of ideology enables the manager to raise fundamental questions about the preservation of status quo or search for alternate arrangements. The two dimensions of ideology, namely, the fundamental and operative, are portrayed as interdependent and interacting, sometimes in conflict and sometimes in harmony. The article describes, through examples, how such conflicts come into being and how they are resolved through mediatory myths that pervade the organizations. The various components of ideology are identified and a model illustrates the interactions among the components and the way myths modify their nature. The various steps involved in ideological analysis are identified and, through examples drawn from real life organizations, the development of a metacontrol system is traced. This is helpful to the manager who seeks to understand more deeply values and ideologies, rather than dealing with them as given.

Finally, to develop some practical guidelines for managerial performance that is in line with the current ideology and values, it is worth remembering that business and society are subject to the same laws, moral and legal; the moral law may not always be clear, while legality can be defined more precisely; when in doubt, act like "a reasonably prudent person." There is a high probability today that one's decisions will be challenged.

## INTRODUCTION

Corporate ideology involves issues of collective perception and commitment which intimately involve ideas, goals, and values. For example, the slogan "What's good for General Motors is good for America" is infused with ideological content. For the manager the "ideological" cannot be divorced from the "practical"; it is both thought and action; ideas and their action consequences. Ideological commitments are expressed in both individual and collective definitions of the situation. Statements such as "Offense is the best form of defense," "An optimal level of conflict is good" and "Work hard; play hard" only make sense within the context of an ideological belief system. What we perceive or experience—whether it is interpreted as a problem, an opportunity, or both—how it comes to be socially shared, its meaning, and the nature of consensus, is conditioned by ideology. Top managers and radicals, formal and informal groups, insiders as well as outsiders can shape ideological settings which reveal or hide opportunities, arouse or depress enthusiasm, and nurture or destroy courage in organizations.

An organization's ideology has profound effect not only on effectiveness but also on determining what effectiveness means and the criteria for its measurement. It determines the way individuals enact organizational structures; it also influences the processes—including how decisions are made, how human resources are used, and how the external and internal environments are perceived. Furthermore, corporate ideology specifies the nature of organizational goals, the criteria for performance evaluation, and the meanings and values ascribed to events, actions, and outcomes. It

# 12

# The Changing Value Set

## The Ideological Character of Organizational Work

HARRY ABRAVANEL

prescribes the limits of appropriate behavior among individuals, and between individuals and the organization; the legitimacy of control and control mechanisms; and the allocation of rewards for "good" behavior.

## THE PROBLEM OF IDEOLOGICAL ANALYSIS

Any interpretation of the collective meaning of actions and their consequences is based on ideology. As participants in organizations and social dramas, we often cannot distinguish between our actions and their ideological grounds—they blend and disappear into one another. This blending conceals the underlying ground of our interest, reduces our uncertainty and tension, and facilitates getting on with our "necessary" activity.

Ideological analysis must seek to uncover preservative practices (what is said) in organizations as well as their underlying grounds (what is not said). The former is nonthreatening, as demonstrated by the extensive interest in control and control systems by organizations and organizational theory. However, the latter is threatening.

The object of ideological analysis is to develop a method to expose our value premises and belief systems to show how they preserve certain organizational practices. For example, business firms usually attempt to be competitive and adopt suitable ideologies to "play the game" at a high standard. The preservation of the "game" excludes considerations of not playing the "game" at all, or just playing a different "game" entirely. Ideological analysis is then interested not only in beliefs about the enhancement of the organization and its competitive standards, but also, in beliefs and myths about why the organization, competitive practice, and organizational methods are desirable in the first place.

### An Example: Unfreezing the Tight Ship

Let me offer an example. I once undertook an organizational development (OD) consulting project in the engineering department of a large United States-based chemical company. It turned out to reflect a typical ideological problem. The senior executive engineers believed that work in the department should be organized in the most efficient way within the prevailing authority structure. The prevailing structure had worked effectively in the past to produce impressive internal growth and a sense of competence. The senior engineers had been with the company a long time and were committed to its paternalistic, rigid, hierarchical structure. They knew that running a tight ship worked.

The chief executive engineer secretly wanted me to confirm that the present structure and methods were best under the circumstances. He believed in matching people characteristics with suitable job characteristics. The fact that given the present organizational design some workers would have boring jobs with little scope for satisfaction was viewed as unfortunate but necessary. Anyway, he correctly believed that not everyone has the aptitude or desire for decision making and responsibility. He believed that those who were motivated would have many opportunities to rise by natural selection to responsible and satisfying jobs. He and some of the other senior executives assured themselves (and wanted me to do the same) that the organization provided numerous and adequate opportunities for advancement. In fact, there were many opportunities, but not enough. Most engineers were actually relegated to monotonous work activity.

In the process of interviewing all the managers in the engineering department, I found some young managers with more egalitarian personal values. They believed that there were more boring jobs than apathetic people to fill them and that satisfying opportunities were scarce. They were privately excited about research studies equating improved work performance with increased responsibility and involvement in decision making. It was evident that such supportive human relations research served to reconcile personal values with their own interests. Although research findings have been equivocal on this subject, the degree of acceptance of such research findings in this case seems to have been based on hierarchical position, personal values, and interests. I found two competing managerial ideologies serving distinct constituencies which coexisted uncomfortably in the same department.

It was my opinion that some of the best young managers subscribed to the counterideology and that, if they were ignored, the company risked damaging turnover among its best and brightest, while retaining the more mediocre performers. Given that the labor market for chemical and project engineers was extremely tight, I felt that it was important for senior executives to be aware of the problem, especially because they had optimistic expansion plans requiring creative and skilled engineers. Bits of interview data were anonymously fed back to the chief executive in a workshop. He was surprised. He slowly accepted the data, acknowledged the problem, and asked what he could do about it.

At first I resisted prescribing a solution since it was not part of the original client contract. Also, expert roles are to be avoided in OD work. The client persisted. I compromised and recommended a process whereby the entire department would have to acknowledge the problem, working together toward its resolution and living with the outcome. Obviously I could not realistically suggest a review of his managerial style and ideology; both he and too many other executives had a vested interest in the status quo.

Since it was unlikely that these executives would change their style, such recommendation would only be upsetting, I recommended that some risk was warranted: that the chief executive openly encourage the articulation of both managerial ideologies without taking sides; that he participate in an extensive, high-level conflict management workshop; that more open and direct communication of conflicts and differences be integrated as part of ongoing work practices; and that more democratic political processes be allowed to determine final outcomes. Thus acknowledgement of the problem and responsibility for final outcomes would be dispersed, creating opportunities for surprising and perhaps innovative resolutions in different circumstances. If you were the chief executive engineer, would you take such a risk?

This example describes three distinct management ideologies: a paternalistic "tight-ship" dominant ideology; an important emerging counterideology; and a proposed alternative that encourages a democratic determination of methods. Ideological choice and commitment is important. In this example, it will determine the department's character, who works there (that is, who leaves), and how decisions are made.

The chief executive engineer, after an impressive history of success and growth, is now confronted with a choice of significant consequence for his subordinates and his department. If he chooses to adhere to the "tight ship" management ideology, to play it safe until he retires, he risks morale problems, turnover, and serious recruiting difficulties. On the other hand, if he should adopt a more egalitarian management ideology, new decision processes may disrupt senior engineers who are satisfied with the present system. Whether he chooses one or the other, his reputation as an effective executive will be undermined by a different and distinct constituency. The proposed third ideological course of action risks antagonizing both constituencies against the chief exectuve.

OD as an intervention strategy is itself infused with a humanistic ideology. The OD practitioner acts as a resource to help and train the client to solve his own problem. It is, in effect, a method of sharing responsibility for finding and implementing solutions among those individuals who have to live and work out the problem and its solution. In this example, I (as consultant) confronted the chief engineer with the responsibility of remaking his ideological commitment. He, in turn, can choose to adopt the OD model and then pass the responsibility of making and resolving ideological commitments to his subordinates. That is, under this approach each manager can choose and negotiate his own preferred management ideology in his area as long as effective performance is maintained. In areas of overlapping jurisdiction, conflict resolution processes can determine final methods without proscribing them in advance.

## DEFINITION OF IDEOLOGY

Organizations cannot rely on an ambiguous underlying belief system. They must make statements and take action in order to accomplish some purpose and enact a role. Ideology serves the purpose of creating and using organizations. It is not any way-of-thinking, but rather, it is a particular way-of-thinking which serves the interests of those who are influential within the organization. It is a system of values combining ideas and their action consequences.

*Organizational ideology is defined as a set of fundamental ideas and operative consequences linked together into a dominant belief system often producing contradictions but serving to define and maintain the organization.*

### Components of Ideology

Corporate ideologies can be viewed as systems in which values, facts, and commitments to ends and means are rationally connected. The pursuit of any organizational policy involving interconnected sequences of action extended over a long time period cannot take place without ideology. Policies are conceived and implemented in some relation to ideals that require moral judgement.

Thus ideology operates in two dimensions: it maintains allegiance to a purity of moral principles (what ought to be) and to practical and immediate considerations (what is being done). Like the Church, ideology must be faithful both to its central beliefs and to its immediate concerns about survival. But when ideology is made to fulfill its functions, to guide concerted action and everyday decisions, it loses its moral purity in deference to practical considerations. For example, no significant political party has ever been able to avoid committing itself to some lines of action which are not at odds with its basic principles and goals. Thus, the logic of central moral principles cannot always account for the logic of actual policies implemented or proposed. A contradiction arises between what ought to be and what is being done that requires bridging. Mediatory myths can effectively bridge the chasm between contradictions. Ideology separates into two dimensions—the fundamental and the operative (see Figure 12-1).

The fundamental dimension includes principles that determine the final goals, the ends towards which the organization is working, the vision of what should be done. The operative dimension (what is) includes principles that underlie actual policies and support the means used to pursue ends that define what can be done immediately. Here, norms of efficiency or expedience may take priority over moral prescriptions.

In practice, there is a basic and simple unity between what organizations do (what is) and what remains to be done (what ought). What remains to be done by an organization (the aspired or ideal) need not necessarily be grounded in the practical, but rather, it is held as that against which the practical (the

achieved) is still recognized as incomplete. What organizations *do* corresponds to operative ideology—that which is dominated by considerations of what is being done and can be done. What remains to be done corresponds to fundamental ideology—that which is dominated by ethical considerations of what should be done.

The fundamental ideology describes organizational commitment to something that is worth pursuing but has not yet been accomplished. Its moral texture provides a basis for evaluating the operative ideology. The operative is the selected means to pursue certain ends defined by the fundamental. The operative and the fundamental form a unity of interdependent beliefs and values: one can be evaluated against the context of the other; the concerns of one can dominate the concerns of the other; one or both can change simultaneously; and contradictions between their separate concerns represent the problematic relationship between ideals and their application. Organizations put ideas into practice. They can never be simply reduced to arguments over technicalities. Priorities must be determined. Essentially, ideological analysis is about the circumstances whereby inherent problematics are kept from interfering with organizational imperatives. That is, the tension between unitary and divisive concerns between the fundamental and the operative is erased, or at least reduced. Sometimes, when circumstances require, the tension between fundamental and operative concerns is allowed to escalate and become public, but this is rare since the dominant process operating is to reduce complexity and achieve social order and control, that is, to get on with the task.

Certain structural components are common to all ideologies, like grammar is common to all modern languages. These components are partisan statements infused with a system of values. They are: description, analysis, moral

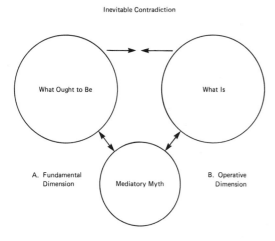

Inevitable Contradiction

What Ought to Be

What Is

A. Fundamental Dimension

Mediatory Myth

B. Operative Dimension

FIGURE 12-1 *The Basic Structure of Ideological Belief Systems.*

prescriptions, technical prescriptions, implements, and rejections (1). Description of phenomena or "what one notices" is determined by direct and practical experience within a given social context. Analysis involves a diagnostic process that identifies what is wrong, inadequate, or demanding—that is, what must be taken seriously in that context. Moral prescriptions or "what should be done" present a value or moral judgement of the description and analysis which may run counter to and prevail over technical prescriptions. Technical prescriptions or "what can be done" are derived from the immediate perception of actual possibilities. Organizations and their methods are implements or means to accomplish "what is to be done". Finally, rejections include what is negated or opposed, in other words, counterideologies.

Briefly, the structural components on the left can be translated to read as a story on the right side from top to bottom as follows:

| description | "we see" |
| analysis | "diagnose" |
| moral prescription | "what should be done" |
| technical prescription | "what can be done" |
| implements | "what is being done" |
| rejections | "that's not us" |

In real life, these components are interdependent and too complex to be formally determined. But they can be given some structure. In agreement with the centrality of ethical values in Weber's sociology, or moral imperatives in Kantian philosophy, moral commitment must be accorded centrality. To illustrate this centrality, and to affirm interdependence between components, we may arrange the components in a circle around the element of moral prescription (what should be done) in the fundamental dimension, and around the element of technical prescription (what can be done) in the operative dimension as shown in Figure 12-2.

FIGURE 12-2 *Bifurcation of Ideology into the Fundamental and Operative Dimensions.*

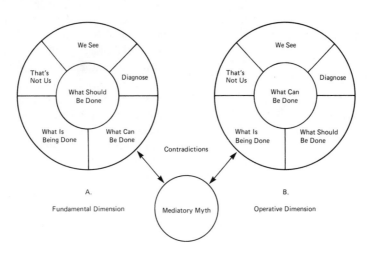

## FEDERAL BUREAU OF INVESTIGATION (FBI): PROTECTOR OF THE AMERICAN WAY OF LIFE

The FBI is an intriguing example of the form and structure of ideological belief systems. J. Edgar Hoover spoke of the FBI as a "we" organization, a team, a human organization, never far from the crossroads of America, either spiritually or physically. The FBI was identified with the higher values of America: law and order as opposed to change and chaos. Such an identification with higher American values was encouraged: law, order, stability, and national security are necessary if America is to survive and thrive. This is part of the FBI's fundamental ideology.

But its operative ideology produced contradictions. The FBI was very concerned about its image and reputation. Hoover has stated the following: "I tell my associates repeatedly that one man did not build the reputation of the FBI—but one man can pull it down" (2). Those who criticized the organization were punished and driven away in disgrace. If they persisted in their criticism after they left, they were considered enemies. Furthermore, as enemies they were equated with outsiders who wished to change, diminish, or expose the Bureau. The FBI's enemies included members of the counterculture of the 1960s, the Nazi Party, the Communist Party, and—in addition to ex-employees—Soviet spies and certain anthropology professors. In terms of organizational rhetoric, "enemies" could include anyone who was designated as "threatening" to America, and especially to the Bureau. How is it that a "we" organization at the crossroads of America can exhibit excessive suspicion as well as mystification and secrecy in its operations? How is it that a "human" organization uses power to disrupt the lives of individuals designated as "enemies"?

The answer is that this is not just any organization. The FBI is no less than the protector of the American way of life. The FBI equates itself with the American ideology. It is this identification with the greater good that transforms license into vigilence. Better to be too careful at the cost of harassing a few suspect individuals than to risk the security of all. Because it stands for America, the FBI is on the side of goodness and "right". It can do no major wrong. That was its mediatory myth under J. Edgar Hoover.

## CHANGING IDEOLOGY

When speaking of organizational ideology, we must normally refer to the dominant ideology, noting that the degree of concensus will vary with time. Often concensus deteriorates under conditions of organizational crisis unless the threat is such that it can unify participants into a common cause in an acceptable way to which all can agree. This is, of course, not always possible. Competing ideologies can be viewed from a life cycle perspective. (See Figure 12-3).

Most attempts to describe how organizational ideology changes assume evolutionary processes in which the deterioration of one ideology contributes to the development of suitable replacements (3, 4). Such a process is depicted in Figure 12-4 in which Ideology 2

129

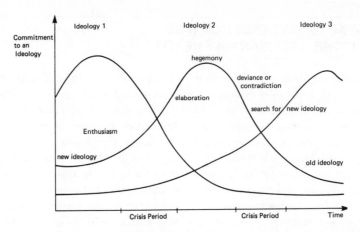

FIGURE 12-3 *Life Cycle and Turnover of Organizational Ideology.*

replaces Ideology 1 in a progressive process followed by Ideology 3. But there are other possibilities. Organizations may adopt new ideologies suddenly when their leaders change (5) or when the organization is faced with a crisis (6).

We can identify a dominant ideology because certain major organizational commitments must be made for the organization as a unit, for example, a commitment to growth. Also certain participants are more influential than others, while some within the system want and need the prescribed incentives and satisfactions that reward good performance or participation.

But organizations contain within them a diversity of ideologies. Sometimes organiza-

tions may be composed of separate parts that are ideologically homogeneous within themselves, but quite different from each other. Ideological differentiation can exist horizontally between functionally distinct groups and vertically between hierarchical levels in the organization; it can be further influenced by geography, professional socialization, culture, interest groups, and politics. Integrating ideological differences may or may not be a problem, but in environments of conflicting but mutually interdependent parts differences will be inevitable. Ideological pluralism will likely be desirable in some complex environments, or, within the same organization, ideological pluralism in one part may coexist with ideological hegemony in other parts.

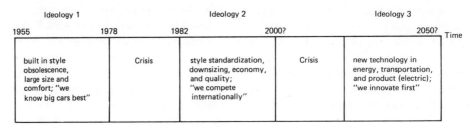

FIGURE 12-4 An Example: *Ideological Change in the U.S. Automobile Industry (Actual and Projected).*

The dominant ideology attempts to convincingly communicate "Be reasonable, do it our way." We know "our way" works, while "your way" may not, especially if *we* don't want "your way" to work as well as "our way."

## A METHOD OF IDEOLOGICAL ANALYSIS

Ideology functions as preservative practice that maintains a given system of values that serves the benefits of getting on with the work at hand in a certain way. Such preservative practices and their underlying grounds constitute an important aspect of the organization. Ideological analysis becomes threatening as it succeeds to increase uncertainty and anxiety by its identification of contradictions that preservative practice effectively hides. If aspects of ideology are hidden, how then can it be analyzed?

The answer to this question will integrate many of the concepts already developed. In this process of ideological analysis, it is useful to think of ideology as a form of communication. The form is the grammar of contradiction and resolution that resourcefully serves the organization (or particular interest groups within the organization) to control or influence. In addition, if we are to proceed with the analysis of an actual case we must identify the following: the content of both the operative and fundamental dimensions; the contradictions that may arise between principles in both dimensions; and the mediatory myths that bridge any contradictions. Also, we must identify whose interests such a system serves by inquiring into what kind of status quo it maintains and what kinds of change would be resisted. At the same time, it is important to identify the nature of your interest as an analyst so that you can monitor or reconstruct your own bias as you proceed.

A procedure and a mode of gathering data is now described. It speaks to the question: "What do you gather, and how do you order it?" and not "What do you do about it?" The procedure provides some guide and structure in an area that is characterized by complex problems. The analyst is her own guide without a tradition, a code of ethics, or a well-defined mode of practice.

*Step 1:* Find contradictions between fundamental and operative dimensions.
- Identify the components of the operative dimension.
- Identify the components of the fundamental dimension.
- Identify contradictions between the fundamental and the operative.

*Step 2:* Find mediatory myths that bridge the contradictions.

*Step 3:* Describe ideology as a metacontrol system.

## A METHODOLOGY FOR DESCRIPTIVE CASES

Mediatory myths are ubiquitous. However, ubiquitousness does not necessarily imply that myths are easy to identify. Identification is sometimes self-evident, while sometimes it requires extensive detective work. Tracing the methodology employed in the following case is recommended practice for the reader who wishes to explore other cases. First, the fundamental and operative ideologies are described; next, any contradictions or inconsistencies between them are identified; and finally, the institutionalized myth that effectively reduces or eliminates contradictions is located.

As an example, International Business Machines (IBM) firmly believes that its employees have freedom and opportunity. Actually the freedom and independence of employees is part of the fundamental ideology. Let us see how it works at IBM according to Ott (7). T. J. Watson Jr., son of the founder of IBM, was fond of telling a story taken from Kierkegaard. It is about ducks flying south for the winter. Someone took pity on them and set out food on a lake that the ducks flew over. While some ducks continued to fly south, others stopped to eat. After some time passed, those ducks who stayed had difficulty flying. The moral was, "You can make wild ducks tame, but you can never make tame ducks wild again." Watson believed that IBM, like any business, needed its wild ducks and would not try to tame them (7).

Operationally, IBM carefully screens and trains its employees to conform to an all-encompassing IBM view of the world. This view and its effects are clearly visible to outsiders, although not necessarily to employees. The suit, dark tie, and black shoes reflect the order and structure which IBM values. The use of alcohol or the hint of sex is avoided in business contexts. Physical handicaps (poor health) usually result in the end of opportunity for advancement and the beginning of retirement. Elaborately landscaped properties with internally controlled environments provide the background for employees who are never idle, even when sitting still. For example, in order to look busy, reading is allowed, but only school books are acceptable.

"Are wild ducks really wild?" asks Ott. In IBM, freedom is the freedom to fly in a particular collective formation, but not to select the migratory route. In other words, employees should not tamper with fundamental or operative ideology. According to IBM rationality, freedom and opportunity are inexorably linked with its brand of structure and conformity. You cannot have one without the other. This constitutes the organizational myth at IBM. It is this myth which allows the employee to reconcile organizational rhetoric—"We do not try to tame wild ducks"—with concrete work requirements such as proper dress and proper behavior. Where there is the chasm of contradiction, there must be the bridge of myth.

## IDEOLOGY AS A META CONTROL SYSTEM

Distinct constituencies within the organization make competing claims. For example, management may have concerns about profit and market share, while the labor union may have concerns about the quality of work life. Official rhetoric may or may not include the interests of all significant participants, while the actual priorities have a moral texture whenever trade-offs must be made. Organizational ideology tacitly refers to the dominant group or groups, those interests that are in control. It will serve those interests because they normally have the influence to define the organization's interest. It is helpful to distinguish the group whose interests are most enhanced by the organization's status quo. It is this dominant group of managers that have the biggest stake in maintaining (or sometimes even changing) organizational ideology.

Ideology is a resource. It is always used by

managers for certain purposes. When top management's values and definitions become internalized and accepted by all as the definitive values of the organization as in IBM or the FBI, they have achieved a most efficient metacontrol system. First, it is internalized by all so that everyone believes that they are making their own decisions. Second, it provides normative orientations and ground rules necessary for the numerous decisions that are made by those far removed from top management. Third, all subordinates are not only "bearers" of the ideology but they also propagate it and are active in socializing new members. Fourth, a mode of rationality can evolve that is patterned by the dominant ideology and is comprehendible to all; thus it integrates diverse individuals or groups. The advantages to such a metacontrol system are numerous. The message "be reasonable, do it our way" is reinforced repetitively in numerous crude and subtle ways unique to each organization.

## CONCLUSION

A method of ideological analysis has been described. Any organizational theory is incomplete if it does not take the belief systems of participants into consideration. The method proposed can be useful in the identification and incorporation of ideological concerns into our thinking about organizations and how they function. More concretely, a large part of managerial work consists of translating ideology into tangibles and in accomplishing concerted collective action directed towards legitimate means and ends.

Managerial skills at putting ideology to work for the organization are highly valued. Effective managers appear to do this successfully. It is my hope that some of the ideas expressed in this paper will encourage a greater concern about organizational ideology, and more importantly, that some of the insights and examples will encourage students of management to sharpen their skills at recognizing ideology at work in organizations.

## REFERENCES

1. M. Selinger, *Ideology and Politics* (London: George Allen and Unwin, 1976), p. 102.

2. R. Ott, "Nobody Shoots Santa Claus" (Working Paper, Organizational Symbolism Conference, 1979b), p. 20.

3. T. S. Kuhn, *The Structure of Scientific Revolutions* (Chicago: University of Chicago Press, 1962).

4. S. A. Jonsson, and R. A. Lundin, "Myths and Wishful Thinking as Management Tools," in *Prescriptive Models of Organizations*, Nystrom and Starbuck, eds. (Amsterdam: North Holland, 1977), pp. 157–70.

5. B. R. Clark, "The Organizational Saga in Higher Education," *Administrative Science Quarterly*, 1972, 17, 178–84.

6. W. H. Starbuck, A. Greve, and B. Hedberg, "Responding to Crises," *Journal of Business Administration*, 1978, 9, pp. 111–37.

7. R. Ott, "Are Wild Ducks Really Wild?" (Working Paper, Northeastern Anthropological Association, 1979a), p. 1.

When we talk about managing people and behavior, we should concentrate on several managerial issues that influence the behavior of people and their performance in the organization. One such issue is motivation.

The article by Pinder deals with the application of motivation theories and raises some questions about premature applications and ethical problems associated with the implementation of some motivational programs in organizations. Pinder claims that most theories of motivation exhibit only limited validity when it comes to prediction and often entertain simplistic assumptions about human nature. As a result, the theories need to undergo more rigorous scientific testing before they are acceptable for public consumption. He advocates controlled application of the theories in real life situations strictly for validation purposes, but he warns against simple-minded application for bringing about changes in existing organizational arrangements in systems.

The manager's influence in an organization goes beyond dealing with individuals. The manager also is expected to understand how groups function and channel their activities toward effective development of the organization in directions that are mutually beneficial to the manager and the managed.

The next article by Waters, Salipante, and Notz takes a much broader approach to the issue of organizational development and change. The authors point out several problems associated with the implementation of change strategies in organizations in the same genre as the Pinder article, and they call for a revised perspective for bringing about change in organizations. The authors emphasize the importance of obtaining diagnostic, implementation, and evaluation information using multiple sources that are independent of each other in order for the change and development programs to take hold and succeed. The article also recommends policy level commitment to pro-

# V

# MANAGING PEOPLE AND BEHAVIOR

grams as opposed to commitment at the operational level. The attention of the reader is drawn toward the need for short and long term feedback, along with clearly established standards of comparison if the program is to work effectively.

In order for a manager to function effectively in an organization, it is not enough to know how individuals and groups behave. He or she should also have a good grasp of what sort of institutional arrangements govern the behavior of people in the institution and how their behavior, in turn, influences the structure and process of the enterprise. This calls for a theory of the firm that is grounded on realistic assumptions.

The article by Petit provides a theoretical perspective for managing our organizations. He reviews the closed system and open system models of the firm and points out the inadequacies of both. Through a process of integration he develops the composite systems view of the firm which incorporates the important assumptions from both earlier conceptions, while avoiding the pitfalls associated with them. The article defines management in terms of managerial actions taken to maintain technical rationality and minimize uncertainty. A three-tier model of the firm with the technical system at the core, the institutional system at the periphery, and the organizational system in between is presented. Based on this model, the ideal characteristics of the managers for the three levels are developed dealing with the nature of the task, viewpoint, technique, time horizon, and decision strategy.

Managers know that they face conflict in their work life from time to time; they often wonder about dealing with conflict. Conflict is an integral part of organizational reality and if a manager has to perform the managerial role well, he or she has to learn how to manage conflict. The first step in learning to manage conflict is to understand its nature, its structure, and the process itself.

The paper by Kilmann and Thomas presents the different ways in which conflict has been conceptualized and identifies the common thread linking the different approaches. The authors develop a metamodel of conflict that incorporates two dichotomies namely 1) internal and external loci of behavior and 2) structure and process of conflict. These two dichotomies yield four different theoretical combinations: 1) Internal structure, 2) Internal process, 3) External structure, and 4) External process. Further, Kilmann and Thomas report the following steps in managing a conflict: 1) Perceiving/experiencing unacceptable conflict, 2) Diagnosing the sources of conflict, and 3) Intervening. Based on the original model, various strategies for the three steps in managing a conflict were also outlined.

No discussion on management is complete without mentioning executive behavior and practices as well as managerial communication. The paper by Belcourt prescribes an executive behavior that is suitable for modern organizations. Belcourt traces the shift in executive values from a militaristic power and aggression orientation toward an emphasis on openess, trust, and social skills. This shift should predispose members in executive ranks to include aspects of both masculinity and femininity in their behavioral repertoire. However, Belcourt also points out that integration of women into the executive ranks has been painfully slow and the major roadblocks lie in our current practices of selection, training, and evaluation. The article points out the problems female managers face in each of the three areas that impede their absorption in the executive cadre. She suggests that "androgyny"—or incorporation of both female and male values—guide executive action toward a possible solution to the problem.

In summary, the different articles in this

section present a balanced picture on the managing of people and behavior from both theoretical and practical points of view. This approach prepares the managers to act in a particular manner; more importantly, it provides them with the frameworks to understand why they act the way they do.

How can I motivate my employees to work harder and more effectively?

This question is one that business leaders, managers, and students of commerce and business administration ask frequently, reflecting both their concern for the important problem of human productivity and as their implicit belief that human beings can (and should) be motivated. The question also reflects the primarily practical orientation of those who ask it—an orientation that is often dissimilar to the orientations of those individuals to whom they direct the question. Similar questions concerning how best to structure one's organization, design jobs, delegate tasks, select employees, and myriad other aspects of managing are directed by advice seekers (such as students and practicing managers) to advice providers (such as academicians and professional consultants) every day. Usually, advice providers answer the questions directed at them and—in the short run, at least—both parties in this exchange can benefit. The advice seekers gain knowledge and insight that *may* help them solve their real problems, while the advice providers stand to benefit from testing the validity, usefulness, and limitations of their ideas. (Advice providers often collect tidy fees for their efforts, as well.)

Sometimes, however, the relationship between advice seekers and advice providers is not so simple and mutually beneficial. It is often the case that the advice given is either too simple to effectively deal with the manager's problem or too complex (or theoretical) for the manager to comprehend and apply appropriately. The result in either case is that inappropriate managerial actions are taken on personnel and organizational problems—actions which are not likely to benefit anyone involved. In fact, instances of premature or inappropriate applications of behavioral science knowledge can be harmful to those who provide such advice, to those who seek it, and to those

# 13

# Human Motivation

*Mutualism Between Management and Behavioral Science: The Case of Motivation Theory*

CRAIG C. PINDER

upon whom managerial action is enacted—the lower participants in the organizations involved.

The purpose of this chapter is to discuss a number of issues related to the application of social and behavioral science to managerial problems. I will make particular reference to the application of theories of human motivation, because of both the importance of the problem of productivity in today's economy and the fact that advice concerning the motivation of employees is probably the type of advice most frequently sought after by managers and business students. In order to begin my analysis, I will present a model that represents a cycle through which new ideas are often developed before they eventually result in practical techniques that managers may use. The cycle reflects the mutualistic relationship that can (or should) exist between behavioral science and the enlightened practice of management. I will use two widely known and yet often misunderstood theories of work motivation to show how failures on the part of behavioral scientists to perform their role in the cycle correctly can result in misunderstandings and oversimplifications by practitioners who then inappropriately (but in good faith) attempt to use the scientists' products in their day to day policy and practice. The focus will then turn to a survey of a few current theories of work motivation, with a view to assessing both their applied validity and their potential for application to organizational problems. The chapter will conclude with a list of criteria that managers and students might apply to new ideas from behavioral science before they adopt such ideas in their daily practice of running organizations.

## THE SCIENCE-APPLICATION CYCLE

Practicing managers and students of business are often unaware that social and behavioral science knowledge results from a cycle of activities that is shared by all sciences. As a result, they often forget that the quality and applied value of that knowledge can be no greater than the quality of the scientific work which created it. The cycle of scientific activities that typically generates new insights concerning social and behavioral phenomena (such as work motivation) is illustrated in Figure 13-1. Also shown in Figure 13-1 is the linkage between the cycle of scientific investigation and the application of new knowledge to practical problems by managers.

The cycle often begins with the observation by someone (such as a practitioner or a scientist) of an event, phenomenon, or problem that is important enough to arouse concern. Poor job performance by employees is an example of such a problem. When the initial observation is made by a social or behavioral scientist or when it is brought to their attention, any of several directions might be taken. In some cases, the scientist may merely set about in an exploratory fashion to observe or reobserve the phenomenon. In other cases, the scientist may have prior hunches about what he will observe and will accordingly develop formalized predictions or "hypotheses" that can be tested by the data he is preparing to collect. Regardless, data are then collected and analyzed. The data come to the researcher by any number of common methods, such as by questionnaires, interviews, experimentation, or structured observation techniques. If the work is purely exploratory, the scientist may do any of several things next, including a return for even further observations of the phenomena (this time with the aid of guiding hypotheses, perhaps). If the

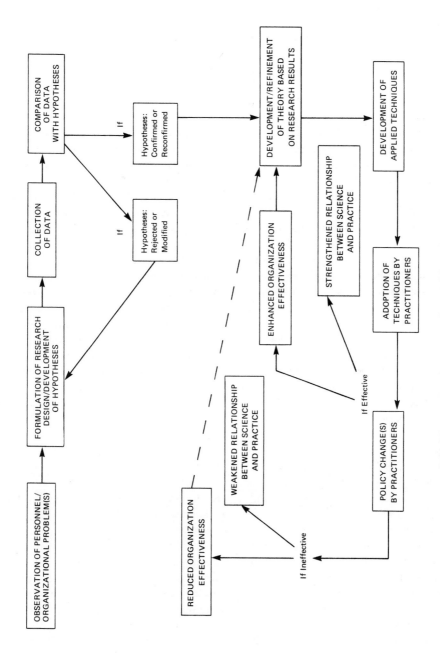

FIGURE 13-1 *The Multualistic Cycle of Science and Application.*

study features testable hypotheses, the results in the data are compared with the results predicted by the hypotheses. If the predictions match the data, the hypothesis (or hypotheses) are said to be "confirmed" (see Figure 13-1) and the scientist has some basis for believing that the phenomenon is at least partially understood. Eventually, after more or less confirmation and reconfirmation, sets of hypotheses are collected and aggregated into formal theories.

Theories are simply symbolic representations of someone's views of the world—they are like templates that are offered as representations or models of the nature of things. "Theory" is often treated as a dirty word by practical people, and many academicians and consultants seem ashamed to use the word when dealing with managers. But the fact remains that much, or most, of our "knowledge" about business and the behavior of people in organizations is based on nothing other than theory.

It should be clear at this point that the scientist's theory can be valid (or correct) only if the research it is founded on has been conducted properly. There are countless ways to do poor research and conduct inappropriate tests of one's hypotheses. Hence, it is sometimes the case that the propositions are not tested "fairly" (as it were), and may be either confirmed or disconfirmed for the wrong reasons. Seldom is a new hypothesis completely accepted or rejected on the basis of only one test, and it is *not* the case that they are always tested incorrectly. The point is that hypotheses that are supported by poor research can accumulate to develop theories of the world that are inaccurate representations of it. On the other hand, valid hypotheses that are not supported by poorly conducted research may be ignored and forgotten, and the knowledge base of the science is not expanded when it might have been.

There are various schools of thought pertaining to the development and testing of social and behavioral theory, but a full treatment of them is beside the purpose of the present chapter. The interested reader is referred to Kaplan (1) and Dubin (2) for two popular perspectives. Regardless of the school(s) to which the scientist or theorist subscribes, however, the theory will undergo more or less further study, usually by people other than those who first developed it.

In many cases, the interest of practitioners with practical problems is aroused, and the principles of the theory are transformed into techniques that are "sold" or otherwise made available for application. Taking theoretical ideas "to the field" is standard practice in the development and maturation of any theory, especially one that is related to organizational behavior.

However, a critical issue at this point pertains to the spirit with which the application is offered and the types and levels of expectations that are aroused at the time (3, 4). On the one hand, the scientist can offer limited promises in terms of what the theory and ideas derived from it might do for the practitioner. On the other hand, great expectations for curing the practitioner's problems may be generated—expectations that are unrealistic and bound to fail.

In many cases, nevertheless, the application of the techniques derived from theory are effective in helping the manager solve the problems. When this happens, everyone in the relationship can benefit. Not only does the practitioner enjoy increased organizational performance, but the people upon whom the theory-guided policies have impact also stand to benefit—through more satisfying work, greater profits to be shared, or whatever. Finally, the academician/scientist also can benefit from the occurrence of effective application of principles from her theories, because their applied value provides further confirmation of their validity (5), as shown in Figure 13-1.

But in far too many cases the application of new theory results in outcomes that are either less spectacular than the practitioner was led to expect or, even worse, harmful to the practitioner's organization and the people in it. In these cases, the credibility of the science in which the application has its roots suffers—not just the reputation of the individuals who provided the application. The only potential benefit from such failures lies in the possible further understanding and refinement for the theory (or theories) which gave rise to the applied techniques. But, as shown in Figure 13-1 by the dotted line, such postmortem analyses are not always done, and when they are, it is usually after significant damage has been done to all parties in the exchange (6, 7).

In short, the development of new ideas in behavioral science involves a series of cycles, each of which entails potential for mistakes and failures. Moreover, the application of new ideas from science to applied problems also is a process that entails risk for those involved. To illustrate one or two of the many possible pitfalls in these cycles, let us look at two of the best known theories of work motivation and examine how problems at various points in the cycles have rendered them either less valid or less useful than they might have been to practicing managers.

## Maslow's Hierarchical Theory of Needs

The most widely known theory of human motivation is, without doubt, the one developed by Abraham Maslow (8). Yet, ironically, while Maslow's theory is the most familiar among practitioners and students, it is probably also the most misinterpreted, misunderstood, and most oversimplified.

Briefly, the theory states that all human beings have a number of basic needs, and that these needs are important determinants of behavior. The needs vary in their relative importance as causes of behavior, according to Maslow, and their relative importance follows a predictable and somewhat universal pattern.

Physiological needs, such as those for nutrition, sleep, water, and sex are the most "prepotent." When these needs are not satisfied, the human being's behavior will be urgently devoted to fulfilling them. Less prepotent are Maslow's so-called "safety" or "security" needs—the needs relating to the protection of one's self from threats and harm. Love needs (or social needs) are seen as next on the hierarchy. This is the set of needs to interact with other people, both giving and receiving interpersonal contact. Even higher (or less prepotent) are human needs for esteem, including both a need for the esteem of other people as well as a need to hold a positive regard for one's self. Maslow's final category is referred to as the need for self-actualization. There is more than one interpretation of what is meant by self-actualization, but the most common is that people have a need to develop themselves to the full extent of their limitations. This need, according to Maslow, is the least urgent of all, and the one that is least commonly fulfilled in our society. In a nutshell, that is Maslow's theory of needs.

So what is the problem? First, the initial observations (see Figure 13-1) which gave rise to the theory were based on the reports of the patients who went to Maslow for psychological therapy. The reports and testimony given by these people were gathered by Maslow and assembled by induction into what was, at the time, an incredibly insightful theory (or template) of the nature of human functioning. But for years the theory was never subjected to the scrutiny of scientific testing (as shown by the cycles in Figure 13-1). Instead, it was more or less accepted as truth—maybe because of its elegance or its intuitively acceptable nature, but certainly not because of any research it generated.

More serious than the lack of objective examination, however, was the fact that the theory was reported over and over by a multitude of authors, often inaccurately. There was a tremendous tendency to oversimplify the theory, presumably to make it more digestible by the many practical people who wished to make use of it. The prepotency feature became translated and represented as a lock-step progression upwards, as in a staircase with five discrete steps. Authors interpreted the theory for users as if Maslow implied that needs at a certain level must be entirely satisfied before needs at the next higher level swing into effect. That is simply not what Maslow intended to say. He spoke, rather, of relative degrees of importance of the various needs, working in combination to affect behavior. As provisions are made to satisfy the "lower" needs, they tend to become *relatively* less important, but they certainly do not shut off or go away!

The difficulties created by the over-simplification of a theory that was never initially intended for application to work settings were compounded by the fact that when researchers *finally* began to test the model, most of them did so inappropriately, reflecting misinterpretations of the theory that were at least as significant as the misinterpretations that had long been made by managers (9). As a result, although there have now been a number of attempts to empirically test the theory (10) only a few studies (11, 12, 13) have legitimately looked at it. It is my opinion that the true validity of Maslow's theory *is still unknown*. Yet everyone in the business of human resource management knows (or thinks they do) about employee motivation based on what they (think they) know about Maslow's theory. In short, inappropriate initial observations, years of grand generalizing without empirical confirmation, inaccurate interpretation for the sake of easy application, and—the crowning touch—inaccurate interpretation for the eventual empirical examination of the theory have left many of us—students, practitioners, and academicians alike—with little better appreciation today for the validity of Maslow's theory than had nearly forty years ago when it was originally reported.

## Herzberg's Two-factor Theory

Next to Maslow's theory, the best-known theory of employee motivation must be that developed by Herzberg, et al (14). As in the case of Maslow's theory, there has been a considerable amount of misinformation arising as a result of the theory. Again, the student is referred to Figure 13-1 to gain a perspective on what went wrong.

Herzberg and his associates started by asking a number of engineers and accountants to recall times when they were either particularly happy or unhappy with their jobs, and to identify the things that they felt caused these experiences of satisfaction or dissatisfaction. The researchers coded and classified these reports (as initial "observations", in the terms of Figure 13-1) in an attempt to seek the causes of positive and negative job attitudes. Based on this attempt, the researchers developed the now-famous motivator-hygiene (or "Two-Factor") theory of job attitudes and motivation. Briefly, the theory holds that certain factors (called "motivators") are associated with positive job attitudes and—by inference—motivation. These factors were interpreted as feelings of responsibility and achievement, recognition and advancement for work well done, and simply doing interesting work. According to the theory however, absence of these features does *not* result in feelings of dissatisfaction; rather, no emotional reaction is seen as resulting. The second set of factors were called "hygiene" factors. These things, when absent from work, were associated with instances of job dissatisfaction, but when present, no particular emotion was seen as resulting. The hygiene factors were things such as favorable company policy, cordial relations with other people in the work place, salary, working conditions, and other aspects of the *context* of the work.

Herzberg's theory was a radical departure from traditional models which had treated job satisfaction and dissatisfaction as opposites; now they were viewed as independent of one another. It was now seen as possible for an employee to be simultaneously satisfied (and presumably motivated) and dissatisfied with his work. Hungry for new ideas concerning how to motivate their employees, managers quickly learned about the theory and attempted to apply it on the job. In fact, it has been pointed out by King (15) that both researchers and practitioners have interpreted the gist of the theory at least five different ways! Again, a theory was oversimplified and misinterpreted.

Unlike the case of Maslow's theory however, a flurry of research ensued to replicate the findings of the original study and thereby test the theory (as is appropriate, according to the model in Figure 13-1). But a great controversy soon developed when it was found that the theory was supported when researchers employed the same observation and coding techniques that Herzberg had used, but not supported when researchers used other methods. Vroom (16) argued convincingly that the two-factor results of pro-Herzberg studies reflected the method of data collection rather than the real nature of job attitudes. His argument was that people are more likely to attribute negative events to outside factors (the hygienes) rather than to the personal relationship between themselves and their jobs (the motivators). Since then, there have been enough other studies conducted that have rejected the two-factor feature of the theory (the key feature that makes it different from other theories) that one can confidently conclude that the theory, in most or all of its five interpretations, is a gross oversimplification of the nature of employee motivation and job attitudes. Readers who are interested in learning more about the so-called "Herzberg controversy" are referred to a balanced summary by Bockman (17).

If the motivator-hygiene theory is not a valid template of the nature of employee attitudes and motivation, why was it mentioned here? There are four reasons. First, the theory

is a second important example of the cycle shown in Figure 13-1 and the problems that can arise when faulty research leads to invalid theory which, in turn, can generate inappropriate implications for managerial policy and action. Herzberg's theory, as I have stated, told us more about his research methodology than about employee motivation. The asymmetry posited in the theory between the factors allegedly associated with positive and negative job attitudes is simply not valid. People can be quite dissatisfied when they fail to receive recognition or advancement from their work. Boring work *is* dissatisfying. Try reducing the responsibility in a person's job or preventing her from gaining feelings of accomplishment and watch the dissatisfaction that results. Herzberg was wrong, but many practical people bought advice based on his notions of asymmetry.

A second reason for raising the two-factor theory in this chapter is that it is instructive to the introductory student of management to see how the self-correcting loop of scientific activity (as shown in Figure 13-1) can, eventually, modify and/or reject theories that were based on poor research. It also shows (as suggested above) that application often occurs too soon, that ideas from theory are sold prematurely— invalid ideas.

My third reason for discussing the theory here is more simple: introductory students simply cannot enter the business world without knowing about it, because the widespread popularity of the theory makes it so that almost everyone encountered in management circles knows about the theory and accordingly believes that they understand employee motivation.

My final reason is to indicate to the student that we need not throw out entire theories when we pursue them with critical research. More recent and more defensible theories of intrinsic motivation and job design have benefitted from the part of Herzberg's work that suggests jobs be designed with responsibility, appropriate levels of challenge (to make achievement possible), and with the provision of positive feedback. Herzberg made a major contribution *to the development of further theory*, but not directly to the practice of management, per se.

My point is simply this: any theory is little more than a summary of someone's view of some part of the world, such as the nature of human motivation at work. Most theories are the result of the observations of those people who advance them, so if the observations are biased or somehow otherwise not truly representative of reality, the theories themselves cannot be valid representations of that reality. There is nothing wrong in forwarding a new theory, in good faith, in the regular process of developing a science. The risk lies in cases where a new theory is put to practical use too soon, before the science cycle illustrated in Figure 13-1 has had a chance to confirm and reconfirm it or—in the case of an invalid theory —to revise or reject it. In the case of the two

theories of motivation discussed above, limitations in the observation processes upon which they were based have severely limited the validity of one of them (the two-factor theory) and have limited our ability to legitimately determine the validity of the other (Maslow's hierarchical model). Yet, in spite of these limitations, almost everyone in the business world thinks he knows a fair bit about the nature of human work motivation on the basis of their understanding of these two popular theories. But can we blame the practitioner alone? I do not think we can. The content of these theories has been taught in schools of business and in psychology departments for years to students with applied interests and to managers with real problems to solve. Most introductory management books are produced, even today, with these theories represented—often badly. Advice seekers tend to seek truths that are practical, solid, and, most of all, simple. Let us take a look at the issue of simplicity.

## PRACTICALITY AND SIMPLICITY OF ADVICE AND IDEAS

It is my experience that most managers and business students are, as I suggested above, very practical people who need practical solutions to "real world" problems. There is nothing inherently wrong with being practical. Frequently, however, the desire for practicality translates—in the demands advice seekers place on advice providers—into a requirement for *simplicity*. Too often advice seekers expect nuts and bolts solutions, stripped of any cautions, caveats, or reservations that advice providers might wish to offer. Advice seekers too frequently require simple solutions to problems that they themselves admit are far from simple. Many advice providers resist the demands placed on them for simplistic answers, often at the cost of scorn and rejection by those

who come to them for help. Many advice seekers prefer, instead, sources of help that will offer one-or-two factor theories of organizations or of the behavior of people within them. Consequently, simple bipolar concepts are appreciated by advice seekers—concepts such as Theory X and Theory Y, the motivator-hygiene theory of motivation, mechanistic versus organic management styles, and so on. Simplicity is a desirable feature in any idea, but when ideas that purport to summarize complex phenomena with too much parsimony are sold to advice seekers who then allow their policies and managerial behavior to be influenced by overly simplistic thoughts, they are dangerous.

The reader is challenged to consider the complexity of human beings by thinking for a minute about the many dozens of factors (or variables) that determine their own behavior. Characteristics of the individual, such as one's intelligence, cognitive style, values, needs, interests, race, sex, culture, religion, education, socioeconomic background, career aspirations, and many others all interact to influence the way one behaves. In addition, characteristics of the work and life settings in which behavior unfolds are important. Consider for example the complexity of features of work and organizational settings, such as the nature of the work group (including such factors as its size, power, degree of cohesiveness, coalitions, and history); the job (including its depth and scope, its healthfulness and safety, for example); and the organization itself (including such things as its size, structure, goals, technology, and the environment in which it operates). These, and countless other factors, have been shown to affect the way people behave in formal organizational settings. Practicing managers readily acknowledge this complexity when it is pointed out to them, yet many of them—in spite of this acknowledgement—continue to expect advice providers to give them simple solutions to problems that involve so much complexity. The sad part is that many advice providers comply with these requests, either because they believe that simple solutions are, in fact, available or because the theories that they prefer are themselves simple. One of the most important lessons a student of business can learn about organizations is that all of the factors listed above, and many others not yet considered, are involved in various multiple combinations to determine employee and managerial behavior. A stance of humility for the

complexity of the behavior of people, organizations, and the behavior of people within organizations is required, as is a healthy skepticism about packages of ideas concerning these thing that feature only one or two factors. I am not saying that advice providers have nothing to offer practical advice seekers, but I wish to repeat my position that simplicity and practicality are not the same thing. What I am suggesting is that the most practical solutions to complex managerial problems may often be complex solutions. Therefore, a thinking manager or student of business should be willing to entertain complex advice from advice providers, and will be wary of those who offer seductively simple solutions. If organization problems were all simple, advice seekers would not need advice providers, and there would be no need for business schools. Common sense would suffice, and all of our organizations would be effective. Clearly, this is not the case.

The educational process in many business schools reinforces in students the expectation for simplicity and deterministic solutions. The content of business courses in mathematics, accounting, and business law, for example, consists of techniques and procedures that are viewed as either right or wrong, correct or incorrect. Certainly, much of business relies on the appropriate use of practical techniques for which there are right and wrong ways of doing things. The problem comes when students and practicing managers expect the same sort of right-wrong simplicity in the solutions they buy from people in the behavioral sciences for solving what they like to call their "people problems."

## SHOULD THE VALIDITY OF A THEORY OF MOTIVATION DETERMINE ITS READINESS FOR APPLICATION?

To this point, I have argued that at least two of our most popular approaches to the understanding of human work motivation are of limited or unknown validity and that, as a result, managerial techniques that make use of these theories have proven to be of limited net usefulness to practical people. In response to an earlier paper I have written on this topic Bobko (18) has suggested that the level of scientific validity of a theory of work motivation is not the most appropriate criterion for deciding whether or not a manager should apply such a theory. He has argued that managers make decisions on a minute-by-minute basis, and—as they do—employ sets of more or less valid *implicit* theories of the nature of human beings and organizations. These implicit theories result in what might be called a "base rate" level of good decisions, a certain proportion of decisions that are effective or ineffective. Therefore, says Bobko, we should assess the value of our formal theories of employee motivation in terms of the added value they can provide over and above the value the manager can achieve without consciously using them. In other words, the marginal utility of the theory rather than its degree of absolute validity should determine whether a manager should attempt to make use of it in the process of managing employees.

Bobko's argument is somewhat compelling, but in practice his "marginal utility" criterion is difficult to apply because of the difficulty in determining what the base rate of "good" decisions is for any given manager in any given work setting. In other words, if we are to use the utility of a manager's decisions as a base against which to compare the utility of decisions guided by theory, we need to know something about the base rate before the application takes place. This is virtually impossible because of the difficulty of assessing the utility or value of decisions in any context. The same manager might be quite successful in leading people on the basis of instinct or "common sense"—what comes naturally. Or he or she might not be very good at energizing human work effort. More likely than either of these possibilities, however, some managers will be more or less successful in some decision-making contexts and at some times more than others. How are we to determine how effective a manager is without

the apparent use of a theory to guide the decisions, and how will we determine whether the apparent increment in quality of decisions that will occur in some circumstances after a conscious application of theory has been attempted is due to the addition of the guidance provided by the theory? Further, it might be said that successful managers are those who unknowingly do the sorts of things that would be prescribed by our best theories anyway.

Aside from the problem of measurement for the sake of determining base rates and marginal utilities, there is, in my opinion, something inherently wrong with a philosophy of technology that is summarized as: "Let's make use of whatever is available!" The rush from scientific discovery to the application of technology has disgraced and hindered the development of many erstwhile respectable sciences, and has led to a growing wariness on the part of the public about both technology as well as basic science itself (19, 20). Medical science provides one of the most dramatic and unfortunate examples of a discipline whose engineering applications have often been premature (21), but the application of knowledge from chemistry, biology, and many other respectable sciences has resulted in sufficient instances of unfortunate consequences to make the public justifiably skeptical (22).

But Bobko's point has some merit and should not be discarded completely. A problem with using validity as a criterion for deciding when application is safe is that validity is a matter of degree. How valid must a theory be so that the applications it generates are safe for sale to advice seekers? And further, is it possible for us to gain accurate understanding of the true levels of validity of our theories? As I suggested earlier, it is often difficult or even impossible to establish or demonstrate the validity of a theory because of the many problems involved in measurement and observation. In fact, it may be that certain of our theories of motivation are actually better representations of the nature of reality than we are capable of showing, given our inherent human limitations as observers and measuring devices.

My point is not that we should not apply and make use of new knowledge by applying the techniques that come from it. I wish to repeat my conviction that it is absolutely necessary for the sake of the science involved for its principles to be extended for application in the field (23). Rather, I am arguing that when ideas are sold to practical people by scientists and advice givers before either party in the exchange understands the possible implications and repercussions from the application, both the buyer and the seller stand to lose. Without sufficient prior understanding of the probable ramifications of an application throughout the greater system in which an organism, a person, a work group, or any other unit is embedded, such an application involves risk for that greater system (24).

When we turn our attention from the physical and medical sciences to the issue of the application of behavioral and social sciences, the same types of risks of systemic repercussion are possible and, while the potential negative consequences seem less drastic (because we are not talking about potential loss of life and limb), they do occur. Sadly, the biggest losers from the premature application of behavioral science to managerial problems are the employees upon whom the applications are perpetrated. It is this group whose jobs are restructured, whose working hours are rearranged, whose work groups are shuffled, or whose pay schemes are changed, usually unilaterally, and often at their expense.

Later, I will discuss a number of reasons for the common premature application of management techniques, but before we turn our attention away from the issue of validity, let us look at a few other current theories of work motivation and the empirical evidence that relates to their scientific validity.

## THE VALIDITY OF SOME CURRENT MOTIVATION THEORIES

How valid are most of our present theories of human motivation? Recent reviews by Locke (25), Campbell and Pritchard (26), and myself suggest that we have only limited grounds for optimism. Some motivation theories make unrealistic or oversimplified assumptions about the basic nature of human beings. Some make predictions of behavior that are valid in the short run but that tend to vanish in the long run. All of these theories are subject to the limitations posed by individual differences (although not all of them recognize this limitation) and many of them make predictions that are in fundamental disagreement with the predictions made by others.

Three of the most popular and scientifically studied theories of human work motivation rely heavily on important assumptions about the nature of human consciousness and rationality that have been shown to be of only limited validity themselves. Accordingly, these same bodies of theory will be limited in the levels of validity they will ever enjoy. The problematic assumptions concern the degree to which humans are rational, contemplative, and capable of processing information. The theories assume that people act on the basis of rational choice after having gathered considerable amounts of information and having processed it with levels of sophistication that are somewhat superhuman. They assume that once the individual has performed such information processing, action is based on conscious choice or intention. Let us look at the major elements of these theories.

## The Expectancy Theories

Among academicians and researchers, probably the most popular theoretical models of work motivation in the past twenty years have been variants of Vroom's "Expectancy Theory" (26, 27). In essence, this theory states that three sets of beliefs on the part of the person combine with one another to determine that person's choice of behavior. One of these beliefs—the so-called "expectancy" perception, involves whether the person "expects" the effort to result in job performance. That is, it deals with the person's anticipation of the odds that, if one tries to perform a task, will one be successful?

The second set of beliefs—called "valences"—consists of the value the person *expects* to derive from whatever outcomes that may accrue from job performance at the various levels chosen.

The third set of beliefs, referred to as "instrumentalities," involves the nature of the person's perceptions concerning the strength of the connection between job performance and the accrual of the aforementioned outcomes. In other words, is job performance at a given level "instrumental" for the attainment of these outcomes?

Countless factors can potentially affect each of these three sets of beliefs for a particular individual. Expectancy perceptions ("Can I perform if I try?") are influenced by the person's experience, self-esteem, and perceptions of the level of difficulty of the task. The nature of the person's need structure and previous experience determine whether he expects various work-related outcomes to be "valent", or of value. Finally, personal experience, vicarious learning from watching the treatment of other people, and the general "wisdom" of the organization all contribute to the degree of strength of the person's beliefs about whether various levels of performance will result in these outcomes (such as pay increases, promotion opportunities, fatigue levels, alienation

from one's spouse, and so on). The theory holds that maximum motivation results when the person believes 1) that high performance is possible and 2) that high performance will lead to desirable outcomes and will prevent the occurrence of undesirable outcomes.

Most tests of the various forms of this basic model have shown it to be of only limited validity, yet most of these tests have themselves been fraught with any of a number of serious methodological problems (28). The precise nature of these methodological mistakes is beyond the scope of this chapter, but suffice it to say that most of the tests of the theory have been—in a sense—"unfair" tests, and that most of those that have been at least minimally fair have still failed to provide overwhelming support for the theory. Nevertheless, it remains one of the most useful and viable approaches we have to understanding (and therfore influencing) employee behavior. Much of the advice given pertaining to the management of people in organizations in recent years has been guided by these expectancy-type theories of motivation.

## Goal-Setting Theory

Another body of theory concerning work motivation—and one which makes assumptions about the rationality of people similar to the assumptions made by expectancy theory—can be referred to as "goal-setting" theory. As before, an exhaustive treatment of this approach is beyond the scope of this chapter, but its fundamental tenets can be reported. This theory holds that most behavior is a result of conscious intentions (or goals). Therefore, to influence a person's behavior, you must first influence her goals and intentions. It follows that "high" goals (or hard goals in a work-related sense) will result in higher levels of performance, but that goals which are too hard will be rejected and therefore result in no effort. Finally, the theory states that specific goals result in higher effort levels than vague goals, such as "Do as well as you can."

The major tenets of goal-setting theory have provided the conceptual underpinnings for a set of managerial techniques referred to under the general rubric "Management by Objectives" (MBO), although the technique itself was developed well in advance of the research on goal setting (29). A full discussion of MBO is beyond the scope and mission of this chapter, but the point needs to be made that MBO may represent the best example of how theories of motivation can be put into practice long before behavioral scientists have developed sufficient understanding of the types of individual and organizational preconditions that are necessary before applications are warranted. The majority of attempts to install MBO in North American organizations have been failures, and it has taken careful postmortem analyses to determine why and when the technique fails. With each failure, the credibility of the science suffers, the effectiveness of the client organization suffers, and the job attitudes and work performance of many working employees is put in jeopardy. Nobody benefits, except possibly the scientist whose only concern is understanding.

Readers interested in learning more about goal setting are referred to Latham and Locke (30) or Steers and Porter (31). Details about MBO programs can be found in Raia (32) or Carroll and Tosi (33). McConsky (34), Jamieson (35) and Levinson (36) describe a number of the problems that have characterized the failure of many MBO programs.

In spite of the many failures of formalized MBO-type programs, there is considerable evidence from both laboratory (37) and field research (38) that goal-setting techniques enjoy not only reasonably high levels of scientific validity but also considerable *potential* applied value. However, the translation of simple goal-setting principles into practice in formalized programs such as MBO seems to be difficult and fraught with potential damage to all of the parties in the exchange.

## Equity Theory

There is a third body of theory that assumes a considerable degree of rationality and information processing on the part of the human being. Referred to as "Equity Theory," this approach assumes that working people hold beliefs about the number and nature of the contributions or "inputs" they provide to their job. Things such as their level of education, prior experience, and effort are three such inputs that a person might consider. Simultaneously, the theory holds that people also consider the consequences or "outcomes" they derive from their jobs. Salary, job satisfaction, fatigue, and hours away from a loved one are examples of the sorts of things a person might view as outcomes. Different people consider different factors as relevant inputs and outcomes. According to the theory, job attitude and the level of effort he or she might elect to expend doing that job result from the person's evaluation of the equity of the psychological ratio he or she perceives between inputs and outcomes, and how this perception compares to the ratio he or she perceives is being experienced by some other person—a comparison other. If the individual perceives a relative equality between his or her ratio of outcomes to inputs relative to that of the comparison standard, satisfaction is hypothesized to result. On the other hand, if the person views these ratios as being sufficiently unequal, the theory predicts job dissatisfaction and, potentially, action perceived necessary to restore a balance (such as working more or less hard, or leaving the organization).

Since the theory was first advanced by Adams (39), it has been tested many times, most frequently in laboratory settings that simulate real work conditions. The results of these studies have been mixed, but mostly nonsupportive of the theory, in spite of the intuitive appeal it holds for many people. There are myriad problems associated with the theory itself (such as the difficulty of determining with whom employees might compare themselves). There are also a number of complex difficulties inherent in creating the experimental conditions necessary for testing it (such as, for example, influencing or even monitoring the types and levels of inputs and/or outcomes a person considers). It may be that equity theory, like expectancy theory, is in fact more valid than behavioral researchers are capable of demonstrating.

The interested reader can find a good summary of the evidence concerning equity theory in Carrell and Dittrich (40).

## Behavior Modification/ Operant Conditioning

Perhaps the motivational technology with the most effective track record in work organizations is that which has been derived from the work on operant conditioning by B. F. Skinner and his followers.

There is more than one variation of the basic model, each differing in the role that cognitive processes (such as those underlying the three theories mentioned above) are seen as playing. In a nutshell, however, these models posit that human behavior is a function of its consequences. If an act results in positive consequences for an individual, the probability increases that the same act will be employed in similar circumstances in the future. The act is said to be "positively reinforced." If a behavior results in adverse consequences for the person, that person is said to be punished and the probability that the punished act will be repeated diminishes. A third consequence for an act is no consequence—the behavior is ignored by others and brings neither positive nor punishing outcomes to the actor. After several such trials, the behavior in question ceases or "extinguishes."

People in organizations serve as sources of both positive reinforcement and punishment for others around them. Supervisors can accordingly encourage or discourage the behaviors of subordinates by responding to their acts with desirable consequences such as praise, promotions, time off, or pay, or undesirable consequences such as reprimands or demotions.

Outcomes are distributed in accordance with what are called "schedules of reinforcement." Schedules which tie the occurrence of behaviors directly to positive outcomes are more powerful as behavior changers than are schedules that see outcomes distributed with no apparent connection to behaviors. Piece rate or commission pay plans are examples of the former, while salary systems (in which the period and amount of pay does not vary with behavior) are examples of the latter.

Due to space limitations, my treatment of the details of behavior modification and operant conditioning techniques must be cursory. The interested reader is referred to articles by Aldis (41) and Nord (42) for two early statements of the relevance of Skinner's principles for the management of employees, and to a chapter by Hamner and Hamner (43) for a review of actual (and generally successful) applications of these principles in work settings. In short, behavior modification programs seem to be effective in influencing a number of work-related behaviors ranging from attendance and tardiness to performance levels, although the role that conscious thought plays in the process is open to dispute (44–46).

## Recapitulation

In the foregoing sections, I have presented brief summaries of some currently popular theories of work motivation. I have tried to highlight the major tenets of each theory as well as provide a quick insight into some of their respective limitations and points of controversy. There are other approaches to work motivation that I have not discussed, such as those that make use of so-called "growth needs" in the design of jobs to make them intrinsically motivating and satisfying. Space limitations prevent their being presented here, but the interested reader is referred to the following sources: Hackman and Oldham, (47), McClelland (48), and Deci (49).

The limited validity of the various approaches discussed above (as well as some not discussed) has prompted at least two authors to argue in favor of models that combine them in various ways and in various circumstances so as to capture the value inherent in each while at the same time acknowledging their respective shortcomings (50, 51). I believe that such balanced, electic approaches are warranted and recommend that students and managers with an interest in the issue of work motivation consider them seriously.

## PRACTICAL PROBLEMS IN USING MOTIVATION THEORIES IN REAL WORK SETTINGS

Even if some or all of our most popular theories of motivation were more valid than they are, and even if they really did accurately reflect the nature of goal-directed work behavior, how easy are they to put into practice? The answer to this question is relatively simple, although the reasons behind the answer are not so simple:

Reward systems in ongoing organizations are typically very limited in the degree to which they can, in practice, implement key principles that are found in theories of motivation.

As an illustration, consider the advice that would derive from three of the theories discussed in the last section—expectancy theory, equity theory, and behavior modification. The first two of these theories would suggest that supervisors attempt to make the distribution of rewards and punishments available to them contingent upon the work behaviors they wish to encourage or discourage among the people who work for them. Further, equity theory would suggest that these rewards and punishments be distributed in a manner that will be perceived by one's staff as equitable (as defined above). In practice, how easily is this accomplished?

Herbert Meyer (52) has addressed the difficult dilemmas faced by the manager who wishes to tie pay (as a specific form of reward) to performance. First Meyer notes that "merit" pay systems contribute little to employee satisfaction with pay, even though contingently-paid employees *may* be more highly motivated to perform than those paid on a flat rate (such as on a salary basis). Results of a study by Schwab (53) also suggest this to be the case.

But other problems emerge when we try to tie pay to performance. First, job performance itself must be measured accurately and with validity if it is to be linked to pay, so that employees can perceive the connection, let alone perceive it as equitably distributed. Achieving reliable and valid assessments of employee performance is a chronic problem of managing for all but production and sales jobs (54). In practice, attempts to tie pay to performance that are *seen* by employees as, in fact, not really doing so are demotivating, so managers who are not aware of who her meritorious people really are run the risk of employing merit pay to their disadvantage.

Another problem noted by Meyer is based

on the likelihood that many or most employees tend to see themselves as above-average in terms of their own job performance. If his findings in this regard are true, it follows that most employees will see merit pay going to co-workers whom they percieve as less meritorious than themselves. In other words, the majority of employees may tend to perceive that differential pay is, in fact, not associated with differences in merit. Again, the result could be the opposite of what was intended.

Additionally, paying people for job performance can generate competition among them—competition that can result in reduced willingness to cooperate and coordinate work effort.

Finally, there is some evidence that pay schemes that tie pay directly to performance may, in some circumstances, reduce the employee's degree of *intrinsic* motivation to perform well (55, 56).

In short, reward systems in organizations typically are very limited in the degree to which they can, in practice, implement the ideas that come from motivation theory. Managers are too busy to monitor performance as effectively as is necessary to structure rewards so that they are, in fact, tied to performance. Even if they could, it is difficult to assure that the employees involved will all perceive that the distribution is equitable. The foregoing analysis is only a brief indication of the difficulties involved in converting theory-based ideas into actual practice in complex work settings—difficulties which magnify the shortcomings of these ideas which result from their limited scientific validity.

## CONSUMING SOCIAL/BEHAVIORAL THEORY AND TECHNIQUES

If most motivation theories enjoy only limited levels of scientific validity, and if practical constraints in organizational settings place further impediments on their applied value, it is reasonable to ask how managers can (and do) decide whether to permit theoretical ideas about employee motivation to influence the way they structure policy and behave toward their subordinates. In this section, I will discuss this question from two perspectives: the descriptive and the prescriptive. That is, I will begin by looking at a number of factors that seem, in practice, to be common influences in managerial decisions about the adoption of theories and/or techniques derived from theories. The second half of this section will feature an alternative set of criteria and considerations that a manager might consider when deciding whether to allow theory to influence practice.

### Criteria in Practice

Few practicing managers seem to be very aware of the validity of most of the theories available to them in social and behavioral science. Instead, other factors seem to be more common influences on the decision of whether to adopt or reject theories or programs derived from them. When we consider a list of these alternative decision criteria, the high rate of instances of premature application that I have mentioned earlier becomes easy to understand. What are some of the more common considerations employed by practitioners?

First, there is cost. Advice seekers are naturally concerned with the issue of how much money they expect it will cost them to implement the advice that comes from social/behavioral scientists. Consultant's fees, equipment, space, managerial time, and the time of others in the organization who might be affected are the most frequent varieties of cost factors considered. Sometimes, (but less frequently), advice seekers also consider the probable costs associated with *not* installing the change.

Second, there are the benefits advice seekers expect will be associated with the adoption of the ideas and programs from advice providers. Benefits seem to be much more difficult to estimate than costs. Competent advice providers can help managers estimate the benefits that *may* be possible as a result of adoptions, but here is a common place where the exchange between advice seekers and providers becomes less fortunate. Too many advice providers, particularly those whose livelihoods depend heavily upon the sale of advice to practicing managers, overestimate the value that managers can expect to derive from the advice they have to offer. Sometimes, the overestimates are a result of innocent zealousness or genuine faith in the products they have to offer. But sometimes their enthusiastic overestimates arise from less noble origins such as the necessity on their part to secure a client and/or experiment at the possible cost of their clients. Advice seekers must consider the motives of advice sellers and be wary of those who promise extreme and unrealistic benefits from the products they offer.

Ease of implementation is a third factor, one that is closely related to the issues of cost mentioned earlier. Many programs can be installed with minimal upset to the client, while others (such as major job enrichment changes, for example) can introduce major redistributions of power within the organization. Changes that entail new organizational designs can also pose major threats to extant power structures and will often encounter significant barriers to installation as a result. Some advice seekers seek help "as long as it does not disrupt things too much."

Risk is another consideration. Some managers are willing to adopt programs and techniques that they believe cannot do too much harm in the event that things do not work out. A common strategy among many managers is to elect a course of action that minimizes the maximum possible risk, so an application which appears the least likely to fail—or if it does fail, to be the least costly—is favored.

A fifth factor is the popularity of the technique among management circles. It is often the case that new programs and techniques enter the scene as "the" solution of the day, and managers—being human—fall prey to the fads. A number of authors over the years have noted the tendency toward faddism in the field (57, 58, 59), but that tendency continues. The role of fads is particularly unfortunate for the scientific disciplines with which they are associated, because they cheapen the image and reduce the scientific credibility of those disciplines in the eyes of people who have fallen subject to them.

To summarize, practicing managers implicitly make use of a number of criteria when they seek the assistance of advice providers and elect to apply techniques that advice providers offer. Most of these criteria are very practical and some of them are unfortunate.

## Some Alternative and Additional Criteria

I believe that enlightened management requires the careful consumption and application by managers of techniques that are rooted in scientific theory and evidence. It follows from this belief that it behooves would-be enlightened managers to be aware of the legitimacy and value (in scientific terms) of the principles and techniques they consider adopting for consideration. Elsewhere, Larry Moore and I have argued that both managers (60) and students (61) should train themselves to become careful consumers of behavioral and social scientific ideas. To be a careful consumer means to make enlightened choices among alternatives—in this case among alternative techniques or the adoption of none. Choice making, in turn, requires the application of choice criteria, so we are faced with the following question: What bases does a manager or a management student have available for deciding whether a piece of research, a theory, or a technique based on theory should be permitted to influence his or her policy and practice? The following list of questions is suggestive of the types of information an enlightened manager might like to know before proceeding with the adoption of a new idea that comes from behavioral research and theory. The list is certainly not exhaustive and the questions are not meant to be independent or mutually exclusive.

When appraising a specific piece of research, the consumer might ask, for example:

1. What was the sample size of the research project on which the results are based? Was it large enough to justify confidence?

2. Was the sample studied similar to the population(s) to which you wish to generalize the results?

3. Did the researcher report the reliability of the research instruments used? How stable and internally consistent were these measures?

4. Did the researcher demonstrate the construct validity of the instruments used?

5. Did the researcher comply with the assumptions underlying the statistical methods used? If not, are the techniques/tests used robust to the violations?

6. How lasting or permanent are the results of the research manipulations? Were the experimental effects found in the research transitory, washing away after a short period of time, or would the changes be more permanent?

7. Are there any viable alternative explanations for the observed results of the research?

8. Was the research design cross-sectional or lon-

gitudinal? Which is more appropriate to adequately (and fairly) test the theory being tested, if any?

9. Is it possible that the researcher has a vested interest in the findings of a research study and that he or she has consequently overinterpreted the results?

10. Even if research results are statistically significant, are they practically significant enough to justify your attention?

11. Do the results of the research and/or the prescriptions of the theory converge with those of other theories?

Likewise, when considering a new theory or a technique that is rooted in theory, a careful consumer might ask questions such as the following:

1. How much empirical evidence is there in favor of the theory?

2. Has the theory been supported by more than one methodological approach?

3. Does the theory have some intuitive appeal? Acceptance and effective implementation by line managers is facilitated if the theory makes some degree of sense.

4. Were samples drawn randomly in the research on which the theory is based, or is it possible that nonrandom sampling limits the generalizability of the findings?

5. Do instruments related to the application of the theory have sufficient face validity to be accepted by those who must use them?

6. How many exceptions to the general rule will occur? In other words, how universally valid is the theory? Does the theory tell you which individual differences variables to include?

7. Can parts of the theory be of value in practice, or must all of it be adopted, intact?

Additionally, there are a number of other more practical considerations that can legitimately be addressed once the prospective application has passed the hurdles listed above. In addition to the issues listed in the previous section, the enlightened (and practical) consumer might ask:

1. How easy would it be to install or apply the theory in your organization? Would application require any cost in the form of changing physical plant, or training of supervisors or other personnel?
2. How easily scuttled are changes and procedures needed to permit the application to be effective, and is it possible that significant people are likely to try to scuttle them?
3. Would application of the theory require changing other support personnel subsystems (such as compensation, recruiting, labor relations)?
4. Would special consultation with the union be advisable before application can proceed?

5. How long will it take until changes based on the theory will show meaningful results? Can you afford to wait that long?

I wish to emphasize that the items in these three lists do not exhaust all of the questions that a careful manager or student might ask—they are meant only to be suggestive of the possibilities. It is my opinion that if more managers of business and government organizations had asked questions such as these more frequently in the past, there would have been fewer cases of premature, inappropriate, and harmful applications of behavioral/social science knowledge than have occurred.

## SUMMARY AND IMPLICATIONS

The majority of those who read this volume will be students of business and administration who, by their very nature, are individuals with particularly applied goals and interests. Many of them will eventually become managers of the multiple resources that contribute to the successful conduct of business. By attending schools of commerce and business administration, they will be attempting to acquire insights into the management of these resources—insights that have their roots in the behavioral, social, and economic sciences and that take longer to acquire without the benefit of formal training. They will be seeking to learn a complex set of principles, practices, conventions, laws, and techniques which their teachers can provide more efficiently than can "the school of hard knocks." Business students, like practicing managers, are applied people, looking for hands-on advice and insight into real, applied problems. On the other hand, authors who write chapters in books such as the present volume are people who purport to possess such

knowledge and insight, as are many other academics and consultants who presume to offer their advice to both business students and managers in practice.

In many ways, the relationship between the academic/theoretician/consultant and the reader/student/manager is a convenient one from which both sides of the relationship stand to benefit. It is a relationship that Garner (62) has referred to as "symbiotic." But there are a variety of forms that symbiosis can take, and I suggest that one of these—mutualism—is the precise relationship that must exist between *enlightened* practitioners and social/behavioral scientists.

Mutualism is defined as "An association whereby two organisms of different species each gain from being together and are unable to survive separately" (63). My argument in this chapter has been that scientists and practitioners need one another in ongoing mutualism, but that occasional mistakes by the former group and the urgency of the needs of the latter have periodically threatened the relationship. Students of business (for whom this chapter is written) must learn to understand and then manage their end of the exchange if they wish to benefit from it.

## REFERENCES

1. A. Kaplan, *The Conduct of Inquiry* (San Francisco: Chandler, 1964).

2. R. Dubin, *Theory Building* (New York: Free Press, 1969).

3. C. C. Pinder, "Concerning the Application of Human Motivation Theories in Organizational Settings," *Academy of Management Review*, 1977, 2, pp. 384–97.

4. G. A. Walter, and C. C. Pinder, Ethical Ascendance or Backsliding?" *American Psychologist*, 1980, 35, pp. 936–37.

5. W. R. Warner, "The Acquisition and Application of Knowledge: A Symbiotic Process," *American Psychologist*, 1972, 27, pp. 941–46.

6. D. Jamieson, "Behavioral Problems with Management by Objectives," *Academy of Management Journal*, 1973, 16, pp. 496–505.

7. P. H. Mirvis, and D. N. Berg, *Failures In Organization Development and Change* (New York: John Wiley, 1977).

8. A .H. Maslow, "A Theory of Human Motivation," *Psychological Review*, 1943, 50, pp. 370–96.

9. V. F. Mitchell, and P. Moudgill, "Measurement of Maslow's Need Hierarchy," *Organizational Behavior and Human Performance*, 1976, 16, pp. 334–49.

10. M. A. Wahba, and L. G. Bridwell, "Maslow Reconsidered: A Review of Research on the Need Hierarchy Theory," *Organizational Behavior and Human Performance*, 1976, 15, pp. 212–40.

11. C. Alderfer, *Existence, Relatedness, and Growth* (New York: The Free Press, 1972).

12. Mitchell and Moudgill, "Measurement of Maslow's Need Hierarchy," pp. 334–49.

13. J. Rauschenberger, N. Schmitt, and J. E. Hunter, "A Test of the Need Hierarchy Concept by a Markov Model of Change in Need Strength," *Administrative Science Quarterly*, 1980, 25, pp. 654–70.

14. F. Herzberg, B. Mausner, and B. Snyderman, *The Motivation to Work* (New York: John Wiley, 1959).

15. N. King, "Clarification and Evaluation of the Two-factor Theory of Job Satisfaction," *Psychological Bulletin*, 1979, 74, pp. 18–31.

16. V. Vroom, *Work and Motivation* (New York: John Wiley, 1964).

17. V. M. Bockman, "The Herzberg Controversy," *Personnel Psychology*, 1971, 24, pp. 155–89.

18. P. Bobko, "Concerning the Non-application of Human Motivation Theories in Organizational Settings," *Academy of Management Review*, 1978, 3, 906–10.

19. T. R. La Porte, and D. Metlay, "Technology Observed: Attitudes of a Wary Public," *Science*, 1975, 188, no. 4183, pp. 121–27.

20. E. Shils, "Anti-science: Observations on the Recent 'Crisis of Science.'" In Ciba Foundation Symposium, London, 1971, *Civilization and Science: In Conflict or Collaboration* (Amsterdam, New York: Elsevier, 1972).

21. E. Stempel, "The Impetus of Thalidomide on Drug Legislation and Regulation," *American Journal of Pharmacy*, 1962, 134, pp. 355–64.

22. J. A. Lauwerys, *Man's Impact on Nature* (Garden City, New York: The Natural History Press, 1970).

23. C. C. Pinder, "The Marginal Utility of the Marginal Utility Criterion: A Reply to Bobko," *Academy of Management Review*, 1978, 3, pp. 910–13.

24. E. P. Willems, "Behavioral Technology and Behavioral Ecology," *Journal of Applied Behavior Analysis*, 1974, 7, pp. 151–65.

25. E. A. Locke, Myths in "The Myths of the Myths about Behavior Mod in Organizations," *Academy of Management Review*, 1979, 4, pp. 131–36.

26. E. E. Lawler, *Motivation in Work Organizations* (Belmont, California: Brooks/Cole, 1973).

27. J. P. Campbell, and R. D. Pritchard, "Motivation Theory in Industrial and Organizational Psychology," in *Handbook of Industrial and Organization Psychology*, M. D. Dunnette, ed. (Chicago: Rand McNally, 1976).

28. *Ibid.*

29. R. G. Greenwood, "Management by Objectives: As Developed by Peter Drucker, Assisted by Harold Smiddy," *Academy of Management Review*, 1981, pp. 225–30.

30. G. P. Latham, and E. A. Locke, "Goal Setting—A Motivational Technique That Works," *Organization Dynamics*, 1979, 8 (2), pp. 68–80.

31. R. M. Steers, and L. W. Porter, "The Role of Task-Goal Attributes in Employee Performance," *Psychological Bulletin*, 1974, 134, pp. 355–64.

32. A. Raia, *Managing by Objectives* (Glenview, Illinois: Scott, Foresman, 1974).

33. S. J. Carroll, and M. L. Tosi, *Management by Objectives* (New York: Macmillan, 1973).

34. D. D. McConsky, "20 Ways to Kill Management by Objectives," *Management Review*, October, 1972, pp. 4–13.

35. Jamieson, "Behavioral Problems."

36. H. Levinson, "Management by Whose Objectives?" *Harvard Business Review*, 1970, 48, pp. 125–34.

37. E. A. Locke, N. Carteledge, and C. S. Knerr, "Studies of the Relationship between Satisfaction, Goal Setting, and Performance," *Organizational Behavior and Human Performance*, 1970, 5, pp. 135–58.

38. B. Latham, and B. Yukl, "A Review of Research on the Application of Goal Setting in Organization," *Academy of Management Journal* 1975, 18, pp. 824–45.

39. J. S. Adams, "Toward an Understanding of Inequity," *Journal of Abnormal and Social Psychology*, 1963, 67, pp. 422–36.

40. M. R. Carrell, and J. E. Dittrich, "Equity Theory: The Recent Literature, Methodological Considerations, and New Directions," *Academy of Management Review*, 1978, 3, pp. 202–10.

41. O. Aldis, "Of Pigeons and Men," Harvard Business Review, 1961, 39, pp. 59–63.

42. W. R. Nord, "Beyond the Teaching Machine: The Neglected Area of Operant Conditioning in the Theory and Practice of Management," *Organizational Behavior and Human Performance*, 1969, 4, pp. 375–401.

43. W. P. Hamner, and E. P. Hamner, "Behavior Modification on the Bottom Line," *Organizational Dynamics*, 1976, 4, pp. 3–21.

44. E. A. Locke, "The Myths of Behavior Mod in Organizations," *Academy of Management Review*, 1977, 2, pp. 543–53.

45. J. L. Gray, "The Myths of the Myths about Behavior Mod in Organizations: A Reply to Locke's Criticisms of Behavior Modification," *Academy of Management Review*, 1979, 4, pp. 121–29.

46. M. Parmerlee, and C. Schwenk, "Radical Behaviorism in Organizations: Misconceptions in the Locke-Gray Debate," *Academy of Management Review*, 1979, 4, pp. 601–7.

47. J. R. Hackman, and G. R. Oldham, *Work Redesign* (Reading, Mass.: Addison-Wesley, 1980).

48. D. C. McClelland, "Achievement Motivation Can Be Developed," *Harvard Business Review*, 1965, 43, pp. 6–24, 178.

49. E. L. Deci, *Intrinsic Motivation* (New York: Plenum Press, 1975).

50. B. T. Mayes, "Some Boundary Conditions in the Application of Motivation Models, *Academy of Management Review*, 1978, 3, pp. 51–58.

51. T. A. Mahoney, "Another Look at Job Satisfaction and Performance," in *Compensation and Reward Perspectives*, T. A. Mahoney, ed. (Homewood, Illinois: Irwin, 1979).

52. H. H. Meyer, "The Pay-for-Performance Dilemma," *Organizational Dynamics*, Winter, 1975, pp. 39–50.

53. D. P. Schwab, "Conflicting Impacts of Pay on Employee Motivation and Satisfaction," *Personnel Journal*, 1974, 53, pp. 196–200.

54. H. G. Heneman, III, *et al*, *Personnel/Human Resource Management* (Homewood, Illinois: Irwin, 1980).

55. Deci, Intrinsic Motivation.

56. B. Staw, *Intrinsic and Extrinsic Motivation* (Morristown, New Jersey: General Learning Press, 1976).

57. M. D. Dunnette, "Fads, Fashions and Folderol in Psychology," *American Psychologist*, 1966, 21, pp. 343–52.

58. D. R. Hackman, "Is Job Enrichment Just a Fad?" *Harvard Business Review*, 1975, 53, pp. 129–38.

59. H. Mintzberg, "Organization Design: Fashion or Fit?" *Harvard Business Review*, 1981, 59, pp. 103–16.

60. L. F. Moore, and C. C. Pinder, "Managers as Consumers of Organizational Behavior: An Historical Perspective on the 'Relevance' Debate," *Relations Industrielles*, 1979, 34, pp. 799–809.

61. L. F. Moore, and C. C. Pinder, "Preparing Students as Consumers of Organizational Behavior: A Call for More Emphasis on Theory," Exchange, 1978, 2, pp. 384–97.

62. W. R. Garner, "The Acquisition and Application of Knowledge: A Symbiotic Relationship," American Psychologist, 1972, 27, pp. 941–46.

*The appropriateness of conventional diffusion-of-knowledge perspectives on the use of behavioral science research is questioned. The need for an experimenting approach to organizational change which emphasizes diagnosis, modification of change strategies during implementation, and organizational commitment to problem-solving rather than to solution-implementation are discussed.*

Of all the problems in which modern managers are interested, it is probably not an exaggeration to place those involving the quality of human performance at work at the top of the list. This managerial interest in human problems has been matched by the interest which behavioral scientists have shown in researching these issues. In 1972, one reviewer conservatively estimated that 3,350 articles and dissertations had been published which studied job satisfaction alone and that the rate was increasing (6). Over 2,000 studies published within the last fifteen years examined the relationship between organizational factors and human performance and satisfaction (9). Even the application of very restrictive standards concerning both quality of research and potential usefulness to policy makers still led those authors to include nearly 700 of these in a subsequent review and evaluation. That review was limited entirely to published research; no effort was directed at scouting out the enormous number of unpublished, "proprietary" studies on these issues. Whatever the standards, it is clear that a very large body of research on these problems has been created over the last quarter century.

Given this great mass of research and the continuously expressed managerial interest, one might expect to find a well-developed body of knowledge, *answers*, about how to achieve productive and harmonious industrial relations. Unfortunately, the reality is quite the opposite. Despite the occasional well-published success, most behavioral science techniques (answers) appear to have suffered from a very

# 14

# Managing Groups

*The Experimenting Organization:*
*Using The Results*
*Of Behavioral Science Research*
JAMES A. WATERS, PAUL F. SALIPANTE, JR., and WILLIAM W. NOTZ

high failure rate when applied to the real-world problems of managers (8).

Why should such a state of affairs exist? Is the research invalid? Or does the source of difficulty lie in the managerial use of behavioral science tools and techniques?

Perhaps part of the problem can be traced to the tendency of managers to want a single, simple answer about how to achieve improved industrial relations. The various behavioral science techniques with which managers have at one time or another been enamored (e.g., employee counselling, participative management, T-groups, job enrichment, etc.) have been adopted as panaceas, usually with disappointing results, and have generally either fallen into disrepute or are in serious danger of doing so (4).

This review suggests that a more fundamental source of the trouble may lie in a mistaken appreciation of the nature of behavioral science research results and that both behavioral scientists and managers are involved. This article questions conventional views on the use of behavioral science research and considers the implications of a revised perspective for organizational change projects.

## IMAGES OF DIFFUSION OF KNOWLEDGE

In discussing the diffusion of knowledge or the application of research, there is often an implicit assumption of a "knowledge flow system" (3) or a "center-periphery" model of dissemination (7). Such models rest on the notion that there exists a body of research findings (generated by behavioral science researchers) and that the use of these findings simply depends on transmitting them to potential users (managers in organizations). Such imagery is very misleading in this context, for at least four major reasons.

### Under-Reporting of "Failures"

Any successful application of a behavioral science technique is much more likely to be reported, in both scientific and more popular journals, than is a failure. The successful General Foods Topeka experiment was reported in several journals, magazines, and on a nationwide television special. Failures seldom become known by the popular media, since neither researchers nor managers are generally eager to have their failures publicized. Furthermore, academic journals rarely publish statistically insignificant results, which generally accompany the failure of a technique such as job enrichment. The net effect is that failures are under-reported. In our review, all but one of 58 job change field experiments reported an improvement in satisfaction or productivity. Under-reporting of negative results may contribute to a bandwagon effect since it leads managers (and others) to overestimate the probability that a given technique will produce the desired results.

### The All Things Equal Fallacy

A pressing criticism of any general behavioral science theory or approach is its implicit "all things being equal" assumption. For a potential user in a complex organizational setting, usually the appropriate assumption to make is that "all things are never equal." Yet, most behavioral science innovations are presented to organizations as a complete idea, *the answer*, the panacea.

Advocates of universal approaches often cite research evidence to support their approach, but examination of the research as a whole rather than selectively yields a different picture. The relationship between any organizational factor and satisfaction or productivity is likely to be a contingent one.

The two general categories of contingency factors in research studies were those related to:

1. *The Work and Work Environment*—Given the multiplicity of technologies that exist in industrial organizations, combined with differences arising from special union-management, organizational structure, market and geographical considerations, the probability that what works in one situation will directly work in another is not likely to be high.
2. *Workers' Characteristics*—Differences among employees such as variations in age, family status, education, cultural norms, relative importance of higher and lower order need satisfaction, etc., will obviously influence the consequences of a change in job design. For instance, democratic supervisory style is related to satisfaction in a positive manner for many subordinates, but not necessarily for those with low need for independence (9).

Thus, a more useful view of the use of research is that situational contingencies will always have a strong impact on whether a particular research finding holds up in practice. The most typical situation will be one in which prescriptions from research findings will have to be modified and tailored to fit the particular situation where they are to be applied.

## Reconstructed Logic Flaw

In applying research findings on the nature of jobs and work life in large organizations, the manager must recognize that published research findings represent an after-the-fact reconstruction of the actual research experience. The research approach and results portrayed in published literature may appear highly logical due to this reconstructed logic (5). Even in the

most controlled laboratory experiment, there is an overload of potentially relevant information. The researcher and subjects in such an experiment respond to a multitude of cues in a variety of ways, not all of them conscious. In field research, which is much less controlled, the cues and responses are even greater in number. The researcher's findings, insights, and conclusions emerge from this complexity through a logic-in-use. However, in attempting to portray these insights to others, the researcher must reduce complexity to manageable proportions through use of a reconstructed logic.

As an example from another field, consider the installation of a new computer system. Accounts of other people's experiences with their own installations can only slightly prepare a manager for the turmoil, chaos and agony involved in attempting to change systems without interrupting operations. When an organization installs its own new system, it finds the reconstructed portrayal of others' installations to be a pale shadow of reality. While the reconstructed portrayal makes the past installation process appear quite "clean," the actual process turns out to be messy and very complex. Similarly, an actual research experience can never be portrayed adequately with all its possible ramifications, so a potential user will always be appraising some idealized version of the actual research experience.

## Abstractness

Because of the variety of work settings and individual differences that exist in industrial organizations, published knowledge about job design is generally at a much more abstract level than might be the case in other fields. For example, the technology to produce ammonia can be specified in some detail, down to special grades of steel, models of compressors, and types of storage tanks. In contrast, the "technology" to change the nature of jobs cannot be specified in such operational detail before confronting the actual situation. Increasing "job challenge" may or may not be a good approach to increasing productivity and satisfaction, but the operationalized meaning of job challenge cannot be established except in regard to particular people in specific work settings. Practitioners must transform the abstract notion, say, of challenge, into specific changes in tasks and responsibilities which employees actually will recognize as increasing their job challenge.

## A New Image: Innovation In Situ

The above discussion implies that the single answer, advocacy approach is glaringly inadequate. Published research under-reports failures, making support for "single-answer" approaches appear unrealistically favorable. Factors upon which any "single answer" depends are underemphasized, leading to lack of concern for the contingencies that must be met for the particular approach to be successful. Further, because of its reconstructed and abstract nature, the portrayal of the research itself will be misleading and inadequate for the practitioner to apply the same technique as the original researcher.

What is required is a more open strategy aimed specifically at the generation of additional knowledge on site so that research results can be tailored to fit a particular context. That "tailoring" process is actually the creation of a change program "in place," i.e., *innovation in situ*. The center periphery or knowledge flow imagery must be discarded, in recognition of the importance of a situational contingencies and the inherent incompleteness of any behavioral science "solution".

Put most simply, the practitioner must be an innovator in his or her own right, an experimenter. This does not mean that the innovator should start from a position of ignorance of current behavioral science theory and research but that he or she must be creative in its application, committed to searching for the additional knowledge that will almost certainly be required to make the innovation successful, and willing to modify the innovation as it proceeds. In short, the innovation in situ model suggests that changes in a particular work setting to achieve specific goals must be created "in place" rather than being "imported".

## A STRATEGY FOR INNOVATION IN SITU

What guidelines can be given to potential innovators in situ? To what traps should the innovator and the organization be alerted? In grappling with these questions, a starting point is to recognize that innovation in situ is essentially a knowledge generating process. Three types of information are essential:

1. *Diagnostic information* on the organization's particular problem from which target variables can be derived (i.e., what specific results are of concern), potentially manipulable variables (action levers) can be specified (i.e., what can be changed that might influence those results), and situational contingencies can be identified.

2. *Implementation information* or short term feedback that can be used to modify the change as it develops.

3. *Evaluation information* or long term feedback to determine whether the innovation is producing the desired results and, if not, whether it is time to implement a previously considered alternative.

## Diagnostic Information

The first step in the process of innovation in situ is to develop a systematic and in-depth understanding of the organization's unique problems.

Such understanding moves beyond the simple awareness that all is not as well as it might be and involves much more than a personal analysis of organizational problems based upon a few quick discussions with key managers. An adequate diagnosis must be based upon hard facts about the particular organization and its problems.

How can the organization generate such a factual data base? Should the process of diagnosis involve systematic, in-depth interviews of managers and employees, questionnaire surveys, structured observations by trained observers, or analysis of archival data (11) (e.g., turnover, absenteeism, productivity, etc.)? No *one* of these techniques, if used strictly by itself, will be likely to yield a valid diagnosis. Each of these measurement procedures contains inherent defects, errors, which if not properly dealt with could lead to a seriously flawed data base, an incorrect assessment of target problems and their causes, and thus a misdirected change strategy. The *only* way to avoid this difficulty is simultaneously to use several different techniques, different in the sense that they possess counterbalancing flaws. The behavioral sciences have not now developed (nor will they ever develop in the future) a single, universally valid method that can be used to diagnose problems any more than they have now developed (or will ever develop) universally applicable solutions to those problems. Only by using several independent methods— self report, observations from several sources, records of past behavior, etc.,—and then triangulating on target problems can the diagnostician have any reasonable confidence in the "hard facts" upon which any action will be based.

Although the principle of multiple methods does not seem to be used often by most practitioners and managers with respect to the human side of organizational analysis and problem solving, it seems to be rather widely applied in other areas. Consider, for example, the many different sources of data routinely used to assess an organization's effectiveness. No modern manager would be willing to make any serious commitment of resources, say the acquisition of another firm, solely on the basis of any single measure of the firm's value (e.g., sales volume *or* growth *or* market share *or* projected cash *or* ROI *or* current ratio, etc.). A rational manager would demand multiple means of measurement and multiple judgments, and a conclusion regarding value would most likely represent convergence of these different modes of evaluation. Yet, in spite of the much greater difficulty involved in attempting to measure the nonfinancial aspects of organizational effectiveness, decisions in these areas are often made on the basis of a single, fallible mode of measurement (e.g., an attitude questionnaire, *or* in-depth interviews, *or* the structured observations of a consultant, etc.).

As a further illustration of the inherent danger involved in overreliance upon a single method of diagnosis, examine the example of using only a questionnaire. There are problems and biases inherent in any self-report method. Even assuming that employees are sufficiently motivated to try to provide accurate self-report data, they may not be able to do so. There is a host of very plausible reasons why employee *perceptions* of their job characteristics might be a systematic distortion of the *objective* features of their jobs. If this were the case, a change strategy directed at a redesign of the actual job characteristics would be unlikely to succeed and could conceivably make matters even worse. If the problems were in the faulty perceptions of employees rather than in the actual jobs, then the faulty perceptions and not the work itself might be a more appropriate target of the change strategy.

There is still another potentially serious, largely unrecognized, problem that may arise from use of self-report methods, particularly standardized questionnaires, in the diagnostic process. All self-report methods are likely to do more than merely measure attitudes and behavior; they are also likely, by themselves, to initiate change. The problem is potentially serious because the changes that these methods generate may be both undesirable and difficult to "undo" at a later date. Research evidence suggests that use of a standardized questionnaire, much of the content of which is likely to appear irrelevant to the personal experience of the employee, not only may miss some crucial information but also may actually decrease the employees' willingness to be open and take risks (1). Since variables like trust, openness, etc., are already problematic in many organizations, it is important to avoid any diagnostic procedures which might unintentionally make matters worse. One way of avoiding this problem is to design an "empathetic questionnaire" that demonstrates some awareness and acceptance of the key (and probably unique) issues facing the organization's members (1). Again, the clear implication is that no diagnostic technique is likely to be universally applicable; most will require fine tuning at least if they are to provide a valid understanding of the organization's problems.

In summary, the process of innovation in situ must begin with the innovative use of several methods, with different strengths and weakness, to produce a truly factual data base for subsequent action. A funneling strategy (in which information generated early in the diagnostic process from "wide-gauge" methods is subsequently used to sharpen the focus of self-report methods) is probably most efficient. To minimize the "change agent effect" of the measurement process itself, a desirable sequence would be to start with analysis of statistical record data, followed by systematic observation and semi-structured interviews, and finally, tailored questionnaires. Such a multimethod diagnosis should identify both the general and the unique characteristics of the organization's problems that are a necessary basis for planning change.

## Implementation Information

No matter how thorough and painstaking the diagnosis, it probably will be incomplete and actual implementation of the innovation will inevitably reveal unanticipated problems. Proposed solutions must always be advanced tentatively, under the assumption that at worst they may not work at all, and at best they will probably require substantial modification. Therefore, the second component of innovation in situ must be short-term feedback which can be used to guide and further shape the innovation itself. Such feedback must provide: (a) information on whether action levers have been successfully manipulated, and (b) information on the extent to which the intervention has produced actual changes.

The first of these, assessment of the innovator's success in actually manipulating the action levers, is generally overlooked. Very few of the 58 experimental studies reviewed reported data to demonstrate that the intended changes had been effectively administered. Yet such data are crucial, since without them, innovators have no way of knowing what, if anything, needs to be modified in their treatment. For example, consider a project in which the target variable was increased productivity and the action lever manipulated was an increase in individual autonomy and discretion. Imagine that subsequent results showed productivity to be unchanged. The meaning of results like these would obviously depend upon whether or not the innovator had actually changed autonomy and discretion. Without a measure of autonomy and discretion, the innovator would have no way of deciding whether the original autonomy/productivity hypothesis was wrong (perhaps because of an unanticipated contingency) or whether the absence of change in productivity simply reflected a lack of change in autonomy and discretion.

With respect to the collection of data on the

effects of the intervention, two issues must be addressed:

1. The innovation must be implemented in such a way that a basis for comparison of its effects is created.
2. Provision must be made for an extensive assessment of the innovation's effects both intended and unintended, and all should be measured with multiple methods.

Feedback on the effects of an innovation is of no value to an innovator in situ unless he has a standard against which to compare it, but frequently no such basis for valid comparison is created. Projects are often implemented, and then, almost as an afterthought, some post hoc effort is made to measure their effects. Such data are completely worthless since "change scores" in this situation can be created only from either the participants' or the innovator's subjective judgments of "what things were like before the project." Obviously, a valid basis for assessing change demands objective "before" measures of target variables, measures which will be readily available *if* the innovation is itself a response to diagnosis.

In many cases, *repeated* "before" measures will be required because of the organizational tendency to select groups with extreme characteristics (e.g., low productivity, high absenteeism, etc.) to receive the innovation first. Extreme measurement scores at a single point can occur because of random factors (including the inevitable measurement error) and are likely to show a subsequent change regardless of the intervention. Feedback, to be interpretable, requires a stable basis for comparison, a time series of "before" measurements.

In a similar way, the use of reasonably comparable control groups which do not receive the intervention often will substantially enhance the interpretability of results. Reductions in absenteeism and turnover may result more from a general decrease in economic activity (with lowered sense of security and alternative employment opportunities) than from the innovation being attempted. Without a control group with which to compare results, the innovator may be led down a false trail based on the apparent "success" of his or her intervention.

In addition to needing a valid comparison basis against which intended effects can be measured, the innovator in situ also needs to be able to assess the unintended consequences of his or her intervention. Organizations consist of subsystems that are richly joined—variables of any sub-system are affected not only by factors within the sub-system, but they both affect and are affected by variables of adjoining subsystems. Thus, a worker's productivity, satisfaction, job involvement, etc., are both a cause and a result of a number of other organizational sub-systems, such as supervisory style, work group climate, pay system, morale of adjacent work groups, etc. As a result, any change of sufficient magnitude to affect the target variables is almost certain to produce unanticipated effects as well.

At first glance, the suggestion that the innovator needs to measure what he or she has not anticipated may seem contradictory. It is not, provided that the innovation has been preceded by an extensive diagnosis in which liberal use has been made of multiple methods and multiple theoretical perspectives. Approaching the problem through an iterative process from several theoretical viewpoints will guarantee an expanded awareness of *potential* contingencies that could affect the projects' outcomes. Diagnostic information that has been generated through several modes of measurement will complement this expanded awareness by providing the innovator with the data base ("before" measures) from which changes in non-target variables, even unanticipated changes can be detected.

During the implementation phase, all of the information must be generated repeatedly and with little delay if it is to be of maximum value in modifying the change strategy in midstream. In general, self-report techniques are not very well-suited to the creation of relatively continuous information. Although questionnaires and interviews are an excellent means of acquiring real-time feedback, they cannot be administered repeatedly without becoming an integral part of the innovation itself. Therefore, during the implementation phase, relatively greater emphasis should be placed on the use of unobtrusive measurement techniques such as structured observation and organization records of productivity, quality, costs, turnover, absenteeism, lateness, early departures, transfer requests, grievances, etc.

## Long Term Evaluation

Even though the process of innovation in situ will produce essentially continuous feedback of results, ultimately a "bottom line" evaluation is required, namely: Did the innovation work? At some point, senior management must decide whether the activity is worthy of further experimentation and investment of resources, perhaps even extension to other parts of the organization, or whether it should be scrapped in favor of a completely different approach to the problem.

Logically, there would appear to be very little difference between the information required for the short-run modification and long-term evaluation of an innovation. The criteria, sources of data, and comparison bases required for both are essentially identical, though the long-term evaluation, like the diagnostic phase, may use self-report methods. Nevertheless, potential consequences of the information generated over the longer-run are such that they cannot be treated as a simple extension of the short-term process.

While most innovators could easily gather the longer-term information that is necessary to evaluate their projects, they may be unlikely to do so. Our contacts with innovators suggest that many managers responsible for work change projects perceive them as pilot projects which must demonstrate to top management that the innovation will be successful. Therefore, to those responsible for carrying out the innovation, the value of accurate, long-run evaluation information may be quite minimal.

The innovator, to use Campbell's concept, becomes *trapped* in a position he or she has championed (2). The advocacy messages delivered in the current management literature encourage the innovator to adopt an advocacy role. Higher management exacerbates the problem by demanding quick results and by constraining the intervention to what was originally proposed; further, it well may be that the innovator's unswerving personal commitment is required to keep the project alive long enough to bear fruit.

This commitment may also be inevitable. Even if initially unbiased and relatively unpressured from above, the innovator is likely to become trapped by the mere commitment to manage the innovation. Considerable empirical evidence indicates that, regardless of long-term outcomes, most change projects are very likely to produce short-term decreases in performance. Further, an emerging body of research indicates that a decision maker's personal commitment to a strategy is more likely to become stronger when the initial outcomes of that strategy are negative than when they are positive (10). Thus, the initially negative results of a change project are very likely to produce a "Viet Nam syndrome" in which the innovator becomes increasingly committed to the particular approach. The message is that innovators are very likely to become trapped in their particular innovations and cannot be expected to perform accurate evaluations of them.

## THE EXPERIMENTING ORGANIZATION

In sum, senior management can expect the trapped innovator to put maximum effort into making his or her innovation successful. The long-run danger is that the change will only be made to *appear* successful. In any event, the presence of a trapped innovator certainly does not increase the likelihood of accurate, unbiased evaluation.

While the innovator may be unavoidably trapped, the organization need not be. The organization (i.e., senior management and worker representatives) can be committed to a larger goal, to *solving a particular problem,* rather than merely to *implementing a particular solution.* While some individuals may become committed to a particular approach, the organization as a whole need not be. The clear implication is that if top management wants hard-headed evaluation of a project, then the responsibility will have to be assigned to someone other than the innovator.

If the long-run evaluator is organizationally independent of the innovator, how can the organization ensure the cooperation between them that is so obviously required? First, senior management can make it clear that independent evaluation is a necessary condition for the innovation to occur. Second, management can make it clear that what is to be evaluated is the *project* and not the innovator. Third, management can help to innoculate the innovator against the disillusionment that accompanies the failure to have a "pet solution" confirmed as worthy by creating a climate in which failure is viewed as a normal part of the *learning* process. In this regard, management can contribute most to the creation of such a climate by demonstrating its own commitment to the process of innovation in situ, a process which helps to prevent failure, since failure can occur only if one has become so committed to a particular

solution in advance that advocacy of an alternative is impossible. Thus, the innovation in situ model refers to an organizational process extended in time. The same model can describe the activities of an individual change agent, but only for a limited time, after which it can be expected that the change agent will become less of an experimenter and more of an advocate.

## How Do Projects Get Started?

One consequence of using the innovation in situ model to consider efforts aimed at changing work designs in an organization is that it raises questions about how such change efforts might get started. If before beginning, one is not exactly sure what one is going to end up doing, how is it possible to appraise the potential benefits of a change effort? And if estimation of the potential benefits (or for that matter, the potential costs) is not possible, how does one decide to begin?

The way to consider this paradox is to confront squarely the notion that a policy level decision rather than an operating level decision is required to begin investing in a work change program. To make the distinction clear, consider the example of corporate contributions to colleges and universities. It would be hocus-pocus to attempt to justify such giving on the basis of a rigorous discounted cash flow analysis. The decision to make such contributions must be a policy level one, based on a broader appreciation of the present culture and on the use of a longer time frame in considering the consequences of corporate activities.

In the same way, a decision to begin investing in human resource development cannot be based on a simple projected cost/benefit analysis. *To do so almost guarantees that the people involved in securing the initial go-ahead will become trapped advocates of a particular solution.* This is especially so since a certain amount of hocus-pocus will be required to conjure up a presentable cost/benefit analysis. Once embarked on a demonstration project, all the pressures are on to prove that the approach selected really does "work"; all the pressures are against asking the crucial questions about other approaches and against being open to all the information available that would allow tailoring the change to the situation.

## Manager and Academic Roles

Finally, if effective work change programs are to take place, rigid and exclusive role definitions for manager and academic researcher must be reconsidered. The latter must be willing to join in the complex world of the manager and to take on some responsibility for helping to produce hard measurable results. Similarly, managers must be willing to put aside their traditional stereotypes of "ivory tower" researchers and open their doors and minds to behavior science researchers and techniques which can facilitate and guide the innovation in situ process. Both academics and managers now tend to view their respective groups as the most important source of valid knowledge (3). Needed organizational change and knowledge generation will await less polarized concern and more collaborative effort in the process of innovation in situ.

## REFERENCES

1. Alderfer, C. P., and L. D. Brown. "Designing an Empathetic Questionnaire for Organization Research." *Journal of Applied Psychology*, Vol. 56 (1971), 456–460.

2. Campbell, D. T. "Reforms as Experiments." *American Psychologist*, Vol. 24 (1969), 409–429.

3. Duncan, W. J. "Transferring Management Theory to Practice." *Academy of Management Journal*, Vol. 17 (1974), 724–738.

4. Hackman, J. R. "Is Job Enrichment Just a Fad?" *Harvard Business Review*, (September–October 1975), 129–138.

5. Kaplan, A. *The Conduct of Inquiry: Methodology for Behavioral Science* (Scranton, Pennsylvania: Chandler, 1964).

6. Locke, E. A. "The Nature and Consequences of Job Satisfaction" in M. D. Dunnette (Ed.), *Handbook of Industrial And Organizational Psychology* (Chicago: Rand McNally, 1976).

7. Schon, D. *Beyond the Stable State* (New York: Random House, 1971).

8. Sirota, D., and A. D. Wolfson. "Pragmatic Approach to People Problems." *Harvard Business Review* (January–February 1973), 120–128.

9. Strivastva, S., P. F. Salipante, Jr., T. G. Cummings, W. W. Notz, J. D. Bigelow, and J. A. Waters, *Job Satisfaction and Productivity: An Evaluation of Policy Related Research on Productivity, Industrial Organization and Job Satisfaction* (Cleveland, Ohio: Case Western Reserve University, 1975).

10. Staw, B. M. "Knee-Deep in the Big Muddy: A Study of Escalating Commitment to a Chosen Course of Action." *Organizational Behavior and Human Performance*, Vol. 16 (1976), 27–44.

11. Webb, E. J., D. T. Campbell, R. D. Schwartz, and L. B. Sechrest. *Unobtrusive Measures: Nonreactive Research in the Social Sciences* (Chicago: Rand McNally, 1966).

*There are three types of managers. Technical managers strive to rationally produce the firm's output. Institutional managers cope with uncertainty in the environment. Organizational managers mediate between technical and institutional managers. The three types of managers differ according to task, viewpoint, technique, time horizon, and decision-making strategy.*

Two major developments in management theory have occurred in recent years. First, there has been a diversity of approaches to the subject. Koontz identifies six separate schools of management theory: the management process, empirical, human behavior, social system, decision, and mathematical schools.[1] Second is the trend toward behavioralism. The behavioral methodology and viewpoint of or-

ganization theory have had an increasing impact on teaching and research in management.

These two developments are interrelated. As theorists focus their attention more sharply on what managers actually do in business organizations, they tend to emphasize one of several possible aspects of management behavior, according to their training, cosmology, and the type of problem that interests them. This diversity does not necessarily mean that there is an undesirable fragmentation of management theory. The subject is vast and calls for many different approaches in this early stage of development. As Simon said, speaking of management theorists, "It is important that we think of ourselves . . . not as representatives of competing or contradictory approaches.[2] Each theoretical approach may be looked upon as a valid but partial explanation of management

[1] Harold Koontz, "The Management Theory Jungle," *Journal of the Academy of Management*, IV, No. 3 (Dec., 1961), 174–188.

[2] Herbert A. Simon, "Approaching the Theory of Management," *Toward a Unified Theory of Management*, ed. Harold Koontz (New York: McGraw-Hill, 1964), p. 79.

# 15

# Managing
# the Organization
## *A Behavioral Theory of Management*
THOMAS A. PETIT

behavior. Eventually one may prove to be more in accord with the facts and eclipse the others.

Another possibility is that there is a conceptual framework within which each approach has a place and where it can be related in a meaningful way to the others. This paper attempts to develop such a conceptual framework. It outlines a behavioral theory of management, based on a behavioral theory of the firm, within which the various approaches to management theory can be integrated.

## THE FIRM AS A SYSTEM

### The Firm as a Closed System

The traditional economic theory of the firm treats the firm as a closed and deterministic system. Closure is accomplished by the device of *ceteris paribus*. Variables that cannot be accommodated within the interlocking assumptions of profit maximization, complete rationality, perfect knowledge, market competition, and identity of firm and entrepreneur are disregarded by assuming "all other things are equal." It is a simple matter then to calculate the profit maximizing price-output relationship by marginal analysis.

Nearly everyone now agrees that this model is not a good one for predicting the actual behavior of firms. That, of course, was never its purpose. As Machlup points out, the theory is "not, as so many writers believe, designed to serve to explain and predict the behavior of real firms; instead it is designed to explain and predict changes in observed prices (quoted, paid, received) as effects of particular changes in conditions (wage rates, interest rates, import duties, excise taxes, technology, etc.)."[3]

Despite the discrepancies between the theory and reality, it offers important insights into the behavior of the firm and its members. Closed deterministic systems have distinct advantages from the standpoint of understanding,

prediction, and control. If the present state of such a system is known, its next state can be predicted without risk of error. This means the system can be rationally manipulated to maximize the value of its goal. Rational behavior consists in selecting the best means to accomplish given ends. Since planned rather than random action is the rule in firms, the concept of rationality is relevant and useful and should be retained in more realistic models of the firm.

### The Firm as an Open System

Some economists have developed biological models of the firm which have the characteristics of open systems. Some of them are based on the physiological concept of homeostasis (i.e., the tendency for living beings to respond adaptively to threatening changes in their environment). Boulding uses this concept to show that when the equilibrium of the firm is disturbed by environmental elements, forces automatically go into action to return it to the homeostasic state. Thus the firm is a reactive entity rather than the active one pictured in the traditional theory of the firm.[4] Knauth has a similar theory in which the maintenance of trade position (i.e., share of the market) is all important to the survival of the firm. When the

[3]Fritz Machlup, "Theories of the Firm: Marginalist, Behavioral, Managerial," *The American Economic Review*, LVII, No. 1 (March, 1967), 9.

[4]Kenneth E. Boulding, *A Reconstruction of Economics* (New York: John Wiley and Sons, 1950), Chapter 2.

firm's trade position deteriorates, homeostasis leads to a return to the original position.[5] Chamberlain's theory of economic process emphasizes the bargaining activities by which the entrepreneur alters environmental forces or adapts to them. Through marketing, pricing, and other bargaining procedures the firm strives to balance cost and revenue flows and to attain its objectives: satisfactory profit, satisfactory market position, and satisfactory growth.[6]

Alchian's work in viability analysis is similar to the homeostasic theories of the firm. His purpose is to explain how firms can survive in an uncertain world. Under uncertainty the outcome of actions cannot be foreseen. Therefore, how does the firm select the profit maximizing course of action? Alchian starts with the fact that some firms do survive for long periods and therefore must have made profits and avoided losses. There are two ways of doing this under conditions of uncertainty: the firm may be "adopted" by the environment or it may "adapt" to it. Adoption occurs when the firm accidentally makes the right choices, given its environmental situation. It is "selected by the environment" to survive just as a plant is selected when it possesses the characteristics necessary to survive in its physical environment. Survival through adaptation to the environment involves imitating the behavior of successful firms.[7]

The homeostasic and viability theories view the firm as a probabilistic open system. There are uncontrollable and unpredictable elements in the environment which have strong effects on the firm in both theories. The behavior of the firm in the homeostasic theory consists of the efforts to cope with external forces of change and to return to the desired equilibrium position. In viability analysis the firm consciously or unconsciously adapts to changing environmental conditions to survive. Rationality and maximization are impossible, and uncertainty and the drive to survive are present in both theories.

## The Firm as a Composite System

The behavioral theory of the firm, analyzed most thoroughly by Cyert and March,[8] views the firm as an open system because it must take courses of action in an environment which does not fully disclose all the alternatives available. The firm is limited in its capacity to gather and process information or to predict the consequences of alternative actions. To operate with any degree of rationality, therefore, the organization must develop processes for searching for information in the environment, for learning from experience which decisions are good and bad, and for deciding upon courses of action in the face of uncertainty.

We said earlier that more realistic theories of the firm should not disregard the concept of rationality simply because there is not the complete rationality assumed in the traditional theory of the firm. Simon's concept of bounded rationality[9] enables us to do this in the behavioral theory of the firm.

Cyert and March show us that the functioning of the firm in an uncertain environment is a highly complex process, so complex, in fact, that if the organization attempted to face up to all the implications of uncertainty it would be overwhelmed. To operate with any degree of rationality, the firm must reduce the complexity and uncertainty to a manageable level. This is done by setting artificial boundaries

[5]Oswald Knauth, *Business Practices, Trade Position, and Competion* (New York: Columbia Univeristy Press, 1956).

[6]Neil W. Chamberlain, *A General Theory of Economic Process* (New York: Harper and Row, 1955).

[7]Armen A. Alchian, "Uncertainty, Evolution, and Economic Theory," *Journal of Political Economy*, LVIII, No. 3 (June, 1950), 211–221.

[8]Richard M. Cyert and James G. March, *A Behavioral Theory of the Firm* (Englewood Cliffs, N.J.: Prentice-Hall, Inc., 1963).

[9]Herbert A. Simon, *Models of Man, Social and Rational* New York: John Wiley and Sons, 1957), pp. 198–200.

around the firm for decision-making purposes. By operating according to the criteria of bounded rationality the number of variables can be reduced so that necessary decisions can be made. Since not all relevant variables are included, rationality is incomplete and maximization is impossible, except by chance.

The behavioral theory of the firm is consistent with the strategic assumptions of both the closed-system and open-system views of the firm. From this viewpoint the firm can be thought of as a composite system. It retains the rationality assumption of the closed-system view (in modified form) and it is consistent with the assumptions of uncertainty and drive for survival of the open-system view. As Thompson says, the composite system organization can be conceived as an open system, *"hence indeterminate and faced with uncertainty, but at the same time as subject to criteria of rationality and hence needing determinateness and certainty."* [10]

## RATIONALITY AND UNCERTAINTY IN THE FIRM

### Structure of the Firm

According to the composite-system view, the firm is unable to operate with complete rationality nor must it face complete uncertainty. This would be impossible if the firm were a homogeneous entity, one part being the same as all others with regard to rationality and uncertainty. But the composite-system firm can be viewed as made up of parts which specialize in coping with uncertainty or striving toward rationality.

According to Parsons' theory of organization[11] there are three levels of responsibility and control in the firm—technical, organizational,[12] and institutional. The technical level is a subsystem which produces the goods or services which are the firm's output. The problems it faces are technical in nature, imposed by the requirements of the task rather than disturbances from environmental elements (e.g., plant layout, production scheduling). The organizational level controls and services the technical level. It procures nec-

essary resources and disposes of the output, and it determines the nature of the technical task, sets the scale of operations, and establishes operating policies. The institutional level deals with the relation of the firm to its environment. It maintains good relations with the public, the industry, government, unions, the community—any group, organization, or institution whose support (or lack of active opposition) is required for the firm's survival.

In Parsons' theory these three levels are qualitatively different. The organizational level does not perform the same functions as the institutional level, only at a lower level in the firm's hierarchy. Furthermore, there is an interdependency between the levels. For example, if the institutional level does not mobilize adequate support for the firm in the environment, the technical level cannot get the resources it requires. On the other hand, the technical level must produce the right output if the institutional level is to have claims on sources of support in the environment.

---

[10]James D. Thompson, *Organizations in Action* (New York: McGraw-Hill, 1967), p. 10.

[11]Talcott Parsons, *Structure and Process in Modern Societies* (New York: The Free Press of Glencoe, 1960), Chapters 1, 2.

[12]Parsons calls the middle level in the organization "the management level." Since we will subsequently argue that there are managers at each of the three levels, the middle level is referred to here as "the organizational level."

## SPECIALIZATION IN RATIONALITY AND UNCERTAINTY

Thompson has linked Parson's structure of organizations to the location in the firm of rationality striving and uncertainty avoidance.[13] Clearly it is the technical level in the firm which emphasizes rationality. It is furthest removed from uncertainties imposed on the firm by the environment, and therefore it has the greatest measure of closure and can be operated with the highest degree of rationality. It is given protection by the organizational and institutional levels in the two activities which tie it to the environment—resource acquisition and output disposal.

tainty as possible and deal with that which cannot be avoided.

The organizational level coordinates the technical and institutional levels. It mediates between the extremes of uncertainty and rationality found in the firm. It irons out disturbances and irregularities from both sources. By coordinating the other two levels, the organizational level makes it possible for the firm to satisfy its rationality criteria and yet remain sufficiently flexible and adaptable to satisfy environmental requirements.

The firm as a composite system is shown in

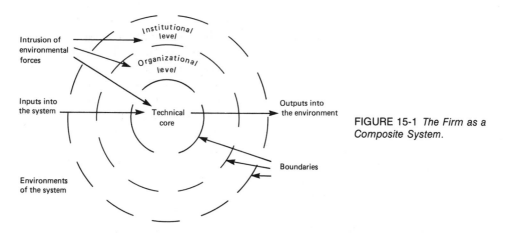

FIGURE 15-1 *The Firm as a Composite System.*

Uncertainty is greatest at the firm's boundary, where the institutional level comes into contact with the environment. The closed-system logic emphasizing rationality is clearly inappropriate here because the firm is subject to the influence of external elements over which it has little or no control. The open-system logic, which permits the intrusion of environmental forces into the operation of the firm, is called for. Therefore, the institutional level specializes in coping with uncertainty. Its particular function is to avoid as much uncer-

Figure 15-1. The technical level has a boundary that does not seal it off entirely from the firm's environment but does have a high degree of closure. The organizational level has less closure and consequently is more susceptible to the intrusion of external elements. The institutional level as a highly permeable boundary and therefore is strongly affected by uncontrollable and unpredictable elements in the environment. Inputs enter the firm, are transposed into outputs in the technical subsystem, and then disposed of in the environment.

[13]Thompson, pp. 11–12.

## TYPES OF MANAGERS

Managers are generally classified according to their level in the firm (e.g., executives, middle managers, supervisors) or the functions they perform (e.g., sales managers, production managers, financial managers). The composite view of the firm suggests that management behavior is qualitatively different at the technical, organizational and institutional levels. Thus this approach offers a different basis for classifying managers, according to the kinds of actions and abilities required to operate the firm as an open system striving for rationality and coping with uncertainty. Technical, organizational, and institutional managers can be differentiated according to task performed, point of view, technique employed, time horizon, and decision-making strategy.

### Technical Managers

The task of managers at the technical level is to produce the firm's output as economically as possible. Their primary target is technical rationality. They are able to operate under conditions of bounded rationality because of protection afforded by the organizational and institutional levels. Technical managers must determine the most efficient method of producing the firm's output, given its technology. They tend to have the engineering point of view and see the technical level as a logical system of action that can be organized and operated with mathematical precision. They are coming more and more to apply the techniques of operations research to their task.

Technical managers tend to have a short-run time horizon. They are mostly concerned with concrete problems that require immediate solutions (e.g., the best combination of resources to produce a given output; optimal re-

lation between production and inventory levels; allocation of limited production facilities when alternative routings are available; criteria for investment in a piece of equipment). These problems are quantitative in nature. They are solved by computing various types of input and output data and then manipulating the data in accordance with the criteria of rationality. That is to say, technical managers use a computational decision-making strategy.

### Institutional Managers

The task of institutional managers is to cope with the uncertainty produced by uncontrollable and unpredictable elements in the firm's environment. Their primary responsibility is to take actions necessary to insure the firm's survival. They have two techniques for doing this. First, they scan the environment for opportunities and threats to the firm (which Thompson refers to as *"opportunistic surveillance"*[14]). Second, they develop cooperative and competitive strategies for dealing with elements in the environment and thus reduce uncertainty (which Cyert and March refer to as *"negotiating the environment"*[15]).

Institutional managers have a philosophic point of view. They must have foresight, a quality that Whitehead defines as the philosophic power of perceiving meaning in the complex flux of human experience.[16] Foresight enables institutional managers to transform observations of qualitative changes in the environment

[14]Thompson, p. 151.

[15]Cyert and March, pp. 119–120.

[16]Alfred North Whitehead, "On Foresight," *The World of Business*, ed. Edward C. Bursk, Donald T. Clark, and Ralph W. Hidy, IV (New York: Simon and Schuster, 1962), 2045–2055.

into quantitive estimates of their impact on the organization.

Institutional managers have a long-run time horizon. They must see environmental changes far enough in advance to do something about them. The future is always hard to read and is highly qualitative; therefore it is interpreted subjectively. Consequently the decision-making strategy of institutional managers is judgmental. They must rely on wisdom, experience, and philosophic insight in making important decisions which guide the firm's destiny.

## Organizational Managers

The task of organizational managers is to coordinate the actions of the technical and institutional managers. Technical managers seek short-run certainty in order to perform well on technical rationality. Institutional managers seek long-run flexibility in order to enhance the firm's survival value in an uncertain future. These goals are often in conflict; if these two groups interacted directly without intermediary the firm would often be in chaos. The organizational managers' task, therefore, is to occupy a middle ground and interpret the technical and institutional managers to one another. They employ the technique of mediation.

Organizational managers use the decision-making strategy of compromise. The best interests of the firm are not served by following either the computational or judgmental strategies exclusively. The organizational managers attempt to influence the balance between the two according to the nature of the problems facing the firm. Since these problems may be either immediate or in the future, organizational managers have both a short-run and a long-run time horizon.

The viewpoint of the organizational manager is basically political. He must always be concerned with what is possible rather than ideal in mediating between technical and institutional managers. He sees the firm as a whole, in terms of both rationality and uncertainty avoidance. His main concern is with organizational viability, which requires both. He must have the politician's ability to resolve conflicting demands.

Table 15.1 shows the differences among technical, organizational, and institutional managers in terms of task, viewpoint, technique, time horizon, and decision-making strategy.

Table 15.1   Differentiation of Managers

| Type of Manager | Task | Viewpoint | Technique | Time Horizon | Decision-Making Strategy |
|---|---|---|---|---|---|
| Technical | Technical Rationality | Engineering | Operations Research | Short Run | Computational |
| Organizational | Coordination | Political | Mediation | Short Run and Long Run | Compromise |
| Institutional | Uncertainty Avoidance | Philosophical | Opportunistic Surveillance, Negotiated Environment | Long Run | Judgmental |

## RELATION OF THE BEHAVIORAL THEORY TO OTHER APPROACHES

Now let us compare the behavioral theory of management with other approaches. The management process school regards management as a unitary process, "regardless of . . . the level in a given enterprise,"[17] but the behavioral theory distinguishes among three enterprise levels and types of managers. The management process school implicitly is based on a closed-system model of the firm, whereas the behavioral theory is based on a composite-system model. Furthermore, the behavioral theory is empirically oriented while the process school is based largely on insights and speculations of individuals which are not subject to empirical test. The two approaches agree in placing major emphasis on the functions of management. However, there is little substantive content to the process school functions of planning, organization, staffing, direction, and control. These functions gain greater meaning when they are thought of as being put to the uses of rationality striving, uncertainty avoidance, and coordination.

The same observation applies to the human behavior school. As Urwick has pointed out, "the unifying 'discipline' is *management*, not human relations . . . Managing, to be sure, is getting things done *through people* . . . But those who specialize in human behavior will forget or minimize the 'things,' the work which human systems of cooperation are created to do, at their peril."[18] The human behavior approach would be much more substantive if it analyzed how interaction processes work to accomplish objectives of rationality, uncertainty avoidance, and coordination.

The behavioral theory of management has most in common with the social system school. The difference between the two is one of focus and emphasis. The social system school focuses on the organization and what we have called the organization level of management, and it generally deemphasizes the roles of management in determining behavior of the organization. The behavioral theory of management focuses on all three types of management behavior from the perspective of organization theory.

The decision theory school "concentrates on rational approach to decision,"[19] and the mathematical school believes that "if management, or organization, or planning, or decision-making is a logical process, it can be expressed in terms of mathematical symbols and relationships."[20] Clearly these schools relate to technical rationality but are not as appropriate for organizational or institutional management.

Mention should be made here of a school of management not mentioned by Koontz but which Gordon[21] includes in his list: the ecological school. This approach analyzes the adaptive behavior of the firm, and it bears a close relation to institutional management.

[17]Koontz, p. 9.

[18]Lyndall F. Urwick, "Management and Human Relations," *Leadership and Organization: A Behavioral Science Approach*, ed. Robert Tannenbaum, Irving R. Weschler, and Fred Massarik (New York: McGraw-Hill, 1961), p. 421.

[19]Koontz, p. 15.

[20]Koontz, p. 16.

[21]Paul J. Gordon, "Transcend the Current Debate on Administrative Theory," *Journal of the Academy of Management*, VI, No. 4 (Dec., 1963), 290–302.

## CONCLUSION

To summarize, the behavioral theory of management has the following characteristics:

1. It is based on a composite-system view of the firm,
2. It defines management in terms of the actions managers take in dealing with the firm's primary needs of technical rationality and uncertainty avoidance, and
3. It differentiates three types of managers according to task, viewpoint, technique, time horizon, and decision-making strategy.

An advantage of this approach to management theory is that it presents a conceptual framework which meaningfully integrates the various approaches to the subject. Another advantage is that it is allied with the behavioral research method that has been used so successfully in organization theory. This opens up the considerable body of organization theory for insights into management behavior, and it offers the student of management a methodology of proven worth for doing original empirical work.[22]

[22]For a thoughtful view of the method and mood of behavioralism see Robert Presthus, *Behavioral Approaches to Public Administration* (University, Ala.: University of Alabama Press, 1965), Chapter 1.

*Diverse explanatory conflict models and intervention strategies reflect key perceptual/attributional choices. Two key choices are used as organizing devices to identify four broad perspectives upon conflict: external process, external structural, internal process, and internal structural. Diagnostic concepts and intervention strategies from the literature are summarized to illustrate each perspective.*

Observers have commented upon the disorganized state of organizational conflict literature (52, 78) and of conflict literature in general (30). This disorganization shows itself in divergent definitions of "conflict," fundamentally different sets of explanatory variables, and recommendations of equally diverse strategies for managing conflict.

As a sample of this diversity, "conflict" has been defined as the condition of objective incompatibility between values or goals (6), as the behavior of deliberately interfering with another's goal achievement (68), and emotionally in terms of hostility (56). Descriptive theorists have explained conflict behavior in terms of objective conflict of interest (4), personal styles (10), reactions to threats (25), and cognitive distortions (57). Normative recommendations range over the establishment of superordinate goals (71), consciousness raising (20), selection of compatible individuals (69), and mediating between conflict parties (83).

This article attempts to organize the richness and diversity of the organizational conflict literature so as to be useful to scholars and practitioners. Its approach is not to value one approach over another, explicitly or implicitly, but rather to legitimize the value of different approaches by placing them in a larger perspective.

Rather than a new conflict model, something more encompassing is needed—a meta model of conflict management. One meta model identifies two key assumptive or attributional choices which run through the diversity of existing models. These assumptive

# 16

# Diagnosing and Managing Conflict

*Four Perspectives on Conflict Management: An Attributional Framework for Organizing Descriptive and Normative Theory*

RALPH H. KILMANN and KENNETH W. THOMAS

choices are used as organizing principles to identify and differentiate four basic perspectives on conflict behavior. These four perspectives are used as integrative mechanisms to identify commonalities which cut across the diversity in conflict definitions, independent variables, and interventions. Each perspective is an equally important component of conflict diagnosis and intervention, whether conflict is between individuals, groups, or broader organizational subsystems.

The scope of this meta model can be clarified by examining the steps involved in managing a conflict. Conflict management is viewed as containing three major interrelated events: (a) perceiving/experiencing unacceptable conflict, (b) diagnosing the sources of the conflict, and (c) intervening. These events are similar to the sequence of conflict management and planned change activities discussed by Robbins (63) and Lippitt et al. (44) and to the events or stages in the conflict models suggested by Pondy (59) and Thomas (78). Within the conflict management cycle, this article is not directly concerned with initial judgment of the acceptability or dysfunctionality of a given conflict—for example, whether there is an optimal level of conflict (63) or whether a given conflict-handling behavior is functional in a given situation (79). These complex functionality issues deserve further explication elsewhere.

This article addresses the subsequent causal attributions (40) involved in diagnosing sources of the conflict and anticipating the leverage of different interventions. The four perspectives developed are applicable regardless of why a given conflict has been judged as dysfunctional—whether one would prefer to escalate or descalate the conflict, to establish collaboration or heighten competition, etc. The specific interventions cited from the literature are slanted towards de-escalate and collaboration only because of the past emphasis within that literature (63).

It is important to distinguish between (a) the process through which a theorist or interventionist diagnoses a conflict and selects an intervention, and (b) the resulting diagnosis and intervention strategy. The four perspectives are concerned with the diagnosis and intervention strategy, not the process of arriving at it—which is necessarily an internal mental process. Thus the process of diagnosis should not be confused with the content of the internal process perspective described later.

## TWO KEY ATTRIBUTIONAL CHOICES

A review of the conflict literature suggested that much of its diversity could be accounted for in terms of two specific attributional distinctions. These two distinctions also seem to be important attributional choices which theorists and practitioners make in trying to comprehend any behavioral phenomena.

### The First Distinction: Process vs. Structural Analyses

Process and structural analyses appear to be fundamentally different methods of perceiv-ing and understanding phenomena. Thomas' (78) synthesis of dyadic conflict theory underscored the distinction, assembling much of that literature into two separate process and structural models of conflict behavior.

Process models of behavior place the parties in a temporal sequence of *events*. Behavior is assumed to be directly influenced by preceding events and anticipation of subsequent events. Structural models focus upon *conditions*, relationships between those conditions, and their influence upon behavior. At a given moment, those conditions are viewed as exerting forces upon behavior. Whereas a process model places parties in a sequence of events, a structural model places them in a web of forces.

A series of verbal threats, acts of physical aggression, and an exchange of evaluative remarks are events. When these events, or a party's anticipation of them, are seen as influencing that party's behavior, the behavior is being explained in process terms. Conflict of interest, norms, beliefs, attitudes, and skills are conditions—things which exist over a period of time. As such, they are structural constructs for explaining behavior.

## The Second Distinction: Internal vs. External Sources of Influence

This distinction refers to two different loci for the origins of behavior. "Internal" models emphasize events and conditions *within* a party which influence behavior. Parties are seen as decision-making entities confronted with alternatives and choice points. Variation in behavior is assumed to be an outcome of differences in the processes and structures of this decision making. By contrast, "external" models focus upon events and conditions *outside* the party which shape behavior. As Bugental (15) notes, the implicit assumption is that parties are fairly interchangeable in their reactions to processes and conditions in their environment—that these processes and conditions are sufficient to explain behavior. Rott (65) found systematic variation among individuals in their tendencies

to attribute behavior to internal or external causes.

Assumptions, perceptions, motives, insights, decision-making styles, and anticipating the other party's responses are phenomena which occur within a party, and are therefore internal constructs for explaining behavior. Examples of external constructs are conflicts of interest, norms, an opponent's threats, an opponent's concessions, and third-party interventions.

## The Four Perspectives

These two distinctions combine logically to identify four perspectives upon conflict, as represented in Table 16.1: "external process," "external structural," "internal process," and "internal structural." Although this scheme was developed independently, it bears a strong resemblance to the scheme used by Clark and Krone (18) to classify their organization development interventions.

Subsequent discussion of each perspective will focus on diagnosis and on intervention strategies. But the four perspectives also help to explain the divergence in definitions of "conflict" in the literature (30): as behavioral interference, threats, or competition (external process); as conflict of interest or objective role conflict (external structure); as experienced frustration or the intent to injure or to interfere with an opponent (internal process); or as personal incompatibilities and antagonistic attitudes or predispositions (internal structure).

## THE EXTERNAL PROCESS PERSPECTIVE

This perspective emphasizes the causal effects of events which impinge upon a party from outside. A party's behavior is seen as a reaction to the behavior of other parties, in "stimulus-response" fashion, and this behavior in turn evokes a behavioral response from them.

### Diagnosis

Sources of conflictful behavior are sought in other stimulus behaviors. More work needs to be done in classifying these behaviors and their effects. Conflict behavior has been asserted to

Table 16.1 The Two Distinctions which Define the Four Perspectives, with Some Examples of Key Diagnostic Variables and the Four Broad Intervention Strategies.

| | Process vs. Structure: Behavior is caused by . . . | |
|---|---|---|
| Internal vs. External Sources of Influence: Behavior is caused by events and conditions . . . | events (Process) | conditions (Structure) |
| outside the party (External) | The External Process Perspective—behavior is shaped by events outside the individual:<br>   threats<br>   negative evaluation<br>   encroachment<br>Intervention strategy: "Interaction management" | The External Structural Perspective—behavior is shaped by conditions outside the individual:<br>   social pressure<br>   conflict of interest<br>   procedures<br>Intervention strategy: "Contextual modification" |
| inside the party (Internal) | The Internal Process Perspective—behavior is shaped by events inside the individual:<br>   frustration<br>   strategies<br>   defense mechanisms<br>Intervention strategy: "Consciousness raising" | The Internal Structural Perspective—behavior is shaped by conditions inside the individual:<br>   motives<br>   attitudes<br>   skills<br>Intervention strategy: "Selection and training" |

be a response to competition (8, 41), threat (25), negative evaluation (34), encroachment (2), and coercion (62). Third party interventions also may be viewed as external events to which the parties react, as in process interventions discussed by Schein (66) and Walton (83).

## Intervention: "Interaction Management"

Since the manner of interaction is seen as the basis of the conflict, the change agent's focus is on changing interactions. This change objective is non-substantive in that the change agent is not especially concerned with the content of the interactions (i.e., the issues of the conflict situation), but with specific behaviors used by the parties in negotiating or otherwise attempting to influence each other.

The class of interventions by which change agents attempt to achieve this objective is termed "interaction management".[2] Change agents may intervene directly into the interaction to control behavior by acting as "referee" to stop unfair behavior, rephrasing statements to make them less provocative, acting as timekeeper and gatekeeper to insure equal time (83), and so on. They may also act as role models (3) to provide an example of effective modes of interaction. For example, a change agent may purposely be non-evaluative and descriptive. The crucial nature of the intervention in this case is the change agent's type of behavior. The parties may adopt similar behavior through identification with the change agent (58), thereby reducing defensiveness and facilitating problem solving.

[2] This term has nothing to do with the Interaction Management Program produced by Development Dimensions, Inc., Pittsburgh.

## THE EXTERNAL STRUCTURAL PERSPECTIVE

The external structural perspective places the causes of behavior in conditions outside the parties. Conditions in the environment are seen as motivating, constraining, or channeling behavior.

### Diagnosis

In a review of the literature on organizational conflict, Thomas (78) identified three clusters of external conditions which influence conflict behavior—conflict incentives, social pressures, and rules and procedures.

"Conflict incentives" is used in a broad sense to include the objectives of the parties and the manner in which satisfaction of those objectives is linked. Two central components discussed have been the stakes involved (11, 29, 31) and the conflict of interest between goals of the conflict parties (4, 23, 68, 71, 85).

Social pressures can be viewed as barriers (83) and forces. Thomas (78) differentiated between pressures from constituents (9, 50, 74) and "ambient social pressure"—social pressure from relatively neutral onlookers who enforce the norms of the larger organization (12, 45, 47) or culture (75).

Finally, the conflict parties can be viewed as interacting within a framework of rules and procedures which shape their negotiations—as well as their opportunities to interfere with each other (68). The conflict behavior of the two parties has been linked to several aspects of established negotiating procedures —frequency of contact (84), barriers to openness (54), formality (49), and sequencing of issues (11). Explicit decision rules evolve to cover sensitive issues (28, 77). Various forms of mediation or arbitration mechanisms may be available when the parties deadlock (32, 70, 73).

### Intervention: "Contextual Modification"

Change objectives focus upon alteration of external conditions which exert forces upon the parties. Interventions which seek to alter this external context of the parties' behavior are labeled "contextual modification." Methods to change the responsibilities of either party, formal and informal rules, job descriptions, incentives, budgets, control mechanisms, social pressures, etc., fit this category. These methods might include: (a) formally dictating a change in policy or goals of either or both parties, (b) mandating a negotiation session between parties in which they have to compromise their budget demands, (c) changing the composition of members belonging to either or both parties, (d) changing the social presssures which other bystanders exert upon the parties, and (e) instituting superordinate goals so that the parties benefit by cooperating with each other. Aspects of contextual modification are now receiving increasing emphasis as the field of organizational behavior leans more heavily toward organizational design (42, 43).

## THE INTERNAL PROCESS PERSPECTIVE

This perspective seeks the source of behavior in the sequence of events which occurs within a party. In the case of individuals, behavior is seen as an outcome of the logic or "psychologic" (57) of perceptions, ideas, and emotions. Whereas the internal structural perspective emphasizes consistencies and personal fixities, this perspective emphasizes the moment-to-moment changes in the individual's phenomenology and the choices which are made at any given moment. The individual is an ongoing process, rather than an object with stable characteristics (15), a view emphasized in humanistic psychology. When the conflict party is a larger social unit (a work group or organization), this focus expands to include the ongoing interpersonal decision processes within the unit which shape its behavior toward other units.

## Diagnosis

Diagnostic efforts center upon understanding the sequence of internal events which are shaping the conflict episode. In his process model, Thomas (78) emphasized the importance of understanding the specific nature of the actual or anticipated frustrations which begin conflict episodes—i.e., the underlying concerns or agendas of the parties. That model also emphasized the importance of the parties' conceptualizations of the conflict situation—their definitions of the issues and their assumptions about possible outcomes.

The change agent operating from this perspective will want to understand the strategic and tactical logic of each party. Parties may adopt political strategies involving coalitions (15, 21, 33), interpersonal strategies involving games or ploys (7, 36, 60), bargaining strategies involving power (67) and so on. Occasionally violence may be understood as a deliberate and rational tactic under this perspective (55), although the parties may also realize the advantages of limiting or managing their conflict (19, 27).

Less rational decision processes also are important from this perspective. Conflict behavior may stem from misperceptions (9, 24), projection (35), selective attention and recall (22), polarization and stereotyping (57), and the inability to recognize alternatives (20).

## Intervention: "Consciousness Raising"

Given the assumption that the parties' conflict behavior stems from their internal processing of decisions, the change agent's objective is to influence the parties' perceptions, cognitions, and emotions regarding the ongoing conflict. Such interventions are termed "consciousness-raising" interventions. Included are many traditional interventions used by the trainer of a sensitivity training group (13), where discussions of "here and now" experiences can lead to new appreciation of an ongoing interpersonal process, awareness of alternative behaviors and their effects, correction of perceptual distortions, and working-through of feelings. Also included are individual or joint counseling sessions aimed at helping the parties to recognize their frustrations and objectives, think through the consequences of alternative paths, and work through ambivalences about a course of action (20).

Although internal process or consciousness-raising interventions may result indirectly in altered modes of interaction between parties, decisions regarding external structural change, or long-run changes in a party's internal structuring, these are not the primary objectives of an internal process intervention. The primary objective is to improve the parties' internal processing of decisions regarding the current conflict episode. Although the term "consciousness-raising" carries connotations of neutral activities intended only to bring some phenomenon into awareness, these interventions may also involve advocacy and persuasion. Nevertheless, consciousness-raising interventions tend to be the most humanistic, in the sense of treating the parties as responsible decision makers.

## THE INTERNAL STRUCTURAL
## PERSPECTIVE

This perspective seeks the causes of the parties' behavior in relatively stable characteristics within them, and in the manner in which these characteristics are organized. The parties' behavior is viewed as an expression of their make-up. This "personality" or "organization" is seen as a compelling influence upon behavior, predisposing parties to characteristic patterns of behavior.

## Diagnosis

An explanation of the general status of a party's relationships with other parties is sought in terms of the party's characteristics, whether based upon instinct (46), culture and socialization (75), or other factors.

To some extent, a party's conflict-handling behavior may be seen in terms of habitual response hierarchies and styles (5, 10). Although trait theories are not currently in vogue, some research evidence indicates a degree of regularity in conflict-related behaviors. For example, Gormly and Edelberg (37) found evidence that an individual's assertiveness is reliable across situations.

The party's general behavior also may be understood in terms of stable underlying attributes which shape behavior: motives and needs (76), value systems (17, 24), information-processing limitations (38), characteristic defense mechanisms (1, 64), and diagnostic and problem-solving skills.

In diagnosing conflict in a specific relationship, attention may be focused upon incompatibilities between styles, needs, etc., of the two parties (53, 69, 83).

## Intervention: "Selection and Training"

As in the internal process perspective, the change agent is concerned with altering things which are internal to the parties. But while the internal process perspective sought to influence decision-related events within the parties during a specific conflict episode, the internal structural perspective is concerned directly with changing the parties themselves—i.e., with making stable changes which will continue to influence the parties' behavior across a number of episodes. The emphasis is upon lasting change rather than facilitating a single here-and-now interaction. Change efforts are therefore likely to be more systematic, involving a *program* of interventions.

One approach to changing the conflict-handling characteristics of individuals in a given organizational position is through the selection of those people—through recruiting and screening managers for initial hiring and for promotion to any given position. Questions about cooperative work relations are common in reference letters and performance appraisals upon which promotions are based. Similar screening procedures may be applied to organizations themselves—for governmental licensing, and for admission to trade organizations and other alliances.

"Training" is used here to denote all interventions directed at producing lasting changes in parties which have already been selected. In the case of individuals, this may include formal or informal socialization of managers into acceptance of organizational norms and values, educational programs directed at cognitive learnings, job rotation practices which facilitate interdepartmental coordination by giving managers a common perspective, laboratory training programs (13) designed to give managers diagnostic and action skills in interpersonal relations, and provisions for individual therapy.

## IMPLICATIONS

This meta model or framework can be used to help potential change agents identify their diagnostic and intervention styles—by surfacing assumptions about the source of conflict, and by classifying their preferred interventions. Development of specialized styles may be functional for a change agent, and the four perspectives help to identify the change agent's strengths. By implication they also help to identify blind spots.

One normative suggestion deriving from this article is that the change agent and practitioner *should* be explicit about their conceptualizations, and explicitly consider the four kinds of diagnoses and intervention strategies in choosing how to deal with an important conflict situation. In effect, these four perspectives can be used as a "checklist" to suggest the full range of possibilities. Having a wider choice of alternatives would enable a more realistic cost/benefit analysis (81)—i.e., an assessment of the costs of each type of diagnosis and corresponding intervention strategy versus the expected short or long range benefits to be derived from the interventions. Even if change agents themselves are not equally skilled in implementing the four perspectives, conscious awareness of all four approaches can allow them to involve appropriate others and prevent them from using their strengths inappropriately.

One can argue normatively for a team of change agents with different perspectives to address important conflict situations. If no single person can be expert in applying more than one or two perspectives, a team can be composed so that all four perspectives will be equally considered, coordinated, and applied as necessary. The present meta model of the four perspectives may give the team a common framework for organizing and appreciating their diversity of approaches, resulting in a true systems approach to conflict management. Such an approach may become more necessary as organizations face more complex, dynamic, and changing environments, where the sources of frequent conflicts are complex and multi-determined.

Although the four perspectives and model emerged from a review of conflict literature, they are easily generalizable to the understanding and influencing of other behavioral phenomena. If management is viewed as a process of influencing others, the four perspectives can be used to classify approaches to management in general: (a) the external process approach is roughly equivalent to close supervision and direct control of others' work; (b) the internal process approach includes counseling and helping individuals to define their own goals, which are basic elements of Management by Objectives (61); (c) the external structural approach involves management through incentives, rules, control systems, and organizational design technologies (42); and (d) the internal structural approach includes recruiting, placement, and training.

In short, this meta model provides a new approach to classifying managerial style—one which emphasizes the individual's implicit philosophy of how people are influenced, rather than inter-personal manner (whether one is considerate, assertive, etc.). This scheme combines a number of important philosophies of management—not only the classic Behavioral Science process distinctions of close Theory X supervision vs. Theory Y counseling and goal setting (48), but also the Management Theory emphasis on incentives and control systems, and Industrial Psychology emphasis on selection and training. Subsequent development of instrumentation to assess managerial reliance upon the four perspectives may provide a means of identifying these managerial philosophies at the level of the individual practitioner, thereby enabling research on the effects of these philosophies upon workers and the organization.

## REFERENCES

1. Adorno, Theodor W., Else Frenkel-Brunswik, Daniel V. Levinson, and R. Nevitt Sanford. *The Authoritarian Personality* (New York: Harper and Brothers, 1950).

2. Ardrey, Robert. *The Territorial Imperative* (New York: Dell, 1966).

3. Argyris, Chris. *Intervention Theory* (Reading, Mass.: Addison-Wesley, 1970).

4. Axelrod, Robert. *Conflict of Interest* (Chicago, Ill.: Markham, 1970).

5. Berkowitz, Leonard. *Aggression: A Social Psychological Analysis* (New York: McGraw-Hill, 1962).

6. Bernard, Jessie. "The Conceptualization of Intergroup Relations," *Social Forces*, Vol. 29 (1951), 243–251.

7. Berne, Eric. *Games People Play* (New York: Grove Press, 1964).

8. Bizenstine, V. Edwin, and Kellog V. Wilson. "Effect of Level of Cooperative Choice by the Other Player on Choice in a Prisoner's Dilemma Game, Part II," *Journal of Abnormal and Social Psychology*, Vol. 67 (1963), 139–147.

9. Blake, Robert R., and Jane S. Mouton. "Reactions to Intergroup Competition under Win-Lose Conditions," *Management Science*, Vol. 7 (1961), 420–435.

10. Blake, Robert R., and Jane S. Mouton. *The Managerial Grid* (Houston, Texas: Gulf Publishing, 1964).

11. Blake, Robert R., Herbert A. Shepard, and Jane S. Mouton. *Managing Intergroup Conflict in Industry* (Houston, Texas: Gulf Publishing, 1964).

12. Blau, Peter M. *The Dynamics of Bureaucracy* (Chicago, Ill.: University of Chicago Press, 1955).

13. Bradford, Leland P., Jack R. Gibb, and Kenneth D. Benne (Eds.). *T-Group Theory and Laboratory Method* (New York: Wiley, 1964).

14. Bugental, James F. T. *The Search for Authenticity* (New York: Holt, Rinehart, and Winston, 1965).

15. Bugental, James F. T. "Someone Needs to Worry: The Existential Anxiety of Responsibility and Decision," *Journal of Contemporary Psychotherapy*, Vol. 2 (1969), 41–53.

16. Caplow, Theodore. *Two Against One: Coalitions in Triads* (Englewood Cliffs, N.J.: Prentice-Hall, 1968).

17. Christie, Richard, and Florence L. Geis. *Studies in Machiavellianism* (New York: Academic Press, 1970).

18. Clark, James V., and Charles G. Krone. "Towards an Overall View of Organizational Development in the Early Seventies," in John M. Thomas and Warren G. Bennis (Eds.), *Management of Change and Conflict* (Baltimore, Md.: Penguin Books, 1972).

19. Coser, Lewis. "The Termination of Conflict," *Journal of Conflict Resolution*, Vol. 5 (1961), 347–354.

20. Culbert, Samuel A. *The Organization Trap and How to Get Out of It* (New York: Basic Books, 1974).

21. Dalton, Melville. *Men Who Manage* (New York: Wiley and Sons, 1959).

22. Dearborn, Dewitt C., and Herbert A. Simon.

"Selective Perception: A Note on the Departmental Identifications of Executives," *Sociometry*, Vol. 21 (1958), 140–144.

23. Deutsch, Morton. "A Theory of Cooperation and Competition," *Human Relations*, Vol. 2 (1949), 129–152.

24. Deutsch, Morton. "Conflict: Productive and Destructive," *Journal of Social Issues*, Vol. 25 (1969), 7–41.

25. Deutsch, Morton, and Robert M. Krauss. "Studies in Interpersonal Bargaining," *Journal of Conflict Resolution*, Vol. 6 (1962), 52–76.

26. Dollard, John, Leonard Doob, Neal Miller, O. H. Mowrer, and Robert R. Sears. *Frustration and Aggression* (New Haven: Yale University Press, 1939).

27. Donnelly, Lawrence I. "Toward an Alliance Between Research and Practice in Collective Bargaining," *Personnel Journal*, Vol. 50 (1971), 372–379, 399.

28. Dunlop, John T. *Industrial Relations Systems* (New York: Holt, Rinehart, and Winston, 1958).

29. Emerson, Richard M. "Power-Dependence Relationships," *American Sociological Review*, Vol. 27 (1962), 31–41.

30. Fink, Clinton F. "Some Conceptual Difficulties in the Theory of Social Conflict," *Journal of Conflict Resolution*, Vol. 12 (1968), 412–460.

31. Gallo, Phillip S. "Effects of Increased Incentives Upon the Use of Threat in Bargaining," *Journal of Personality and Social Psychology*, Vol. 4 (1966), 14–20.

32. Galtung, Johan. "Institutionalized Conflict Resolution," *Journal of Peace Research*, Vol. 4 (1965), 348–397.

33. Gamson, William A. "Experimental Studies of Coalition Formation," *Advances in Experimental Social Psychology*, Vol. 1 (1964), 81–110.

34. Gibb, Jack R. "Defensive Communication," *ETC: A Review of General Semantics*, Vol. 22 (1965), 221–229.

35. Gladstone, Arthur. "The Conception of the Enemy," *Journal of Conflict Resolution*, Vol. 3 (1959), 132–137.

36. Goffman, Erving. *Strategic Interaction* (Philadelphia: Penn.: University of Pennsylvania Press, 1969).

37. Gormley, John, and Walter Edelberg. "Validity in Personality Trait Attribution," *American Psychologist*, Vol. 29 (1974), 189–193.

38. Hayakawa, S. I. *Language in Thought and Action*, 2nd ed. (New York: Harcourt, Brace and World, 1963).

39. Kahn, Robert L., Donald M. Wolfe, Robert P. Quinn, J. Diedrick Snoek, and Robert A. Rosenthal. *Organizational Stress: Studies in Role Conflict and Ambiguity* (New York: Wiley, 1964).

40. Kelley, Harold H. "The Processes of Causal Attribution," *American Psychologist*, Vol. 28 (1973), 107–128.

41. Kelley, Harold H., and Anthony J. Stahelski. "Social Interaction Basis of Cooperators' and Competitiors' Beliefs About Others," *Journal of Personality and Social Psychology*, Vol. 16 (1970), 66–91.

42. Kilmann, Ralph H. *Social Systems Design: Normative Theory and the MAPS Design-Technology* (New York: Elsevier North-Holland, 1977).

43. Kilmann, Ralph H., Louis R. Pondy, and Dennis P. Slevin. *The Management of Organization Design* (Volumes I and II (New York: Elsevier North-Holland, 1976).

44. Lippitt, Ronald, Jeanne Watson, and Bruce Westley. *The Dynamics of Planned Change* (New York: Harcourt, Brace and World, 1958).

45. Litwin, George H., and Robert A. Stringer, Jr. *Motivation and Organizational Climate* (Boston, Mass.: Harvard University, 1968).

46. Lorenz, Konrad. *On Aggression* (New York: Harcourt, Brace and World, 1966).

47. March, James G., and Herbert A. Simon. *Organizations* (New York: Wiley and Sons, 1958).

48. McGregor, Douglas M. *The Human Side of Enterprise* (New York: McGraw-Hill, 1960).

49. McKersie, Robert B., and W. W. Shropshire, Jr. "Avoiding Written Grievances: A Successful Program," *The Journal of Business*, Vol. 35 (1962), 135–152.

50. Megginson, Leon C., and C. Ray Gullett. "A Predictive Model for Union-Management Conflict," *Personnel Journal*, Vol. 49 (1970), 495–503.

51. Murray, Henry A. *Exploration in Personality* (New York: Oxford University Press, 1938).

52. Murray, V. V. "Some Unanswered Questions on Organizational Conflict," *Organization and Administrative Sciences* Vol. 5 (1975), 35–53.

53. Myers, Isabel B. *The Myers-Briggs Type Indicator* (Princeton, N.J.: Educational Testing Service, 1962).

54. Newcomb, Theodore M. "Autistic Hostility and Social Reality," *Human Relations*, Vol. 1 (1974), 69–86.

55. Nieburg, H. L. "Uses of Violence," *Journal of Conflict Resolution*, Vol. 7 (1963), 43–54.

56. Nye, Robert D. *Conflict Among Humans* (New York: Springer, 1973).

57. Osgood, Charles E. "An Analysis of the Cold War Mentality," *Journal of Social Issues*, Vol. 17 (1961), 12–19.

58. Peters, David R. *Identification and Personal Change in Laboratory Training Groups* (Ph.D. dissertation, Massachusetts Institute of Technology, 1966).

59. Pondy, Louis R. "Organizational Conflict: Concepts and Models," *Administrative Science Quarterly*, Vol. 12 (1967), 296–320.

60. Potter, Stephen. *The Complete Upmanship* (New York: Holt, Rinehart and Winston, 1971).

61. Raia, Anthony P. *Managing by Objectives* (Glenview, Ill.: Scott, Foresman, 1974).

62. Raven, Bertram H., and Arie W. Kruglanski. "Conflict and Power," in Paul Swingle (Ed.), *The Structure of Conflict* (New York: Academic Press, 1970), pp. 69–109.

63. Robbins, Stephen P. *Managing Organizational Conflict: A Nontraditional Approach* (Englewood Cliffs, N.J.: Prentice-Hall, 1974).

64. Rokeach, Milton. *The Open and Closed Mind* (New York: Basic Books, 1960).

65. Rotter, Julian B. "Generalized Expectancies for Internal Versus External Control of Reinforcement," *Psychological Monographs*, Vol. 80 (1966), 1–28.

66. Schein, Edgar H. Process Consultation: *Its Role in Organization Development* (Reading, Mass.: Addison-Wesley, 1969).

67. Schelling, Thomas C. *The Strategy of Conflict* (New York: Oxford University Press, 1963).

68. Schmidt, Stuart M., and Thomas A. Kochan. "Conflict: Toward Conceptual Clarity," *Administrative Science Quarterly*, Vol. 17 (1972), 359–370.

69. Schutz, William C. "The Interpersonal Underworld," *Harvard Business Review*, Vol. 36 (1958), 123–135.

70. Scott, William G. *The Management of Conflict: Appeal Systems in Organizations* (Homewood, Ill.: Irwin-Dorsey, 1965).

71. Sherif, Muzafer. "Superordinate Goals in the Reduction of Intergroup Conflict," *The American Journal of Sociology*, Vol. 63 (1958), 349–356.

72. Simon, Herbert A. *Administrative Behavior* (Glencoe, Ill.: Free Press, 1957).

73. Stagner, Ross, and Hjalmar Rosen. *Psychology of Union-Management Relations* (Belmont, Calif.: Brooks/Cole Publishing Co., 1965).

74. Stern, Irving, and Robert F. Pearse. "Collective Bargaining: A Union's Program for Reducing Conflict, *Personnel*, Vol. 45, No. 3 (1968), 61–72.

75. Storr, Anthony. *Human Aggression* (New York: Antheneum, 1968).

76. Terhune, Kenneth W. "The Effects of Personality in Cooperation and Conflict," in Paul Swingle (Ed.), *The Structure of Conflict* (New York: Academic Press, 1970).

77. Thibaut, John W., and Harold H. Kelly. *The Social Psychology of Groups* (New York: Wiley and Sons, 1959).

78. Thomas, Kenneth W. "Conflict and Conflict Management," in Marvin D. Dunnette (Ed.), *Handbook of Industrial and Organizational Psychology* (Chicago, Ill.: Rand McNally, 1976), Chapter 21, pp. 889–935.

79. Thomas, Kenneth W. "Toward Multi-Dimensional Values in Teaching: The Example of Conflict Behaviors," *Academy of Management Review*, Vol. 2, No. 3 (July 1977), 484–490.

80. Thomas, Kenneth W. and Ralph H. Kilmann.

"The Social Desirability Variable in Organizational Research: An Alternative Explanation for Reported Findings," *Academy of Management Journal*, Vol. 18 (1975), 741–752.

81. Thomas, Kenneth W., Richard W. Walton, and John M. Dutton. "Determinants of Interdepartmental Conflict," in Matthew Tuite, Roger Chisholm and Michael Radnor (Eds.), *Interorganizational Decision Making* (Chicago, Ill.: Aldine, 1972).

82. Toch, Hans B. *Violent Men* (Chicago: Aldine, 1969).

83. Walton, Richard E. *Interpersonal Peacemaking; Confrontations and Third Party Consultation* (Reading, Mass.: Addison-Wesley, 1969).

84. Walton, Richard E., John M. Dutton, and H. Gordon Fitch. "A Study of Conflict in the Process, Structure, and Attitudes of Lateral Relationships," in Albert H. Rubenstein and Chadwick J. Haberstroh, *Some Theories of Organization* (Homewood, Ill.: Irwin, 1966).

85. Walton, Richard E., and Robert B. McKersie. "Behavioral Dilemmas in Mixed-Motive Decision-Making," *Behavioral Science*, Vol. 2 (1966), 370–384.

For most people, learning that the leadership in organizations is male-dominated is like learning that we speak in prose. Just as the fish assumes that water is *the* environment, so the organizational member assumes that what is, should be. What is the male norm in organizational life? It is competitiveness, achievement orientation, suppression of feelings, autonomy, logical problem-solving, and a value for extrinsic rewards. This is very much a description of organizational life. One only realizes it is also a description of masculine values when it is contrasted with a list of feminine norms: cooperation, affiliation orientation, awareness of feelings, supportiveness, and intuitive problem-solving. The student of organizational behaviour recognizes in the male norm—the manager in the grey flannel suit—an accurate description of organizational life in the fifties. In the seventies, however, the value of feminine norms became apparent as organizations attempted to open up their managers to awareness of feelings, trust and cooperation by sending them to encounter groups. Now, in the eighties, the pendulum is swinging towards the middle as people recognize the merits of both masculine and feminine norms. The result: the androgynous manager.*

However, the rise of women in the corporate hierarchy is slow. It is estimated that approximately five percent of the female labor force are managers. Why does this paradox exist? This paper shall attempt to explain why, and how the perceptions of females as managers block the successful integration of women into management positions.

*Androgyny, coined by the Greeks, indicates the presence of both male and female characteristics in a single organism.

# 17

# Executive Behavior, Personality, and Communications

*So You Want To Be
An Executive:
Be Androgynous!*
M. BELCOURT

# PERCEPTIONS OF WOMEN
## AS MANAGERS

It has been well documented (1, 3) that managers, both male and female, believe that women make inferior managers. Schein (4) has documented that the perceived characteristics of successful middle managers are similar to those of males in general, and dissimilar to those of females in general.

There are two factors involved in the judgment of managerial performance. One is objective. What did the person actually do or achieve: sales increase of 10 percent? quality improvement of 2 percent? The second operational factor is how this performance is perceived.

What does the objective evidence show? Dealing with the first factor of real performance, Day and Stogdill (5), Chapman (6), Bartol (7), Osborn and Vicars (8), and Crozier (9) have concluded from their own research and reviews of the literature, that sex does not affect leadership style. Osborn and Vicars note that laboratory studies support the effect of stereotyping on selection and evaluation, but field studies have not found differences between male and female leaders. Bartol, in reviewing laboratory studies which had an objective measure of job performance, concluded that the sex of the leader does not appear to be a useful predictor of job performance either in the case of individual performance as managers, or as leaders in tasks involving group performance.

If female managers perform as well as male managers, how is this performance perceived? Not as equally, according to many studies.

Some differences in the satisfaction of subordinates with male and female leaders has been found (10). Male supervisors are generally perceived more favorably than female supervisors, and the tendency is true regardless of the rater's sex (11). Haccoun et al. found that subordinates (actually, subjects were read cases and pretended that they were subordinates) rated the effectivenss of and satisfaction with different leadership styles depending upon the sex of the leader. For example, the directive style was rated least favorably when it was displayed by female supervisors. They concluded that the contingency view of leadership should include the sex of the leader and the sex role appropriateness of the leadership style.

Pheterson, Kiesler, and Goldberg (12) reported that male performances are rated more highly than female performances, even when performances are held constant in a laboratory situation. Rosen and Jerdee (13) found that, even when job performances are similar, women are less likely to be promoted than men.

The process of judging a person according to the degree to which he or she acts according to sex role stereotype was also noted by Jacobson and Effertz (14). They found that males are judged more harshly than females when they are leaders, but more leniently than females when they are followers. If the performance does not meet the rater's expectations, the individual is negatively evaluated.

Because the stereotype of a woman does not include the adjective "power", her leadership style may be influenced (15). Her lack of power outside the organization in the larger societal environment may mean more limited power within the organization. One study which documented differences in leadership style, but not effectiveness, of female managers, supports the notion of powerlessness affecting behavior. Wexley and Hunt (16) described female leaders as engaging in more accommodative behaviors. For example, they would exhibit more tension-realizing behavior (jokes), agree more often, and ask for more suggestions. Hennig's research (17) confirms that the strategies chosen by female executives tend to minimize the authoritarian use of power. Instead, they tried to maximize subordinate autonomy and learning through delegation. Further support comes from Megargee's research (18) which showed that women are reluctant to assume the leadership role. If a high dominant female was paired with a low dominant male, she made the decision (as was to be expected) as to who would be the leader, by appointing the man 91 percent of the time!

The conclusions that could be drawn from the above review suggest that there is no significant difference in the effectiveness of male versus female leaders, that subordinates perceive them differently in some cases, and that there may be some differences in style.

## PERSISTENCE OF STEREOTYPES

Given the lack of evidence of real differences between males and females, and the real evidence that they are perceived to be different, one begins to understand why the stereotypes persist. These perceptions are reinforced culturally, and they also serve individual needs.

Fransella and Frost (19) argue that stereotypes are maintained culturally through children's books and advertising. Children's books still have more male figures. Males are active and females are passive.

Rosen and Jerdee (20) report some reasons why sex role stereotypes persist. First, stereotypes help provide a framework for viewing the world. By preordering events and relationships, the individual does not have to judge every event, and therefore, has some stability in life. Secondly, stereotypes serve a variety of functions for individuals—ego defense, for example. By projecting negative qualities onto one group, one does not have to see this in oneself. These attitudes also reinforce status and authority relationships.

But what happens when one encounters a highly successful woman, one who does not match the stereotype? According to Williams (21), we assume that the woman comes from an enriched background, had a pattern of development different from other women, or was in a unique position (wartime, or death of husband). All these hypotheses serve to reinforce the stereotype that a successful woman is a deviant in an idiosyncratic position. Managers in organizations further this discreditation process, as will be seen in a later section.

## BARRIERS TO INTEGRATION

If few relevant sex differences exist, and yet people continue to perceive men and women in stereotypical ways, what effect does this have on female work performance? The research presented below focuses on the selection, socialization, and evaluation of women workers, particularly those in the professions and management.

Traditionally, the range of jobs open to men numbered in the thousands; those open to women were limited to service categories: nurse, secretary, and so on. Despite the apparent freedom of choice, organizations continue to sex-type positions. Sex-typing in organizations occurs when a very large majority of those in certain positions are of one sex, and when there is a normative expectation that this is as it should be (22). These expectations not only determine the type of jobs males and females may enter, but also the hierarchical ordering of these jobs (23). Males are not expected to take orders from females, and therefore males, in general, have more power.

It was noted earlier that female traits, in general, were valued less than male traits. This effect tends to ripple into the area of occupational prestige. Touhey (24) found that the prestige and desirability of professions decreased for both male and female raters when increased proportions of women entering the profession were anticipated. (One amusing anecdote illustrating the pervasiveness of this occupational devaluation was told by one working mother who, incidentally, was a judge. She asked her son what he wanted to be when he grew up. He replied: "A truck driver." She, having the ambitions of all parents, asked: "Why not a judge?" His reply: "Nah, that's just for girls").

Because jobs tend to be sex-typed, and those associated with females tend to be devalued, we can predict that these two factors are important in the selection, training, and evaluation of performance on the job.

## SELECTION

Consistent with the research that shows that males and females are viewed in distinct stereotypical ways is the research that shows that females are not perceived as having leadership capabilities (25). This view is held by both males and females. In one study, Bowman, Worthy and Greepli found that 41 percent of male executives look on the idea of women executives with some disfavor. Ninety percent feel that a woman has to be overqualified to succeed. Nearly 200 male managers in another study indicated that they felt people want male managers, that they themselves would be uncomfortable with a female supervisor, and that women are not dependable. These attitudes are reflected in the channeling and controlling of employees in organizations. Add stereotyped perceptions to the mix and a powerful, but covert, controlling mechanism is unleashed.

In fact, Schein (26) argues that one can conceive of the organization as a multidimensional filtering system which allows or obstructs the movement of individuals within the organization. As will be seen below, each major step of an individual's organizational life can be a potential filtering point. These many steps can be grouped into three major ones: selection, which includes preentry training; the actual interview selection, and the assignment to the first job; training which includes formal training, informal training and informal links with communication networks; and evaluation, which includes the formal appraisal process, informal judgments of supervisors, peers and subordinates, and promotion decisions.

As overt barriers to entry into traditionally male careers are broken down, more females are prepared and willing to compete for jobs on an equal footing. However, there is evidence that, at the selection interivew stage, there is a tendency for interviewers to discriminate against women (27). Tully (28) found that male interviewers try to convince women that the job would be too demanding, or unrewarding, or unmatched to their qualifications.

Heilman and Saruwatari (29) found that women were penalized for their appearance when they sought managerial jobs. Attractive women were thought too feminine (and feminine does not click with manager), while attractive men were judged as more masculine than unattractive men. To be successful as a manager is to be masculine. Women are seen as needing a pleasant appearance and skills. Men are seen as needing motivation, ability, and interpersonal relations skills (30).

And thus, through covert and sometimes unconscious practices, women are channeled into traditional jobs.

## TRAINING

Training is a term referring, in this paper, to the initiation of the candidate into the corporate norms. This is accomplished in organizations both formally, through the use of administrative manuals and, more importantly, informally. By being sensitive to organizational cues such as size of desk, who interrupts whom, physical distance between individuals, and so on, an individual can decide who has the real power, and what are the real, as opposed to stated, objectives. In order to play the game, one must understand the formal (and often ignored) rules and the informal rules.

Again, at preentry stage women are seriously disadvantaged as Harragan argues so successfully in her book *Games Mother Never Taught You* (31). Males are taught to play as part of the team, whether they like the other players or not. They learn to value an individual who has one special, but needed, talent even though he would be rated as undesirable in other traits. Females, on the other hand, play only with those they like, and much activity is spent getting others to like them. This dichotomy between liking or respecting your colleagues is just one of the many factors that influence the effectiveness of individuals within the organization, and it is an area where females are seriously disadvantaged.

Attitudes of others also have a direct effect on the socialization of females. Most managers assume that women should not be given extra work or travel assignments and that they are not mobile (32). This particular attitude ("Let me carry those heavy reports for you, dear.") may be one of the more successful ways in which organizations regularly channel women into maintenance and noncritical jobs.

The confusion between the role of female (let the man pay for dinner) and the role of manager (let the manager pay for the client's dinner) creates an uncomfortable atmosphere for many. Many female executives have handled this by avoiding these situations, and in effect, isolating themselves (33). The results of this isolation mean that female managers were not getting the kind of training, which is largely informal and after-hours, basic to becoming an executive.

The confusion of roles hampers one's being chosen as a protégé. In a completely male environment, it is quite acceptable for the star performer to be groomed by his boss. This grooming means spending many hours together, on and off the job, and receiving privileges such as interesting assignments. These same circumstances, when a woman is a protégé, lead to speculations of the degree of intimacy and exchange of favors. (Mary Cunningham was a recent victim.) This forces many women to become overeducated for their work, on the assumption that a Bachelor of Commerce at night school is equivalent to the kind of tutored training that their peers are receiving.

The role of the informal organization is not to be underestimated. The informal organization consists of those networks of people who exchange information over coffee and lunch. Zacharias (34) has documented the specific characteristics of these informal networks that ensure the exclusion of women. According to him, in informal networks, people prefer to speak to high-status people who will help them. They prefer to talk to others who make them feel secure and good about themselves. They will avoid people who threaten them. Furthermore, members of an organization communicate as if they were trying to improve positions. Given the low status of women, and their potential threat as another minority group demanding rights, one can begin to understand why women are not normally part of this informal exchange. (It should be noted that most of these barriers are probably operating at an unconscious level. However, in one antiquated book, *Managing Women in Business*, Ellman suggests that if possible, managers should keep women in groups to themselves. He offers no explanation for this advice. He also counsels, in the section on recruitment, that women are prone to lie about their age, and so managers should consider whether the woman appears younger or older than her age!)

## EVALUATION

Assuming that the female executive has passed the first two hurdles—entry and training—she comes to that part of the career process where she has the least control over her fate, and the stereotyped perceptions of her evaluators are less obvious, but still pervasive.

In the professions and the field of management, the evaluation of employees tends to be based on peer assessment, and not on objective standards. At the lower levels, where some objective criteria exist, women tend to excel and, unfortunately, become irreplaceable as technical specialists (35). At higher levels, and in professional occupations, objective standards are much more difficult to obtain. Is a Chief Executive Offier who increases sales a better manager than one who maximizes today's profits? Likewise, it is difficult to get agreement on the quality of an academic paper. Judgments tend to be based on the professional's sensitivity to his peers, the bonds of common background, continual association, and affinity of interests (36). These ambiguous reference points are open to interpretation by others, which research has shown to work to the disadvantage of women.

At this point, we are not concerned with the objective effectiveness of managers. What concerns us is how influential individuals within the organization perceive and react to male versus female leaders.

A curious phenomenon in this area has been well documented. Researchers have listed four basic reasons why people may have performed successfully: luck, ease of task, effort and ability. When women were clearly successful in organizations, raters attributed this success to luck, ease of task, and effort, whereas men's success is attributed to ability (37). Therefore, when a woman is successful, she is not necessarily rewarded for it because it is seen as being due mainly to circumstances outside her control (luck, effort, ease of task), which are considered to be unstable factors. A male is more likely to be rewarded because his performance is due to ability, which is considered, at a subconscious level, to be a stable internal factor.

Compounding this attribution process is the tendency of women themselves to attribute their performance to luck or to ease of the task. Heilman and Kram (38) report that women see themselves as responsible for negative performance. This ties in neatly with the generally-held self-contempt and low expectations of females. Harragan warns would-be female

managers to beware of people who are enthusiastic and complimentary about some tasks
they have completed, particularly if it is a normal part of the job. The implicit assumption is
that it is good work—for a woman!

Not only does a woman tend to disclaim her
own successful performance, she tends to de-
value the performance of other women (39, 40).
This tendency tends to inhibit the career advancement of women.

But there is some hope. There is some
evidence that the discrimination exists because
of the attribution of casual factors, not discrimination because of sex alone. When Heilman and Guzzo manipulated the experimental
conditions so that men's performances were attributed to luck, the males too were discriminated against. Furthermore, Benson and Jerdee (41) report that although women employees
are discriminated against in decisions involving
promotion and development, male employees
were discriminated against in decisions involving competing role demands from family circumstances. (Those who saw the film *Kramer
vs. Kramer* will recognize this situation.) The
important point here is that discrimination occurs when a male or female is not acting according to his or her sex role stereotype.

As was noted, both males and females tend
to have low expectations of the performance of
female managers. Expectations of how we think
people should behave often overpower our observations of how they do behave. We look, but
we do not see. We label the same behavior
differently, depending on whom we are observ-
ing, in accordance with our stereotypes. "Jane's
report was good because she was lucky enough
to get that confidential information." "John's
report was good because he knows how to present ideas logically." But these expectations of
behavior are not confined simply to labeling
and attribution of casual factors. They are communicated subtly in our interactions, and they
actually influence what others may do. The
classic example of this was Rosenthal's study
(42) with elementary school children. Teachers
were told (falsely) that some children would
become intellectual bloomers, and the children
did, as evidenced by their higher grades. This
effect, which Rosenthal called the Pygmalian
effect, was replicated in hundreds of studies in
both field and experimental situations. What
you believe, you see. It is an unconscious process that subtly influences objective evaluations
of employee performance.

## CONCLUSION

The evidence presented in the preceding section attempts to establish that, although there
were no differences in male/female leadership
behavior, raters perceive a difference which
leads to subtle discriminatory acts. People, in
general, still hold stereotyped views of sex
roles. Those males and females who do not
behave according to their sex role stereotype
are negatively evaluated.

These traditional sex role expectations have
led us to believe that the model of the manager

is masculine, and the standard is male (43). Yet,
the conclusions drawn from research on the
psychology of sex differences indicate that there
are more differences among the sexes than between the sexes. Tavris (44) states that "current
research in psychology and physiology is moving away from the polarized view of male and
female to an appreciation of the fact that most of
us live with elements of each sex."

The concept of androgyny, referring to the
presence of both female and male characteris-

tics in a single organism, reflects this fact. To modern researchers, androgyny probably refers to the flexibility of the sex role (45).

Sandra Bem is credited with the advancement of the concept of androgyny to replace the confining male and female stereotypes. Her research shows that approximately 35 percent of today's undergraduates are androgynous (50 percent are appropriately sex-typed; 15 percent are cross-typed) (46). She argues that people should exhibit either masculine or feminine behaviors, depending on the situational appropriateness of these behaviors. She further states that playing only the correct sex role has dysfunctional consequences. Bem found that high femininity in females has been correlated consistently with high anxiety, low self-esteem, and low social acceptance. During adulthood, high masculinity in males has been correlated with high anxiety, high neuroticism, and low self-acceptance. Cross sex-typing has been correlated quite consistently with greater intellectual development (47). She makes a strong case for androgyny on a mental health basis.

Organizationally, would androgyny work? Shepard (47) traces the development of organizations as a result of societal values. In the 1940s and 1950s, anyone who survived high school, which emphasized obedience, competition, pleasing the authorities, meaningless tasks, and feelings of self-worth associated with status symbols, would do quite well in an organization.

In the 1960s, the demands of an organization upon men and women began to shift. Experiments such as the T-Group deemphasized the traditional "masculine" values, and opened the door for the anima—openness, trust, expression, and use of emotion. Authority and obedience no longer guaranteed success. A wide range of interpersonal strategies were needed to cover the situation in which one would have to work—matrix plans, work with minorities, consumer activists, encroaching unions, and old-timers who liked the pace of assembly lines.

At the same time that organizations were demanding a wider range of interpersonal skills from its managers, certain segments of society were questioning the validity of the traditional sex-role stereotypes. These two movements may have forced into creation the androgynous executive.

One major problem remains: will those in power see male and female managers as they are, or as they are supposed to be?

## REFERENCES

1. Bernard Bass, Judith Krussel, and Ralph S. Alexander, "Male Managers' Attitudes toward Working Women," *American Behavioral Science*, 1971, 15, pp. 221–36.

2. Garda Bowman, N. Beatrice Worthy, and Stephen A. Greepli, "Are Women Executives People?" *Harvard Business Review*, July/August 1965, 43.

3. Edgar S. Ellman, *Managing Women in Business* (Waterford, Connecticut: Prentice-Hall, 1963).

4. Virginia Schein, "Think Manager: Think Male," *Atlantic Economic Review*, March/April 1976, pp. 21–24.

5. David R. Day, and Ralph M. Stogdill, "Leader Behavior of Male and Female Supervisors: A Comparative Study," *Personnel Psychology*, 1972, 25, pp. 353–60.

6. J. Brad Chapman, "Comparison of Male and Female Leadership Style," *Academy of Management Journal*, 1975, 18, pp. 645–50.

7. Kathryn M. Bartol, "The Sex Structuring of Organizations: A Search for Possible Causes,"

*Academy of Management Review,* October, 1978, pp. 805–12.

8. Richard N. Osborn, and William M. Vicars, "Sex Stereotypes: An Artifact in Leader Behavior and Subordinate Satisfaction Analysis," *Academy of Management Journal,* 1976, 19, pp. 439–49.

9. Michael Crozier, *The World of the Office Worker,* translated by David Landau (Chicago: University of Chicago Press, 1971).

10. Bartol, "The Sex Structuring of Organizations."

11. Dorothy M. Haccoun, Robert R. Haccoun, and George Sallay, "Sex Differences in the Appropriateness of Supervising Styles: A Non-Management View," *Journal of Applied Psychology,* 1978, 3, pp. 124–27.

12. Gail J. Pheterson, Sara B. Kesler, and Philip A. Goldberg, "Evaluation of the Performance of Women as a Function of Their Sex, Achievement," in *Woman: Dependent or Independent Variable?* R. K. Under and F. L. Denmark, eds. (New York: Psychological Dimensions, Inc., 1975).

13. Benson Rosen, and Thomas H. Jerdee, "Sex Stereotyping in the Executive Suite," *Harvard Business Review,* March/April 1974, pp. 45–58.

14. Marsha Jacobson, and Joan Effertz, "Sex Roles and Leadership: Perceptions of the Leaders," *Organizational Behavior and Human Performance,* 1974, 12, pp. 383–96.

15. Barbara Bunker, Benedict and Edith W. Seashore, "Power, Collusion, Intimacy-Sexuality, Support: Breaking the Sex-Role Stereotypes in Social and Organizational Settings," *Beyond Sex Roles,* Alice B. Sargent, ed. (New York: West Publishing Co., 1977).

16. Kenneth N. Wexley, and Peter J. Hunt, "Male and Female Leaders: Comparison of Performance and Behavior Patterns," *Psychological Reports,* 1974, 35, pp. 867–72.

17. Margaret Hennig, and Anne Jardim, *The Managerial Woman* (New York: Pocket Books, 1978).

18. Edwin J. Megargee, "Influences of Sex Roles on the Manifestation of Leadership," *Journal of Applied Psychology,* 1969, 53, pp. 377–82.

19. Fay Fransella, and Kay Frost, *On Being a Woman* (London: Tavistock Publications, 1977).

20. Benson Rosen, and Thomas H. Jerdee, "The Psychological Basis for Sex Role Stereotypes: A Note on Ierbargand Ilgens' Conclusion," *Organizational Behavior and Human Performance,* 1975, 14, pp. 151–53.

21. Martha Williams, "Women and Success in Organizations," in *Women in Management: Proceedings of the Conference,* M. Gerrard, J. Oliver, and M. Williams, eds. (Austin: University of Texas, 1975).

22. Cynthia Epstein, "Encountering the Male Establishment: Sex Status Limits on Women's Careers in the Professions," *Women: Dependent or Independent Variables?* (New York: Psychological Dimensions, Inc., 1975).

23. Joan Acker, and Donald Van Hauten, "Differential Recruitment and Control: The Sex Structuring of Organizations," *Administrative Science Quarterly,* 1974, 19, pp. 152–63.

24. John C. Touhey, "Effects of Additional Women Professions on Ratings of Occupational Prestige and Desirability," *Journal of Personality and Social Psychology,* Nov. 7, 1974, 29, pp. 86–89.

25. J. Brad Chapman and Fred Luthans, "The Female Leadership Dilemma," in *Women in Management,* B. A. Stead, ed. (Englewood Cliffs, New Jersey: Prentice-Hall, 1978).

26. Edgar Schien, "The Individual, the Organization, and the Career: A Conceptual Scheme," Organizational Psychology, D. A. Kabb, J. M. Ruben, and J. M. McIntyre, eds. (Englewood Cliffs, New Jersey: Prentice-Hall, 1974).

27. Schien, "The Individual, the Organization, and the Career."

28. J. Tully, "Recent Data on Informal Barriers," in *Women in Management: Proceedings of the Conference,* M. Gerrard, J. Oliver, and M. Williams, eds. (Austin: University of Texas, 1975).

29. Madeline Heilman, and Lois B. Saruwatari, "When Reality is Beastly: The Effects of Appearance and Sex on Evaluation of Job Applicants for Management and Non-Managerial Jobs," *Organizational Behavior and Human Performance,* 1979, 23, pp. 360–72.

30. Williams, "Women and Success in Organizations."

31. Betty Lehan Harragan, *Games Mother Never Taught You* (New York: Warner Books, 1977).

32. Tully, "Recent Data on Informal Barriers."

33. Harragan, *Games Mother Never Taught You.*

34. Donald W. Zacharias, "Women and the Informal Organization," in *Women in Management: Proceedings of the Conference* M. Gerrard, J. Oliver, and M. Williams, eds. (Austin: University of Texas, 1975).

35. Hennig and Jardim, *The Managerial Woman.*

36. Epstein, "Encountering the Male Establishment."

37. Madeline Heilman, and Richard Guzzo, "The Perceived Cause of Success as a Mediator of Sex Discrimination in Organizations," *Organizational Behavior and Human Performance*, 1978, 21, pp. 346–57.

38. Madeline Heilman, and Kathy Kram, "Self-Perogating Behavior in Women-Fixed or Flexible: The Effects of Co-Workers' Sex," *Organizational Behavior and Human Performance*, 1978, 22, pp. 497–507.

39. Heilman and Kram, "Self-Perogating Behavior."

40. Pheterson, Kessler, and Goldberg, "Evaluation of the Performance of Women."

41. Rosen Benson, and Thomas H. Jerdee, "Sex Stereotyping in the Executive Suite," *Harvard Business Review*, March/April 1974, 47.

42. Robert Rosenthal, *Experimenter Effects in Behavioral Research* (New York: Appleton-Century Crofts, 1973).

43. Rosalind Loring, and Theodora Wells, *Breakthrough: Women in Management* (New York: Van Nostrand Reinhold, 1972).

44. Carol Tavris, "Stereotypes, Socialization, and Sexism," *Beyond Sex Roles*, Alice B. Sargent, ed. (New York: West Publishing Co., 1977), p. 186.

45. Alexandra G. Kaplan, and Joan P. Bean, eds., *Beyond Sex-Role Stereotypes: Readings toward a Psychology of Androgyny* (Boston: Little, Brown, 1976).

46. Sandra Bem, "Psychological Androgyny," in *Beyond Sex Roles*, Alice B. Sargent, ed. (New York: West Publishing Co., 1977).

47. Sandra Bem, "Sex-Role Stability: One Consequence of Psychological Androgyny," *Journal of Personality and Social Psychology*, 1975, 31 (4), pp. 634–43.

48. Herbert A. Shepard, "Men in Organizations: Some Reflections," in *Beyond Sex Roles*, Alice B. Sargent, ed. (New York: West Publishing Co., 1977).

So far we have explored the various aspects of management and outlined for our use selective bits of knowledge developed in each area of management. In this section, we extend our observations into the future and speculate on the appropriate profile of the future manager as well as the future of management theory. From our understanding of the trends that are emerging we feel that the future manager is likely to be liberated from the strait jackets of conventional wisdom and uncritical acceptance of any established mode of management. The liberated manager is likely to absorb different ideas from various disciplines without any predetermined commitment to any one way of thinking. The liberated manager likes to select problems that interest him to utilize his trained capabilities, and to seek visibility. He may look upon conflict as a means of clarifying issues and of achieving personal growth and development.

The new manager expects independence and detachment, prefers maximum choice and mobility, and welcomes conflict on strategic issues. What the liberated manager wants is more joy in his work, to live and work more fully, and to have authentic relations with those who work with him.

The modern environment requires an essentially bilingual (information and existentialism) and bicultural (linear and nonlinear) perspective. People in our society want both affluence and achievement, on the one hand, and awareness and authenticity on the other. For liberated managers, intention and decision making are central.

Executive life demands strength of ego, for an executive can rarely make a decision which is certainly correct. He can only reduce the degree of uncertainty, not eliminate it. Given this situation, managers opt for the best decision and hope for consensus from superiors and colleagues.

The existential executive tries to supplement his own analytic skills. This requires an effort in lateral or divergent thinking.

# VI

# MANAGING THE FUTURE

Instead of moving vertically, the existential executive tries to move laterally in a mental context where intelligence and hunches count, to try and find the real problem.

The most important thing for the existential executive is to realize his own personal destiny. In the last three decades, the belief has grown that one can become a more active force in shaping one's destiny. In order to accomplish this, a new ethos, pathos, and logos must be introduced into the study of people. Ethos, which refers to the moral frame of reference, is considered with the ethic of intention, based on the tenet that each individual is responsible for his own actions and the effects of that action. Pathos is the ability to move people emotionally. Existentialism also has its own logos, its own specific intellectual infrastructure.

Nearly two decades ago, Harold Koontz wrote a famous article called "The Management Theory Jungle" which described six different theoretical points of view. Now Koontz has returned with "The Management Theory Jungle Revisited"; the implication is that the jungle may be becoming more dense and impenetrable.

In the final analysis, to try and develop a new perspective on management, one should examine management as a combination of theatre, information, and existentialism. Management does not emerge from the simple addition of structure, process, and values together in an imaginative fashion that will get things done.

Efficacy in management is preferred to either efficiency or effectiveness. While efficiency reflects the performance of functions in the best possible and least wasteful manner, effectiveness is the achievement of a desired purpose. Efficacy, on the other hand, is the capacity of producing a desired result and effect.

The various schools of or approaches to management theory that I identified nearly two decades ago, and called "the management theory jungle," are reconsidered. What is found now are eleven distinct approaches, compared to the original six, implying that the "jungle" may be getting more dense and impenetrable. However, certain developments are occurring which indicate that we may be moving more than people think toward a unified and practical theory of management.

Nearly two decades ago, I became impressed by the confusion among intelligent managers arising from the wide differences in findings and opinions among academic experts writing and doing research in the field of management. The summary of these findings I identified as "the management theory jungle" [Koontz, 1961]. Originally written to clarify for myself why obviously intelligent academic colleagues were coming up with such widely diverse conclusions and advice concerning management, my summary was published and widely referred to under this title. What I found was that the thinking of these scholars fell into six schools or approaches in their analysis of management. In some cases, it appeared that, like the proverbial blind men from Hindustan, some specialists were describing management only through the perceptions of their specialties.

Judging by its reception over the years, the article and the concept of the "jungle" must have filled a need. In fact, so many inquiries have been made over the intervening years as to whether we still have a "management theory jungle" that I now believe the "jungle" should be revisited and reexamined. What I now find is that, in place of the six specific schools identified in 1961, there are at least eleven approaches. Thus, the jungle appears to have become even more dense and impenetrable. But various developments are occurring that might in the future bring a coalescence of the various approaches and result in a more unified and useful theory of management.

# 18

# The Liberated Manager

## The Management Theory Jungle Revisited
HAROLD KOONTZ

## THE ORIGINAL MANAGEMENT THEORY JUNGLE

What I found nearly two decades ago was that well-meaning researchers and writers, mostly from academic halls, were attempting to explain the nature and knowledge of managing from six different points of view then referred to as "schools." These were: (1) the management process school, (2) the empirical or "case" approach, (3) the human behavior school, (4) the social system school, (5) the decision theory school, and (6) the mathematics school.

These varying schools, or approaches (as they are better called), led to a jungle of confusing thought, theory, and advice to practicing managers. The major sources of entanglement in the jungle were often due to varying meanings given common words like "organization," to differences in defining management as a body of knowledge, to widespread casting aside of the findings of early practicing managers as being "armchair" rather than what they were—the distilled experience and thought of perceptive men and women, to misunderstanding the nature and role of principles and theory, and to an inability or unwillingness of many "experts" to understand each other.

Although managing has been an important human task since the dawn of group effort, with few exceptions the serious attempt to develop a body of organized knowledge—science—underpinning practice has been a product of the present century. Moreover, until the past quarter century almost all of the meaningful writing was the product of alert and perceptive practitioners—for example, French industrialist Henry Fayol, General Motors executive James Mooney, Johns-Manville vice-president Alvin Brown, British chocolate executive Oliver Sheldon, New Jersey Bell Telephone president Chester Barnard, and British management consultant Lyndall Urwick.

But the early absence of the academics from the field of management has been more than atoned for by the deluge of writing on management from our colleges and universities in the past 25 years. For example, there are now more than 100 (I can find 97 in my own library) different textbooks purporting to tell the reader—student or manager—what management is all about. And in related fields like psychology, sociology, system sciences, and mathematical modeling, the number of textbooks that can be used to teach some aspect—usually narrow—of management is at least as large.

The jungle has perhaps been made more impenetrable by the infiltration in our colleges and universities of many highly, but narrowly, trained instructors who are intelligent but know too little about the actual task of managing and the realities practicing managers face. In looking around the faculties of our business, management, and public administration schools, both undergraduate and graduate, practicing executives are impressed with the number of bright but inexperienced faculty members who are teaching management or some aspect of it. It seems to some like having professors in medical schools teaching surgery without ever having operated on a patient. As a result, many practicing managers are losing confidence in our colleges and universities and the kind of management taught.

It is certainly true that those who teach and write about basic operational management theory can use the findings and assistance of colleagues who are especially trained in psychology, sociology, mathematics, and operations research. But what dismays many is that some professors believe they are teaching management when they are only teaching these specialities.

What caused this? Basically two things. In the first place, the famous Ford Foundation (Gordon and Howell) and Carnegie Foundation

(Pearson) reports in 1959 on our business school programs in American colleges and universities, authored and researched by scholars who were not trained in management, indicted the quality of business education in the United States and urged schools, including those that were already doing everything the researchers recommended, to adopt a broader and more social science approach to their curricula and faculty. As a result, many deans and other administrators went with great speed and vigor to recruit specialists in such fields as economics, mathematics, psychology, sociology, social psychology, and anthropology.

A second reason for the large number of faculty members trained in special fields, rather than in basic management theory and policy, is the fact that the rapid expansion of business and management schools occurred since 1960, during a period when there was an acute shortage of faculty candidates trained in management and with some managerial experience. This shortage was consequently filled by an increasing number of PhD's in the specialized fields noted above.

## THE CONTINUING JUNGLE

That the theory and science of management are far from being mature is apparent in the continuation of the management theory jungle. What has happened in the intervening years since 1961? The jungle still exists, and, in fact, there are nearly double the approaches to management that were identified nearly two decades ago. At the present time, a total of eleven approaches to the study of management science and theory may be identified. These are: (1) the empirical or case approach, (2) the interpersonal behavior approach, (3) the group behavior approach, (4) the cooperative social system approach, (5) the sociotechnical system approach, (6) the decision theory approach, (7) the systems approach, (8) the mathematical or "management science" approach, (9) the contingency or situational approach, (10) the managerial roles approach, and (11) the operational theory approach.

### Differences between the Original and Present Jungle

What has caused this almost doubling of approaches to management theory and science? In the first place, one of the approaches found nearly two decades ago has been split into two. The original "human behavior school" has, in my judgment, divided itself into the interpersonal behavior approach (psychology) and the group behavior approach (sociology and cultural anthropology). The original social systems approach is essentially the same, but because its proponents seem to rest more heavily on the theories of Chester Barnard, it now seems more accurate to refer to it as the cooperative social systems approach.

Remaining essentially the same since my original article are (1) the empirical or case approach, (2) the decision theory approach, and (3) the mathematical or "management science" approach. Likewise, what was originally termed the "management process school" is now referred to more accurately as the operational theory approach.

New approaches that have become popular in the past two decades include the sociotechnical systems approach. This was first given birth by the research and writings of Eric Trist and his associates in the Tavistock Institute in 1951, but did not get many followers to form a clear-cut approach until the late 1960s. Also, even though the systems approach to any science or practice is not new (it was recognized in the original jungle as the "social systems" approach), its scholarly and widespread approach to management theory really occurred in the 1960s, particularly with the work of Johnson, Kast, and Rosenzweig [1963].

The managerial roles approach has gained its identification and adherents as the result of the research and writing of Henry Mintzberg [1973, 1975], who prefers to call this approach the "work activity school."

The contingency or situational approach to management theory and science is really an outgrowth of early classical, or operational, theory. Believing that most theory before the 1970s too often advocated the "one best way," and often overlooking the fact that intelligent practicing managers have always tailored their practice to the actual situation, a fairly significant number of management scholars have begun building management theory and research around what should be done in various situations, or contingencies.

Many writers who have apparently not read the so-called classicists in management carefully have come up with the inaccurate shibboleth that classical writers were prescribing the "one best way." It is true that Gilbreth in his study of bricklaying was searching for the one best way, but that was bricklaying and not managing. Fayol recognized this clearly when he said "principles are flexible and capable of adaptation to every need; it is a matter of knowing how to make use of them, which is a difficult art requiring intelligence, experience, decision, and proportion" [1949, p. 19].

## The Current Approaches to Management Theory and Science

I hope the reader will realize that, in outlining the eleven approaches, I must necessarily be terse. Such conciseness may upset some

adherents to the various approaches and some may even consider the treatment superficial, but space limitations make it necessary that most approaches be identified and commented on briefly.

**The empirical or case approach**  The members of this school study management by analyzing experience, usually through cases. It is based on the premise that students and practitioners will understand the field of management and somehow come to know how to manage effectively by studying managerial successes and failures in various individual cases.

However, unless a study of experience is aimed at determining *fundamentally* why something happened or did not happen, it is likely to be a questionable and even dangerous approach to understanding management, because what happened or did not happen in the past is not likely to help in solving problems in a most certainly different future. If distillation of experience takes place with a view to finding basic generalizations, this approach can be a useful one to develop or support some principles and theory of management.

**The interpersonal behavior approach**  This approach is apparently based on the thesis that managing involves getting things done through people, and that therefore the study of management should be centered on interpersonal relations. The writers and scholars in this school are heavily oriented to individual psychology and, indeed, most are trained as psychologists. Their focus is on the individual, and his or her motivations as a sociopsychological being. In this school are those who appear to emphasize human relations as an art that managers, even when foolishly trying to be amateur psychiatrists, can understand and practice. There are those who see the manager as a leader and may even equate managership and leadership—thus, in effect, treating all "led" activities as "managed." Others have concentrated on motivation or leadership and have cast important light on these subjects, which has been useful to managers.

That the study of human interactions, whether in the context of managing or elsewhere, is useful and important cannot be denied. But it can hardly be said that the field of interpersonal behavior encompasses all there is to management. It is entirely possible for all the managers of a company to understand psychology and its nuances and yet not be effective in managing. One major division of a large American company put their managers from top to bottom through sensivitiy training (called by its critics "psychological striptease") only to find that the managers had learned much about feelings but little about how to manage. Both research and practice are finding that we must go far beyond interpersonal relations to develop a useful science of management.

**The group behavior approach** This approach is closely related to the interpersonal behavior approach and may be confused with it. But it is concerned primarily with behavior of people in groups rather than with interpersonal behavior. It thus tends to rely on sociology, anthropology, and social psychology rather than on individual psychology. Its emphasis is on group behavior patterns. This approach varies all the way from the study of small groups, with their cultural and behavioral patterns, to the behavioral characteristics of large groups. It is often called a study of "organization behavior" and the term "organization" may be taken to mean the system, or pattern, of any set of group relationships in a company, a government agency, a hospital, or any other kind of undertaking. Sometimes the term is used as Chester Barnard employed it, meaning "the cooperation of two or more persons," and "formal organization" as an organization with conscious, deliberate, joint purpose [1938, p. 65]. Chris Argyris has even used the term "or-

ganization" to include "*all* the behavior of *all* the participants" in a group undertaking [1957, p. 239].

It is not difficult to see that a practicing manager would not likely recognize that "organizations" cover such a broad area of group behavior patterns. At the same time, many of the problems of managers do arise from group behavior patterns, attitudes, desires, and prejudices, some of which come from the groups within an enterprise, but many come from the cultural environment of people outside of a given company, department, or agency. What is perhaps most disturbing about this school of thought is the tendency of its members to draw an artificial and inaccurate line between "organization behavior" and "managing." Group behavior is an important aspect of management. But it is not all there is to management.

**The cooperative social system approach** A modification of the interpersonal and group behavior approaches has been the focus of some behavioral scientists on the study of human relationships as cooperative social systems. The idea of human relationships as social systems was early perceived by the Italian sociologist Vilfredo Pareto. His work apparently affected modern adherents to this school through his influence on Chester Barnard. In seeking to explain the work of executives, Barnard saw them operating in, and maintaining, cooperative social systems, which he referred to as "organizations" [1938, pp. 72–73]. He perceived social systems as the cooperative interaction of ideas, forces, desires, and thinking of two or more persons. An increasing number of writers have expanded this concept to apply to any system of cooperative and purposeful group interrelationships or behavior and have given it the rather general title of "organization theory."

The cooperative social systems approach does have pertinence to the study and analysis of management. All managers do operate in a cooperative social system. But we do not find what is generally referred to as managers in *all* kinds of cooperative social systems. We would hardly think of a cooperative group of shoppers in a department store or an unorganized mob as being managed. Nor would we think of a family group gathering to celebrate a birthday as being managed. Therefore, we can conclude that this approach is broader than management while still overlooking many concepts, principles, and techniques that are important to managers.

**The sociotechnical systems approach**   One of the newer schools of management identifies itself as the sociotechnical systems approach. This development is generally credited to E. L. Trist and his associates at the Tavistock Institute of England. In studies made of production problems in long-wall coal mining, this group found that it was not enough merely to analyze social problems. Instead, in dealing with problems of mining productivity, they found that the technical system (machines and methods) had a strong influence on the social system. In other words, they discovered that personal attitudes and group behavior are strongly influenced by the technical system in which people work. It is therefore the position of this school of thought that social and technical systems must be considered together and that a major task of a manager is to make sure that these two systems are made harmonious.

Most of the work of this school has consequently concentrated on production, office operations, and other areas where the technical systems have a very close connection to people and their work. It therefore tends to be heavily oriented to industrial engineering. As an approach to management, this school has made some interesting contributions to managerial practice, even though it does not, as some of its proponents seem to believe, encompass all there is to management. Moreover, it is doubtful that any experienced manager would be surprised that the technology of the assembly line or the technology in railroad transportation or in oil companies affects individuals, groups, and their behavior patterns, the way operations are organized, and the techniques of managing required. Furthermore, as promising and helpful as this approach is in certain aspects of enterprise operations, it is safe to observe that there is much more to pertinent management knowledge than can be found in it.

**The decision theory approach**   This approach to management theory and science has apparently been based on the belief that, because it is a major task of managers to make decisions, we should concentrate on decision making. It is not surprising that there are many scholars and theorists who believe that, because managing is characterized by decision making, the central focus of management theory should be decision making and that all of management thought can be built around it. This has a degree of reasonableness. However, it overlooks the fact that there is much more to managing than making decisions and that, for most managers, the actual making of a decision is a fairly easy thing—if goals are clear, if the environment in which the decision will operate can be fairly accurately anticipated, if adequate information is available, if the organization structure provides a clear understanding of responsibility for decisions, if competent people are available to make decisions, and if many of the other prerequisites of effective managing are present.

**The systems approach**   During recent years, many scholars and writers in management have emphasized the systems approach to the study and analysis of management thought. They feel that this is the most effective means by which such thought can be organized, presented, and understood.

A system is essentially a set or assemblage

of things interconnected, or interdependent, so as to form a complex unity. These thing may be physical, as with the parts of an automobile engine; or they may be biological, as with components of the human body; or they may be theoretical, as with a well-integrated assemblage of concepts, principles, theory, and techniques in an area such as managing. All systems, except perhaps the universe, interact with and are influenced by their environments, although we define boundaries for them so that we can see and analyze them more clearly.

The long use of systems theory and analyses in physical and biological sciences has given rise to a considerable body of systems knowledge. It comes as no surprise that systems theory has been found helpfully applicable to management theory and science. Some of us have long emphasized an arbitrary boundary of management knowledge—the theory underlying the managerial job in terms of what managers do. This boundary is set for the field of management theory and science in order to make the subject "manageable," but this does not imply a closed systems approach to the subject. On the contrary, there are always many interactions with the sytem environment. Thus, when managers plan, they have no choice but to take into account such external variables as markets, technology, social forces, laws, and regulations. When managers design an organizational structure to provide an environment for performance, they cannot help but be influenced by the behavior patterns people bring to their jobs from the environment that is external to an enterprise.

Systems also play an important part within the area of managing itself. There are planning systems, organizational systems, and control systems. And, within these, we can perceive many sub-systems, such as systems of delegation, network planning, and budgeting.

Intelligent and experienced practicing managers and many management writers with practical experience, accustomed as they are to seeing their problems and operations as a network of interrelated elements with daily interaction between environments inside or outside their companies or other enterprises, are often surprised to find that many writers regard the systems approach as something new. To be sure, conscious study of, and emphasis on, systems have forced many managers and scholars to consider more perceptively the various interacting elements affecting management theory and practice. But it can hardly be regarded as a new approach to scientific thought.

**The mathematical or "management science" approach** There are some theorists who see managing as primarily an exercise in mathematical processes, concepts, symbols, and models. Perhaps the most widely known of these are the operations researchers who have often given themselves the self-annointing title of "management scientists." The primary focus of this approach is the mathematical model, since, through this device, problems—whether managerial or other—can be expressed in basic relationships and, where a given goal is sought, the model can be expressed in terms which optimize that goal. Because so much of the mathematical approach is applied to problems of optimization, it could be argued that it has a strong relationship to decision theory. But, of course, mathematical modeling sometimes goes beyond decision problems.

To be sure, the journal *Management Science*, published by the institute of Management Sciences, carries on its cover the statement that the Institute has as its purpose to "identify, extend, and unify scientific knowledge pertaining to management." But as judged by the articles published in this journal and the hundreds of papers presented by members of the Institute at its many meetings all over the world, the school seems to be almost completely preoccupied with mathematical models and elegance in simulating situations and in developing solutions to certain kinds of problems. Consequently, as many critics both inside and outside the ranks of the "management scientists" have observed, the narrow mathematical focus can hardly be called a complete approach to a true management science.

No one interested in any scientific field can overlook the great usefulness of mathematical models and analyses. But it is difficult to see mathematics as a school of management any more than it is a separate school of chemistry, physics, or biology. Mathematics and mathematical models are, of course, tools of analysis, not a school of thought.

**The contingency or situational approach** One of the approaches to management thought and practice that has tended to take management academicians by storm is the contingency approach to management. Essentially, this approach emphasizes the fact that what managers do in practice depends on a given set of circumstances—the situation. Contingency management is akin to situational management and the two terms are often used synonymously. Some scholars distinguish between the two on the basis that, while situational management merely implies that what managers do depends on a given situation, contingency management implies an active interrelationship between the variables in a situation and the managerial solution devised. Thus, under a contingency approach, managers might look at an assemblyline situation and conclude that a highly structured organization pattern would best fit and interact with it.

According to some scholars, contingency theory takes into account not only given situations but also the influence of given solutions on behavior patterns of an enterprise. For example, an organization structured along the lines of operating functions (such as finance, engineering, production, and marketing) might be most suitable for a given situation, but managers in such a structure should take into account the behavioral patterns that often arise

because of group loyalties to the function rather than to a company.

By its very nature, managerial practice requires that managers take into account the realities of a given situation when they apply theory or techniques. It has never been and never will be the task of science and theory to prescribe what should be done in a given situation. Science and theory in management have not and do not advocate the "best way" to do things in every situation, any more than the sciences of astrophysics or mechanics tell an engineer how to design a single best instrument for all kinds of applications. How theory and science are applied in practice naturally depends on the situation.

This is saying that there is science and there is art, that there is knowledge and there is practice. These are matters that any experienced manager has long known. One does not need much experience to understand that a corner grocery store could hardly be organized like General Motors, or that the technical realities of petroleum exploration, production, and refining make impracticable autonomously organized product divisions for gasoline, jet fuel, or lubricating oils.

**The managerial roles approach** Perhaps the newest approach to management theory to catch the attention of academics and practitioners alike is the managerial roles approach, popularized by Henry Mintzberg [1973, 1975]. Essentially this approach is to observe what managers actually do and from such observations come to conclusions as to what managerial activities (or roles) are. Although there have been researchers who have studied the actual work of managers, from chief executives to foremen, Mintzberg has given this approach sharp visibility.

By systematically studying the activities of five chief executives in a variety of organizations, Mintzberg came to the conclusion that executives do not act out the traditional classification of managerial functions—planning, organizing, coordinating, and controlling. Instead they do a variety of other activities.

From his research and the research of others who have studied what managers acutally do, Mintzberg has come to the conclusion that managers act out a set of ten roles. These are:

A. **Interpersonal Roles**
   1. Figurehead (performing ceremonial and social duties as the organization's representative)
   2. Leader
   3. Liaison (particularly with outsiders)

B. **Informational Roles**
   1. Monitor (receiving information about the operation of an enterprise)
   2. Disseminator (passing information to subordinates)
   3. Spokesperson (transmitting information outside the organization)

C. **Decision Roles**
   1. Entrepreneur
   2. Disturbance handler
   3. Resource allocator
   4. Negotiator (dealing with various persons and groups of persons)

Mintzberg refers to the usual way of classifying managerial functions as "folklore." As we will see in the following discussion on the operational theory approach, operational theorists have used such managerial functions as planning, organizing, staffing, leading, and controlling. For example, what is resource allocation but planning? Likewise, the entrepreneurial role is certainly an element of the whole area of planning. And the interpersonal roles are mainly aspects of leading. In addition, the informational roles can be fitted into a number of the functional areas.

Nevertheless, looking at what managers actually do can have considerable value. In analyzing activities, an effective manager might wish to compare these to the basic functions of managers and use the latter as a kind of pilot's checklist to ascertain what actions are being overlooked. But the roles Mintzberg identifies appear to be inadequate. Where in them does one find such unquestionably important managerial activities as structuring organization, selecting and appraising managers, and determining major strategies? Omissions such as these can make one wonder whether the executives in his sample were effective managers. It certainly opens a serious question as to whether the managerial roles approach is an adequate one on which to base a practical theory of management.

**The operational approach** The operational approach to management theory and science, a term borrowed from the work of P. W. Bridgman [1938, pp. 2–32], attempts to draw together the pertinent knowledge of management by relating it to the functions of managers. Like other operational sciences, it endeavors to put together for the field of management the concepts, principles, theory, and techniques that underpin the actual practice of managing.

The operational approach to management recognizes that there is a central core of knowledge about managing that exists only in management: such matters as line and staff, departmentation, the limitations of the span of management, managerial appraisal, and various managerial control techniques involve concepts and theory found only where managing is involved. But, in addition, this approach is eclectic in that it draws on pertinent knowledge derived from other fields. These include the clinical study of managerial activities, problems, and solutions; applications of systems theory; decision theory; motivation and leadership findings and theory; individual and group behavior theory; and the application of mathematical modeling and techniques. All these subjects are applicable to some extent to other fields of science, such as certain of the physical and geological sciences. But our interest in them must necessarily be limited to managerial aspects and applications.

The nature of the operational approach can perhaps best be appreciated by reference to Figure 18-1. As this diagram shows, the operational management school of thought includes a central core of science and theory unique to management plus knowledge eclectically drawn from various other schools and approaches. As the circle is intended to show, the operational approach is not interested in all the important knowledge in these various fields, but only that which is deemed to be most useful and relevant to managing.

The question of what managers do day by day and how they do it is secondary to what makes an acceptable and useful classification of knowledge. Organizing knowledge pertinent to managing is an indispensable first step in developing a useful theory and science of management. It makes possible the separation of science and techniques used in managing and those used in such nonmanagerial activities as marketing, accounting, manufacturing, and engineering. It permits us to look at the basic aspects of management that have a high degree

FIGURE 18-1 *The Scope of Operational Science and Theory. Operational management science and theory is that part of the diagram enclosed in the circle. It shows how operational management science and theory has a core of basic science and theory and draws from other fields of knowledge pertaining to management. It is thus, in part, an eclectic science and theory.*

of universality among different enterprises and different cultures. By using the functions of managers as a first step, a logical and useful start can be made in setting up pigeonholes for classifying management knowledge.

The functions some theorists (including me) have found to be useful and meaningful as this first step in classifying knowledge are:

1. Planning: selecting objectives and means of accomplishing them.
2. Organizing: designing an intentional structure of roles for people to fill.
3. Staffing: selecting, appraising, and developing people to effectively fill organizational roles.
4. Leading: taking actions to motivate people and help them see that contributing to group objectives is in their own interest.
5. Controlling: measuring and correcting activities of people to ensure that plans are being accomplished.

As a second step in organizing management knowledge, some of us have found it useful to ask basic questions in each functional area, such as:

1. What is the nature and purpose of each functional area?

2. What structural elements exist in each functional area?
3. What processes, techniques, and approaches are there in each functional area and what are the advantages and disadvantages of each?
4. What obstructions exist in effectively accomplishing each function?
5. How can these obstructions be removed?

Those who, like me, subscribe to the operational approach do so with the hope of developing and identifying a field of science and theory that has useful application to the practice of managing, and one that is not so broad as to encompass everything that might have any relationships, no matter how remote, to the managerial job. We realize that any field as complex as managing can never be isolated from its physical, technological, biological, or cultural environment. We also realize, however, that some partitioning of knowledge is necessary and some boundaries to this knowledge must be set if meaningful progress in summarizing and classifying pertinent knowledge is ever to be made. Yet, as in the case of all systems analyses where system boundaries are set, it must be kept in mind that there is no such thing as a totally closed system and that many environmental variables will intrude on and influence any system proposed.

## THE MANAGEMENT THEORY JUNGLE: PROMISING TENDENCIES TOWARD CONVERGENCE OF THEORIES

As can be seen from the brief discussions above of the schools and approaches to management theory and science, there is evidence that the management theory jungle continues to flourish and perhaps gets more dense, with nearly twice as many schools or approaches as were found nearly two decades ago. It is no wonder that a useful management theory and science

has been so tardy in arriving. It is no wonder that we still do not have a clear notion of the scientific underpinnings of managing nor have we been able clearly to identify what we mean by competent managers.

The varying approaches, each with its own gurus, each with its own semantics, and each with a fierce pride to protect the concepts and techniques of the approach from attack or change, make the theory and science of management extremely difficult for the intelligent practitioner to understand and utilize. If the continuing jungle were only evidence of competing academic thought and research, it would not much matter. But when it retards the development of a useful theory and science and confuses practicing managers, the problem becomes serious. Effective managing at all levels and in all kinds of enterprises is too important to any society to allow it to fail through lack of available and understandable knowledge.

At the same time, there appears to be some reason to be optimistic, in that signs exist indicating tendencies for the various schools of thought to coalesce. Although the convergence is by no means yet complete, there is reason to hope that, as scholars and writers become more familiar with what managers do and the situations in which they act, more and more of these schools or approaches will adopt, and even expand, the basic thinking and concepts of the operational school of management.

While acknowledging that these are only indications and signs along the road to a more unified and practical operational theory of management, and that there is much more of this road to travel, let us briefly examine some of these tendencies toward convergence.

## Greater Emphasis on Distillation of Basics within the Empirical Approach

Within the many programs utilizing cases as a means of educating managers, there are indications that there now exists a much greater emphasis on distilling fundamentals than there was two decades ago. Likewise, in the field of business policy, by which term most of these case approaches have tended to be known, there has been increased emphasis in teaching and research toward going beyond recounting what happened in a given situation to analyzing the underlying causes and reasons for what

happened. One major result of all this has been a new emphasis on strategy and strategic planning. This has been nowhere more noteworthy than at the Harvard Business School, which is regarded as the cradle of the case approach. This has led many empiricists to come up with distilled knowledge that fits neatly into the operational theorist's classification of planning.

## Recognizing that Systems Theory Is Not a Separate Approach

When systems theory was introduced into the management field some two decades ago, it was hailed by many as being a new way of analyzing and classifying management knowledge. But in recent years, as people have come to understand systems theory *and* the job of managing better, it has become increasingly clear that, in its essentials, there is little new about systems theory and that practicing managers as well as operational theorists had been using its basics (although not always the jargon) for a number of years. Nonetheless, as those in the field of operational management theory have more consciously and clearly employed the concepts and theory of systems, their attempts at developing a scientific field have been improved.

## Recognizing that the Contingency Approach Is Not a New or Separate Approach

Although perceptive and intelligent managers and many management theorists have not been surprised by the realization, it is now clear that the contingency view is merely a way of distinguishing between science and art—knowledge and practice. As I pointed out earlier, these are two different things, albeit mutually complementary. Those writers and scholars who have emphasized contingency approaches have, to be sure, done the field of management theory and practice a great service by stressing that what the intelligent manager actually does depends on the realities of a situation. But this has long been true of the application of *any* science.

That contingency theory is really application in the light of a situation has been increasingly recognized, as is evidenced by a recent statement by one of its founders. Jay Lorsch recently admitted that the use of the term "contingency" was "misleading" [1977, pp. 2–14]. He appeared to recognize that an operational management theorist would necessarily become a situationalist when it came to applying management concepts, principles, and techniques.

## Finding that Organization Theory Is Too Broad an Approach

Largely because of the influence of Chester Barnard and his broad concept of "organization" as almost any kind of interpersonal relationships, it has become customary, particularly in some academic circles, to use the term "organization theory" to refer to almost any kind of interpersonal relationships. Many scholars attempted to make this field equal to management theory, but it is now fairly well agreed that managing is a narrower activity and that management theory pertains only to theory related to managing. Management theory is often thought of as being a subset of organization theory and it is now fairly well agreed that the general concept of organization theory is too broad.

This sign offers hope of clearing away some of the underbrush of the jungle.

## The New Understanding of Motivation

The more recent research into motivation of people in organizational settings has tended to emphasize the importance of the organizational climate in curbing or arousing motives. The oversimplified explanations of motives by Maslow and Herzberg may identify human needs fairly well, but much more emphasis must be given to rewards and expectations of rewards. These, along with a climate that arouses and supports motivation, will depend to a very great extent on the nature of managing in an organization.

Litwin and Stringer [1968] found that the strength of such basic motives as needs for achievement, power, and affiliation, were definitely affected by the organizational climate. In a sample of 460 managers, they found a strong relationship between highly structured organizations and arousal of the need for power, and a negative relationship with the needs for achievement and affiliation. Likewise, in a climate with high responsibility and clear standards, they observed a strong positive relationship between this climate and achievement motivation, a moderate correlation to power motivation, and an unrelated to negatively related relationship with affiliation motivation.

The interaction between motivation and organizational climate not only underscores the systems aspects of motivation but also emphasizes how motivation depends on what managers do in setting and maintaining an environment for performance. These researches move the problem of motivation from a purely behavioral matter to one closely related to and dependent on what managers do. The theory of motivation, then, fits nicely into the operational approach to management theory and science.

**The melding of motivation and leadership theory**    Another interesting sign that we may be moving toward a unified operational theory of management is the way that research and analysis have tended to meld motivation and leadership theory. Especially in recent years, leadership research and theory have tended to emphasize the rather elementary propositions that the job of leaders is to know and appeal to things that motivate people and to recognize the simple truth that people tend to follow those in whom they see a means of satisfying their own desires. Thus, explanations of leadership have been increasingly related to motivation.

This melding of motivation and leadership theories has also emphasized the importance of organization climate and styles of leaders. Most recent studies and theories tend to underscore the importance of effective managing in making managers effective leaders. Implied by most recent research and theory is the clear message that effective leaders design a system that takes into account the expectancies of subordinates, the variability of motives between individuals and from time to time, situational factors, the need for clarity of role definition, interpersonal relations, and types of rewards.

As can be readily seen, knowledgeable and effective managers do these things when they design a climate for performance, when goals and means of achieving them are planned, when organizational roles are defined and well structured, when roles are intelligently staffed, and when control techniques and information are designed to make self-control possible. In other words, leadership theory and research are, like motivation, fitting into the scheme of operational management theory, rather than going off as a separate branch of theory.

## The New Managerially Oriented "Organization Development"

Both "organization development" and the field ordinarily referred to as "organization behavior" have grown out of the interpersonal and group behavior approaches to management. For a while, it seemed that these fields were far away and separate from operational management theory. Now many of these scientists are seeing that basic management theory and techniques, such as managing by objectives and clarifying organization structure, fit well into their programs of behavioral intervention.

A review of the latest organization behavior books indicates that some authors in this field are beginning to understand that behavioral elements in group operations must be more closely integrated with organizational structure design, staffing, planning, and control. This is a promising sign. It is a recognition that analysis of individual and group behavior, at least in managed situations, easily and logically falls into place in the scheme of operational management theory.

## The Impact of Technology: Researching an Old Problem

That technology has an important impact on organizational structure, behavior patterns, and other aspects of managing has been recognized by intelligent practitioners for many years. However, primarily among academic researchers, there has seemed to be in recent years a "discovery" that the impact of technology is important and real. To be sure, some of this research has been helpful to managers, especially that developed by the socio-technical school of management. Also, while perceptive managers have known for many years that technology has important impacts, some of this research has tended to clarify and give special meaning to this impact.

The impact of technology is easily embraced by operational management theory and practice. And it should be. It is to be hoped that scholars and writers in the area of technological impacts will soon become familiar with operational management theory and incorporate their findings and ideas into that operational framework. At the very least, however, those who subscribe to the operational approach can incorporate the useful findings of those who emphasize the impact of technology.

## Defections Among "Management Scientists"

It will be recalled that in the discussion of schools or approaches to management, one of them is identified as the mathematical or "management science" approach. The reader has also undoubtedly noted that "management science" was put in quotation marks; the reason for so doing is that this group does not really deal with a total science of management but rather largely with mathematical models, symbols, and elegance.

There are clear signs among the so-called management scientists that there are defectors who realize that their interests must go far beyond the use of mathematics, models, and the computer. These especially exist in the ranks of operations researchers in industry and government, where they are faced daily with practical management problems. A small but increasing number of academics are also coming to this realization. In fact, one of the leading and most respected academics, one widely regarded as a pioneer in operations research, C. West Churchman, has (in conversations with me) been highly critical of the excessive absorption with models and mathematics and, for this reason, has even resigned from the Operations Research Society.

There is no doubt that operations research and similar mathematical and modeling techniques fit nicely in the planning and controlling areas of operational management theory and science. Most operational management theorists recognize this. All that is really needed is for the trickle of "management science" defectors to become a torrent, moving their expertise and research more closely to a practical and useful management science.

## Clarifying Semantics: Some Signs of Hope

One of the greatest obstacles to disentangling the jungle has long been, and still is, the problem of semantics. Those writing and lecturing on management and related fields have tended to use common terms in different ways. This is exemplified by the variety of meanings given to such terms as "organization," "line and staff," "authority," "responsibility," and "policies," to mention a few. Although this semantics swamp still exists and we are a long way from general acceptance of meanings of key terms and concepts, there are some signs of hope on the horizon.

It has become common for the leading management texts to include a glossary of key terms and concepts and an increasing number of them are beginning to show some commonality of meaning. Of interest also is the fact that the Fellows of the International Academy of Management, composed of some 180 management scholars and leaders from 32 countries of the world, have responded to the demands of its members and have undertaken to develop a glossary of management concepts and terms, to be published in a number of languages and given wide circulation among many countries.

Although it is too early to be sure, it does appear that we may be moving in the direction necessary for the development of a science— the acceptance of clear definitions for key terms and concepts.

## THE NEED FOR MORE EFFORT IN DISENTANGLING THE JUNGLE

Despite some signs of hope, the fact is that the management theory jungle is still with us. Although some slight progress appears to be occurring, in the interest of a far better society through improved managerial practice it is to be hoped that some means can be found to accelerate this progress.

Perhaps the most effective way would be for leading managers to take a more active role in narrowing the widening gap that seems to exist between professional practice and our college and university business, management, and public administration schools. They could be far more vocal and helpful in making certain that our colleges and universities do more than they have been in developing and teaching a theory and science of management useful to practicing managers. This is not to advocate making these schools vocational schools, especially since basic operational management theory and research are among the most demanding areas of knowledge in our society. Moreover, these schools are *professional* schools and their task must be to serve the professions for which they exist.

Most of our professional schools have advisory councils or boards composed of influential and intelligent top managers and other leading citizens. Instead of these boards spending their time, as most do, in passively receiving reports from deans and faculty members of the "new" things being done, these boards should find out more of what is going on in managerially related teaching and research and insist that some of these be moved toward a more useful operational science of management.

## REFERENCES

Argyris, C. *Personality and organization.* New York: Harper & Brothers, 1957.

Barnard, C. I. *The functions of the executive.* Cambridge, Mass.: Harvard University Press, 1938.

Bridgman, P. W. *The logic of modern physics.* New York: Macmillan, 1938.

Fayol, H. *General and industrial management.* New York: Pitman, 1949.

Gordon, R. A.; & Howell, J. E. *Higher education for business.* New York: Columbia University Press, 1959.

Johnson, R. A; Kast, F. E.; & Rosenzweig, J. E. *The theory and management of systems.* New York: McGraw-Hill, 1963.

Koontz, H. The management theory jungle. *Academy of Management Journal,* 1961, 4 (3), 174–188.

Litwin, G. H., & Stringer, R. A., Jr. *Motivation and organization climate.* Boston: Harvard Graduate School of Business Administration, 1968.

Lorsch, J. W. Organization design: A situational perspective. *Organizational Dynamics,* 1977, 6 (2), 12–14.

Mintzberg, H. *The nature of managerial work.* New York: Harper & Row, 1973.

Mintzberg, H. The manager's job: Folklore and fact. *Harvard Business Review,* 1975, 53 (4), 49–61.

Pierson, F. C. *The education of American businessmen: A study of university-college programs in business administration.* New York: McGraw-Hill, 1959.

## LIST OF CONTRIBUTORS

Kamran Khozan is a Ph.D. student of Management at Concordia University, Montreal, Canada.

J. Pierre Brunet is an assistant professor of Management at Concordia University, Montreal, Canada.

Laird W. Mealiea is an associate professor of Organization Theory and Behavior, School of Business Administration, at Dalhousie University, Halifax, Nova Scotia.

Dennis Lee is an assistant professor of Organization Theory and Behavior, School of Business Administration, at Dalhousie University, Halifax, Nova Scotia.

Walter R. Nord is a professor of Organizational Psychology at the Graduate School of Business Administration at Washington University, St. Louis, Missouri.

George Strauss is an associate dean of the College of Business Administration, University of California, Berkeley.

Michael B. McCaskey is an assistant professor of Organizational Behavior at the Harvard Business School, Boston, Massachusetts.

J. Richard Hackman is a professor of Organizational Studies and Management at Yale University, New Haven, Connecticut.

A. Bakr Ibraham is a Ph.D. student of Management at Concordia University, Montreal, Canada.

Richard S. Blackburn is an assistant professor of Organizational Behavior in the School of Business Administration, at the University of North Carolina at Chapel Hill.

Geert Hofstede is professor of Organizational Behavior at the European Institute for Advanced Studies in Management, Brussels, Belgium, and at INSEAD, Fontainebleau, France.

Theodore T. Herbert is an associate professor of Management at the University of Akron, Akron, Ohio.

Ralph W. Estes is Elmer Fox Professor of Accounting at Wichita State University, Wichita, Kansas.

Harry Abravanel is a professor of Organizational Behavior at Bishop's University, Quebec, Canada.

Craig C. Pinder is an associate professor of Management at the University of British Columbia.

James A. Waters is an assistant professor of Organizational Behavior and Policy of the Faculty of Management at McGill University, Montreal, Canada.

Paul F. Salipante, Jr. is an assistant professor of Industrial Relations of the School of Management, Case Western Reserve University, Cleveland, Ohio.

William W. Notz is an associate professor of Business Administration of the Faculty of Administrative Studies, University of Manitoba, Winnipeg, Canada.

Thomas A. Petit is a professor of Management at the University of North Carolina, Greensboro, North Carolina.

Ralph H. Kilmann is an associate professor of Business Administration at the University of Pittsburgh, Pittsburgh, Pennsylvania.

Kenneth W. Thomas is an associate professor of Industrial Relations and Organizational Behavior in the School of Business Administration, Temple University.

Monica Belcourt is a lecturer in Management at Concordia University, Montreal, Canada.

Harold Koontz is Mead Johnson Professor of Management Emeritus, Graduate School of Management, University of California, Los Angeles and Chancellor of the International Academy of Management.

A practical, thought-provoking, and yet entertaining treatment of business and the golden rule in management, this reference guide offers proven-effective techniques to help you recognize problems, mobilize facts, and implement a lucrative plan for action.

THE NEW MANAGEMENT SCENE reveals how you can easily integrate structure, process, and value to develop the right executive ethos and enhance your charismatic leadership skills.

Moreover, you'll discover what every manager should know to maximize your managerial skills and achieve corporate efficacy, including information about:

- the new optic and perspective in management

- how to reconcile existential and system values

- model-building skills

- political skills

- schools of management

- and much more.